10/5

THIS LAND
THESE VOICES

A different view of Arizona history in the words of those who lived it

by Abe Chanin with Mildred Chanin

MIDBAR PRESS • TUCSON

Reprinted in Paperback
by Midbar Press
1988

ISBN 0–87358–164–4
Library of Congress Catalog Card Number 77–79071
Composed and Printed in the United States of America

To Beth, Lance and Sean,
our link to the future as well as the past

Contents

Illustrations

Preface

WHEN WE SAT DOWN to tape the first voice for this book, we knew this project should have been started many years ago. For already too many voices have been stilled and too many great stories from the course of human events in this frontier state have gone unrecorded.

While the voices transcribed in this book are those of Arizonans, the stories they have told give a broad picture of the development of the Southwest. And yet this is not another history of the Southwest; rather it is a word picture of the social history and development of a frontier state that is typical of the region. On the pages ahead are the personal experiences of those who lived this history or had stories passed down to them by parents and grandparents. The emphasis here is deliberately on the events that narrate the human experience and this, then, sets this book apart from southwestern histories of dates and facts.

Thus while southwestern histories record the Long Walk, those dates and facts remain cold when placed alongside the retelling of that disgraceful event by Annie Wauneka, daughter of the last Navajo chief, Chee Dodge. After all, her father and others of her family were in that tattered line of Indians who were marched 300 miles away from their homes and into an internment camp. History books cannot match the words of a former Apache tribal chairman who tells of the day he stopped hating the white man.

The technique for the taping of these conversations was planned to be simple. There were no prepared questions, and thus there are no prepared answers on the pages ahead. We have made a point of keeping narrations true to the original tapings; only minimal editing was done so that as many voices as possible could be recorded in this book.

Two other points we would like to make. First, we were warned at the outset that it would be difficult, perhaps impossible, to talk to some of the oldtimers, that the eighty- and ninety-year-olds would not be able to tell their stories. The warning was empty. We found they wanted to talk, these oldtimers, perhaps out of some feeling of having been passed by, and in most cases they were excited about having their stories retold for the generations ahead.

Second, in crisscrossing this state to meet the people and to record their voices, we gained a new appreciation of the hardships of the pioneers—hardships eloquently described in the pages ahead. And if some are losing their faith in people today, we could only wish they had accompanied us into the homes of these Arizonans. Not only were we warmly accepted, but there was a genuine appreciation of what we were trying to accomplish with this book. And so these people, with their voices and vivid narrations, have given us a greater concept of the making of a frontier state. As you read these stories we believe you, too, will feel you have entered their homes, their lives, and you will discover, as we did, the courage, fortitude and remarkable abilities of these delightful people.

BOOK ONE
THE FIRST SETTLERS

*The three most important
Precolumbian tribal groups
in Arizona were the Hohokams,
the Anasazi and the Mogollon. . . .
The Hohokam lived in the desert
regions of southern Arizona; the
Mogollon centered in the mountain
belt; and the Anasazi inhabited
the Colorado Plateau.*

JAY J. WAGONER
IN *Early Arizona*

The Stars That Guided Her Life

STATE HIGHWAY 264 is a ribbon of asphalt cutting across the high desert of northern Arizona. It is a moving ribbon, undulating up and around, down, then up and around again until it has traversed the First, Second and Third Mesas. This is the land of the Hopi Indian tribe, the descendants of the "Ancient Ones" who built the great cliff dwellings throughout the Southwest.

Traveling east you come first to Hotevilla, the old village atop the Third Mesa. Not far down the road is Oraibi, the cliffside Hopi village which is one of the oldest continuously inhabited towns in the United States. Archaeologists have evidence dating Oraibi to A.D. 1150. At the foot of the Third Mesa is New Oraibi; it was established after a dispute between conservatives and liberals over education for their children.

In New Oraibi one of the greatest of liberal Hopi teachers makes her home. She is Elizabeth White, a remarkable woman who has been teacher to her people, artist to the world. At the time of the taping of her story she was living in a newly constructed home. The living room was still bare, furnished only with two chairs and an old, worn table. Only recently the house had been rebuilt on the foundation of the home her husband had built for her, and which she loved so much. In 1974 the home had burned down to the foundation. It was a tragic event that came not long after Elizabeth White had been badly hurt in an automobile accident. That accident had left her hands without the strength to mold clay.

"Of this period in my life," said the eighty-four-year-old woman, "I do not want to talk. I do not understand the meaning of what has happened."

She was, at first, reluctant to talk at all. So many times she had been asked to relate her life story and now she was weary. Too, she worried about the recent happenings in her life which she believed carried some mystic message for her. But once she began to talk the words and stories flowed. In the taping that follows she recalls her home at Old Oraibi where she was born in 1892.

Throughout her life milestones were commonplace: she was one of the first Oraibi girls to go to school, the first to become a teacher, the first of the teachers on the reservation to institute progressive methods. Elizabeth White was never ready to accept the easy way of life in learning or teaching; nor was she a follower. In the classroom she was a pioneer, and in her second career as a potter in her own style, she was a classic artist.

It was when she retired as a teacher at the age of sixty-five that she turned to a new career, and today her pottery graces museum shelves throughout the Southwest. Her lifetime of teaching won her many honors, including a Bronze Medal and an Honor Award from the United States Department of the Interior. In 1974 the Museum of Northern Arizona paid tribute to her with the unveiling of a bronze bust executed by the English sculptor, Una Hanbury. Two years later the Heard Museum at Phoenix invited her to a rich ceremony at which Elizabeth White was named Artist of Excellence.

A NEW WORLD FOR A HOPI GIRL

Elizabeth White looked at the tape recorder, and it was obvious she considered it no friend. This was a period in her life which she was reluctant to talk about. When we convinced her that we wanted only to hear about her earlier days, she brightened. Now there was no sag to her shoulders and she began speaking in a voice that was so soft, so dramatic that the empty room seemed to become a stage. . . .

"I grew up in the old village of Old Oraibi. I would say it was very simple, very earthy in every form because there weren't any of the things we have today. The clay and the rocks were our supplies, clay dishes to eat from and rocks to build from; everything was very earthy.

"And we knew very little about white man, though our grandparents used to tell us that he would appear some day. Then he did appear and since then everything seems to have taken place so quickly—the change, or method of living . . . the pattern of living."

You were among the first of the Hopi girls to go to school weren't you?

"No, I was not the first. There were others before me. I was, however, the only Hopi girl who ventured on my own desire and will away from the mesa. I don't know why I ventured so far. I don't know. It's just curiosity, desire, and I think it probably was all due to my father's experience with the first missionary, H. R. Voth. Our family were conservative people; we would have blended with conservative Hotevilla [another village on the Third Mesa] at the time. But father became a friend to the first missionary, a very ambitious man. He is the one that I believe has kind of stirred my curiosity within me."

Was it then that you decided to become a teacher?

"No, that stems back before that . . . while I was up on the mesa. We were very, very poor . . . very poor. And we had, I imagine, one or two-room house; eight people lived in that. And it was during the time, I believe, one evening, our house leaked because of the rain and I sat out in the dark, had my feet in the little baking pit my mother had used that evening to bake some of her corn cakes. And it was warm and I was sitting out there with a little blanket around me. I remember that.

"All of a sudden, why the stars appeared and I saw these stars while my feet were warm in that little hole while the rest of the children, yes, brothers, were in the house with the parents. And there was just a corner where the floor didn't get soaked from the leaks of the roof, and there wasn't enough room so I went out there, I remember. And that was the night that I felt, as I sat in the dark and I saw these stars . . . 'Hmmm, beautiful!' . . . and I became very curious. 'I hope some day when I grow up, maybe I'll know what those little holes, bright holes, in the sky, opening to some unknown world . . . maybe I'll understand that when I grow up.'

"And then I thought of the folks in the house and I thought . . . if we had a bigger home there'd be room for all of us and maybe it wouldn't leak like it did. And all these little childish thoughts ran through my mind: 'And with that mysterious thing up above,' I said to myself, 'when I grow up I'll understand. And when I grow up I'm going to build a big home, a very large home, big enough for my whole family, my relatives.'

"You know how a child dreams. That was my childhood dream that developed there. Little did I know that this was a mysterious dream, because when I left from there on any little thing that was of value, I always thought, 'Maybe I will think of the future connected with it.' "

Now we understand why she had placed such a premium on her big house, why she had been so desolate when it burned to the ground. Elizabeth White's mysticism had overtaken us, and for a long while we sat

In a dry wash below the high mesas Hopi youth take part in a traditional foot race.

his old photograph was taken at the finish line, a rope stretched across the sandy wash.

ARIZONA HISTORICAL SOCIETY

quietly. Then the sounds of the playing children filtered through the window, and she began to speak again.

"And when I was at Sherman [the Indian institute then at Riverside, California] I was chosen to become a house girl to a certain couple. They paid me . . . I think it was about twenty-five cents a day. And I remember going over there with this idea—it didn't leave me—I was going to save that money. And I used to tell this man when he handed me the money, I said, 'You save it for me.' And he did. So before I left Sherman he gave me all that I had saved. I came home with money, excepting I remember of buying some dishes in nearby town of Winslow for my mother. But aside from that I brought that money home."

The touch of education excited her, and she could not stay on the mesa until she had more. She went to Tuba City to learn and teach with missionaries, and then she went for an extended period at Newton, Kansas, Academy and College. She studied for three and a half years and then returned, first to teach at Tuba City and then closer to her people at Hotevilla.

"There I was with this little group up there at Hotevilla. There were forty of them, beginners in the first grade, mainly beginners. And it was my own life when I first started there. At Tuba I realized how confusing, frustrating it was to be among the people, Anglos, who didn't understand your language. There at Hotevilla I saw myself as a Hopi in my first experience in a classroom so I could understand them—these little children.

"I said to myself, 'I'm not going to let these little children suffer. We're going to understand each other.' So that is when this new idea came in: to live, to talk, to take the children on their level of interest from day to day. Never mind about the books. Never mind about anything that's a little foreign to them—that will come.

"So I just started right in that classroom with that many children— forty to sometimes forty-five children from two villages. And we just had a wonderful time from day to day right from the start. At first they didn't know what it is all about. Anything that is said in English they look at you a second time. I didn't give myself away that I was Hopi. I was there to teach them the English so therefore I would just look at them; I knew exactly what was going on inside of them. So my first few days and few weeks objects, actions, everything I could get hold of, this and that—and if there are any abstract situation or words come up, well, I would take that aside—we talked about. I did not once let them know that I am Hopi because they would expect me to tell them in Hopi. But they struggled with English because I didn't let them know.

"Oh, it must have been a month or two that I play this game with them. And I saw to it that all the first learnings were objects that they know, are familiar with around the school, with anything they bring from their homes. I visited their homes. That was one of the things I did to get acquainted with each child's parents, which was very important. It helped me to understand the children. Well, this is the way I started."

In those days Elizabeth's teaching was revolutionary, especially for a government school on a reservation. There were times when her teaching style came under attack, but she persisted until she became a model for other teachers. We asked her now if on retirement she had felt fulfillment of that dream she had had up there on the mesa as a youngster.

"I had. I was very, very happy. I debated even the last year. I had let out that I was going to resign and a mother called and said, 'Heard you are retiring. Could you stay another year?'

" 'Well, I don't know. I don't think so. Why?'

" 'I would like to send one of my little girls to school with you. I want you to start her in.'

"And I said, 'Well, there are other teachers that are competent and that she would be happy with.'

" 'But,' she said, 'my other children learned so much and we learned so much from them.'

"I always see to it that the children had something to take home from the classroom, any new word that they had learned. Well, a lot of these mothers learned, too, and you know how they take pride in their children.

"So I hesitated for a while. No, there are many, many things I wanted to go into. I wanted to do some writing and I wanted to do some more music. I didn't have too much music, but I had an inkling that I would like to compose Indian music if possible, which I tried. But then I just composed one and then let it go. It's too difficult; it's not for me. But anyway these are the things. . . ."

After retirement she had studied, she had composed Indian music, written a book and then she became, at age sixty-five, Elizabeth White the potter. How did this come about?

"Oh, yes, I had never thought about pottery until a year after I retired. That was the last thing that came to my desire, wanting to do this.

I know that a lot of pots were going on, that everybody was having a sale for it. And I thought, 'Leave it to them; that's their art.' But I became very restless and probing around during one of my idle days I walked in on the potters down at Sedona [an art colony in central Arizona]. I wanted to continue writing and I heard they were giving a course in art and writing and a few other things there down at Sedona in the Art Barn. I had intended to take up writing and instead, why as I walked in, there was Charles and Otellie Loloma [distinguished Hopi artisans] right near the door working with the clay. And they were happy to see me and threw a ball of clay in my hand.

" 'What are you doing around here?' they said. And I got stuck with the clay. That's when I first started. That's how I became a potter."

But not just a potter as she was not just a teacher. Elizabeth White put a touch of greatness to all her experiences and even in her lifetime her works have become legacies for the future.

The Unique Life-style of a Hopi

JUST OFF HIGHWAY 264 as it crosses the Third Mesa, a few hundred yards from the village of Hotevilla, lives Charles Loloma. To interview the Hopi artist we had to wait more than twenty-four hours. The day before our taping session, a hot Saturday afternoon in August, we watched Loloma the traditionalist shuffle through the dust of Hotevilla with clansmen of the Snake Society.

They were performing the Snake Dance ritual as once their fathers and grandfathers had danced. They had purged themselves of outside influences by spending a week underground in the kiva (the ceremonial pit). Now they were dancing under the hot sun, chanting and handling the snakes in what Anglos like to call the Hopi Snake Dance. For the Hopis, as Loloma was to explain the next day, the dance was more than a prayer for rain; it was a continuing struggle to retain the Hopi way of life.

When the dance was over Loloma went back into the kiva with his clansmen. The next morning he returned to his home—to the Loloma way of life, and to talk with us.

Despite his disclaimers Loloma is a unique man, unique by his own design. He is artist and poet, recorder of traditional Hopi music and dancer of the Snake Society. He is a farmer in the old manner of his people, and a philosopher, too. But Charles Loloma also is the artist whose jewelry has been displayed in New York, London and Paris; jewelry so valued that even in his time Loloma pieces are in museums and purchased not only for wearing but for collecting.

Charles Loloma is a man of contrast. There is no running water in his modest home, yet outside there is a sleek Jaguar that can outrun anything on the ground in Hopi country. On a bright morning on the Third Mesa Loloma will tend his cornfield on a dry, sandy slope (the Hopis use no

11

fertilizer, no irrigation even in an arid land); in the afternoon he will climb into a friend's plane and fly off to a distant city for an art show or to a party given in his honor.

It was in Hotevilla, where Elizabeth White once taught the little ones, that Loloma was born in 1921. It was painting, not jewelry, that won him early acclaim. He painted murals at the Golden Gate Exposition in San Francisco and at other sites under the direction of Fred Kabotie, the "father" of Hopi art. In 1945 Loloma studied and taught both at Arizona State University and the University of Arizona, holding Whitney and Rockefeller fellowships. In 1961 he helped found the Institute of American Indian Art at Santa Fe, New Mexico. One of his great honors came in 1976 when he was named a Fellow of the Collegium of Craftsmen of the American Crafts Council.

Loloma is the complete artist, working in clay, oils, silver, gold and glass. He sees nothing unusual in the contrast of his lifestyles—snake dancer one day, jeweler to the artistic and the wealthy the next. It is the Hopi way of life that interests Loloma the most, and he frets that the remaining 6,000 Hopis may lose their beautiful traditions to the lure of the white man's world and "progress."

TAKING THE BEST FROM TWO WAYS OF LIFE

If Charles Loloma was tired from participating in the Snake Dance the day before, he didn't show it. Rather, he was anxious to talk, for he enjoys his position as spokesman both for his art work and for the traditional Hopi way of life. Loloma's house and studio are simple, the beauty locked into the works of art. We sat on sheepskins placed on the floor alongside a long, low table. We began by asking Loloma to explain why he chose to stay on the mesa when he could have walked away to live in New York or Paris.

"I find myself totally as a person here because in order to participate, like in a drama, for me to be a poet, for me to make music, for me to dance, if I lived elsewhere I'd have to be some other kind of a professional. And I never would have survived; I couldn't have done this kind of art work. This is where everything is.

"This understanding comes through from our participating in the ways of the past. I'm benefiting from this way of life because I understand what this is all about . . . not all about it because it takes maturity

The religious Snake Dance of the Hopis, pictured in this early photograph, is a part of the way of life the Hopis are fighting to retain. ARIZONA HISTORICAL SOCIETY

to understand all. I don't think anybody totally understands. Maybe you understand just enough of it, but if you really try to understand then you have a richer life.

"When it comes to [Hopi] philosophy you cannot really interpret a true philosophy because lots of things are discussed through our songs and through our ceremonial situations. This is where the true philosophy is coming from. Sometimes there's no way of reaching the young people because in order for me to reach them they'd have to participate in the songs and ceremonials; this is the only way that you will come to know. You have to experience some of these things to realize what this way— this Hopi way—of life is all about.

"Some of the people still care, but when they don't care they don't get the full understanding from what they have participated in. You've seen that with other people. Lots of people that I know, good friends of mine, have gone through various universities and they never come out doing anything better. They keep coming around, trying to search for more. All through their life they're searching and they probably will keep searching the rest of their life."

Loloma pushed back from the low table, brushed hair from his forehead and continued . . .

"Well, I think any way of life is a struggle because it is an effort and because of the way we are brought up, or at least the younger generations are being brought up. It seems like there is no more physical philosophy that exists among the Hopi people. At one time the younger people weren't even allowed to sleep before the sun came up. It was like this: Everybody wakes up at night and you run—that's part of your duties. The young ones run so many miles and come back and take a bath at some springs. Then the body is kept cool, and as a result you are immune, and you don't need any medicine, no stimuli of any kind to keep you going through the day because your body is such that you never feel sleepy at all.

"That is the way it was. Today is it different with much of the younger generation. The young people would rather have a Honda or Yamaha to get their thrills. Some of them don't get up until way late in the day. They're up practically all night just meandering around, wandering around. And so this philosophy, this physical philosophy, that existed at one point is not there much any more. Oh, they have a race now every year, but they're not probably as fast runners as in the older days. In the older days it was a completely different thing.

"Of course, I believe our age group was misled by the Christian influence, such as in my father's time when there was a split of thought of Christianity versus Indian understanding. I think lots of our people who took the route of Christianity, and other Indian people throughout the United States, have lost a great deal and they can't, at this point, even identify themselves as Indians. Lots of the Indian groups are in that situation, and it's a pretty sad thing. Out here our past is still quite alive, but even so there is conflict—the same type that grew when the Bureau of Indian Affairs got in on it. At this point so many of our young people are depending on government jobs for salaries and things like that, they cannot say very much against the BIA. When you take those salaries I think you are taking something you really don't believe in, but you just go along with this particular type of thing.

"Some Indians have turned dead around and couldn't care less that they take these things. To them life doesn't mean any longer what it means to us. But I think, too, that some of the younger Indians are beginning to be aware of what is happening around them. They all of a sudden woke up to the facts: Where are we? Who are we? And what is our purpose here?

"What is the Hopi purpose? Well, the purpose of being here is to survive and to observe what is beautiful. And the purpose is to also enjoy the deeper concepts of the way of life—like raising corn and to participate in the drama of dancing. Dancing is not only for rain, it is part of our way of life, part of the drama of our life which to me is the purpose of any group of people who understand or want to have a direction. It's because the life must go on and this is really the purpose.

"What is really here? I think that is what many of the young are asking, but nobody can really explain. It is difficult because we are speaking today in two different languages. Lots of this cannot be interpreted into white society because there are things, words and thoughts that cannot be understood in the deeper sense the way they should. Lots of this must come through in songs and dance forms, lots of it through many, many other ways of our traditions.

"The purpose . . . this is what I'm saying. . . . the purpose is present. How shall I put it? Well, what I'm saying is that everything, everything about life is present within the ceremonial because it discusses the whole way of life. Everything is there. There is nothing that we don't have. I believe in our way of life. I think it works for us. It is not just because of our ceremonial things but because of the effort that must be made to retain our way of life. It's an effort to make something good and I think this is the valuable thing to preach."

Loloma began to weave art into the discussion. He, like so many other artisans, is upset over the flood of "tourist art" and the direction of much of Indian art.

"It has gone very stereotyped which is too bad. What can be done about it? I think the artists should concentrate on the depth and go back to the roots of everything—understand that part of it, grow up a little more. Some of the younger artists are doing good things because of their searching for a way of life. In their search they are suddenly beginning to appreciate the older ways. They see there is a finer way that other people are living. Some of them are turning back to the old ways.

"And some of the young people we can get into our ceremonials, our traditions; some we can't. I imagine that in a lot of cases they're too close to it. They couldn't appreciate it because they've not come to the maturing point of appreciating anything. We all grow on maturity levels.

"The arts are a Hopi tradition. All Hopis are exposed to the arts because ceremonial things are an art form. I think any life is an art, any life-style is an art form. Certainly the Anglo way of life can be an art form, too—I mean like good sculptures, good architecture, you know, very fine creative ways of doing things."

We asked Loloma whether he felt he could continue to live the Hopi way and still take those luxuries he does from the white man's world. Can old rituals and driving a Jaguar go together?

"Well, I think there is a right way to having the nicest things you can afford. This is what I can afford. Luxuries exist in everything, and it's the person who has imagination and is not lazy to use it who can have luxuries. You are determined to get the finest no matter what it is. If it was the old way of doing things I would probably want something really great, not necessarily things that you own, but maybe a nice field, or something that is really great."

Loloma concluded with a sarcastic shot:

"And it's what I tell other people about art: It must not be difficult because even the Indians can do it."

The Daughter of the Last Navajo Chief

ANNIE DODGE WAUNEKA lives out on the reservation, away from the cities and towns. Her home is off the highway that joins State 264 to Interstate 40. Perhaps there is no more than twenty minutes of driving separating her from the rush of cars and trucks on the freeway, but Annie Wauneka, daughter of the last Navajo tribal chief, is years away from them.

She is a stunning woman and large—both tall and broad. Her skin is fair, her gray hair gathered at the back in traditional Navajo style. Her dress is Navajo, worn proudly even when she comes before groups of whites. When she walks into a room she exudes strength and self-confidence; those traits carried her to leadership among her people, the *Diné*. She learned leadership from her father, and she became the first woman elected to the Navajo Tribal Council.

We first heard the rustle of her long, gathered dress as she entered the room for the taping session. She smiled softly and extended a hand. And as she stood there it was obvious that she would be in command, not only of this taping session, but in command of any situation. It is that strength that carried her through a difficult family situation during childhood, that helped her to care for the sick and needy through a lifetime and to push and cajole her people to accept higher standards of living.

Those who have worked with Annie Wauneka in the Public Health Service or on the Navajo Tribal Council describe her as a very remarkable person. Many honors have come to her through the years; many more will come as she steps down from leadership as she predicted in this interview she would do soon.

Throughout the taping Annie spoke reverentially of her father, referring to him always as "Mr. Dodge." It was in 1863–64 that Colonel Kit

Carson began his push to round up the Navajos and take them to an internment camp at Bosque Redondo, New Mexico. That was to become known as the Long Walk. When she remembered the days of the Long Walk, there was anger in her voice, even as softly as she spoke.

Strangely the interview got off to a slow start. We asked a question and instead of replying, Mrs. Wauneka said, "An' what else?" We asked another question and again she asked, "An' what else?" After still another exchange without an answer, we decided to sit back and listen, and let Annie Wauneka begin at the beginning. . . .

THE TIME OF THE LONG WALK

Annie Wauneka rested in the chair and began to turn her mind back. Minutes passed until her lips parted in a small smile and she began her story . . .

"As I understan' the story that is told about my father, he was born at the old Fort Defiance which is all modernized now. I understan' he was born there durin' the difficulties of tryin' to get the government an' the Navajo people to understan' the problems . . . for the Navajos to understan' what the government intended to do with the Indian tribes. All this time the Navajos were havin' troubles with the people comin' through the country. The Navajos tried to keep these intruders away an', of course, that created all kinds of trouble an' fightin', an' killin', an' burnin' each other's property up. I don't think the Navajos ever realized there is this group of people that are comin' about to create a government.

"If they [the whites] done it a little better than what they've done in those days, maybe things would have been better. But this was with force that was done. You know, Navajos try to get themselves free like they have always been before. Of course, they had enemies before . . . with Utes an' some other Indian tribes. Especially with Utes we had problems because of the land an' property an' what have you. Jealousy, I imagine. An' then here comes these white people want to get hold of the Navajos or settle them, or whatever way it was. So the best they can do is round up the Navajos an' get them somewhere where they won't be troublesome. An' they did, partially at least.

"An' Mr. Dodge was born February 22, 1860, I think it was. An' when he was four years old an' they [the Navajos] were bein' treated rudely: the food was taken away from them, which was livestock; they had some farm, raisin' corn an' what have you. It was all destroyed. So maybe it was to kill them off with starvation, whatever the plan was. The only group that they know that has food was the Hopis. So a lot of Navajos had gone to the Hopis to get whatever they could eat from the Hopis, which was corn meal, peaches, or whatever they had. Some of them return an' some of them never returned.

"So his mother an' his aunt an' some very close relatives, as I understan', were starvin' an', of course, they had to have some food for the only baby they had was this little boy. This is Chee Dodge. They call him Chee because he was sort of very light color an' they called him Chee. So they had to have some food for him. So the mother advised the other two sisters that she is goin' into the Hopi country to get some food, to ask that the Hopis give them some food so the boy can have some food. An' she took off just a little ways an' the two sisters caught up with her an' said, 'Now, look, you cannot take the little boy,' because he was sittin' on his mother's back.

"The two sisters says, 'No, you cannot take the little boy.' But the sisters already knew that she'll never return an' encouraged her not to take the boy. Another advice was that if 'you happen to get some food, you'll be carryin' it on your back an' where you goin' to put the little fellow?' So they took the boy off her back an' told her that they'd keep him until she returns. So off she went an' they kept waitin' for her. She never returned. . . ."

Annie Wauneka's voice had trailed off. She began again by relating the events of the Long Walk.

"Well, the Navajos are asked to come in to Fort Defiance, that they'd be taken care of, you know. Just voluntarily come in; if they don't they'd be destroyed . . . they were troublesome an' so forth. An' so there was a terrific war that was goin' on between the Navajos an' these intruders. An' the Navajos knew their way around in all these big mountains an' washes, an' Canyon de Chelly, an' Navajo Mountain; they were pretty rough to get at. So the army decided to use the Utes; they did all the fightin' by bow an' arrow. But the army came forth with ammunition an' delivered it to the Utes to kill off all the Navajos. The Navajos gave the Utes trouble, an' that didn't satisfy the army so they brought in the Comanches an' also gave them ammunition to get all the Navajos they can get.

"My father never mentioned the Zuñis, but he mentioned these two tribes, the Utes an' the Comanches. An' he said, 'Boy, did they go to town. Everyone kill all the Navajos they possibly can.' "

After the army victories in Canyon de Chelly and elsewhere, the Navajos were rounded up at Fort Defiance.

"So these two ladies [the sisters of Chee Dodge's mother] decided to go to Fort Defiance. So they came in, were accepted an' began to be part of the band, were fed until they were ready to be moved to Fort Sumner, New Mexico, that they have called it as Bosque Redondo. So my father was part of the Long Walk when he was four years old. He was on this wagon, on this ox-driven wagon, an' he remembers just which direction they went because he was a little one that was on the wagon. The aunts an' some old people—there was quite a number of Navajos that marches —an' remained at Fort Sumner, until he was eight years old. Four years old over there, so it made him eight years old. Of course, they had a terrible price to pay at Fort Sumner, too—no shelter, no food, no water, no sanitation . . . no nothin'.

"He used to tell me, Mr. Dodge, that the old ones, the weak ones, the sick ones that were tryin' to participate in the march, they was just destroyed, an' sometimes just fell over an' died. The same thing took place over at Fort Sumner. People were sick, hungry an' cold, an' disease. An' they were lonesome.

"I remember, Mr. Dodge used to tell me that before they went to Sumner a large group of Navajos—medicine men—would get together an' they used to advise an' sing. I guess probably that was their last enjoyment. An' there, he used to say, the leaders in those days tried to encourage the young men, the young Navajo men, to stop their savage type of attack. An' they wouldn't do it. So they would yell through into the night, sayin' that they're ready to attack another group of people, these intruders.

"An' the Navajo leaders would just advise them, 'Don't do that.' They warned that the white man would take all the Navajo away. In the next year or two, they would say, all you will find is the tracks of coyotes on this particular area. An' Mr. Dodge used to say that did happen because everybody was shipped away, an' he said there was really empty space for about four years. My father used to say, 'Sure enough there was nothin' but coyotes through that country for about four years.' "

She related the return of the Navajos to their land after the signing of the Peace Treaty of 1868—"an' everybody was happy, no matter how hungry, how poor, whatever they was without, shoes, or whatever." *Then*

The Long Walk of 1864 when Navajos were marched some 300 miles to internment at Bosque Redondo in New Mexico is vividly portrayed in these two photographs. The mother and child were posed just before they were taken from Canyon de Chelly and the young child alone sat for the camera in the camp at Bosque Redondo. The Treaty of 1868 permitted the Navajos to return to their homes in the Arizona Territory. ARIZONA HISTORICAL SOCIETY

Annie began to narrate how Chee, adopted "by a person by name of Henry Dodge," began, even as a little boy, to be used as a messenger. The young boy learned English and Spanish, and with his knowledge of Navajo he soon became an interpreter, a go-between for the Navajos and the government agents.

"So the more he was closer to those agents, those administrators, the more he learned, more than all the Navajos did. They wanted to be away; they don't want to be any closer. They wanted to get back to their homes, but he say he didn't. He remained close to them, an' so I guess he was taught how to do things. He was used as an interpreter most of the time between the Navajos an' the government. So finally, he said, they used to trust him. He took care of their belongin's, you know, took care of their homes an' their papers an' what have you. They trusted him very much, an' they decided to put him in school at Menaul in Albuquerque. He was one of the students there for about four months, an' that's why he used to accuse us, you know, those of us that went to school. He asks us questions; we don't answer. He says, 'What did you go to school for? I went to school for four months in Menaul, an' I've learned more than you folks.'

"An' he said, 'I would have stayed in school if the Navajos just left me alone. But the Navajos say, 'We want that little Chee back 'cause he's the only guy that can deliver the message, an' we can trust his views an' his advice and his interpretation.' So he was called to the camp to be interpreter 'cause he's the only one who can deliver the two messages [in English and Navajo] an' three with the Mexican. So really when you think about it, he's purely a made leader. He became a chief 'cause these old Navajos remember just where he came from an' what family he was born. He was born from a really respected family, but they were killed out. So he was all that was left except his aunts were still out somewhere; he did reunite with them later. His father, as he used to tell us, was Juan Ignacio; the Apache scouts killed him just before they went to Fort Sumner, when Chee Dodge was a little baby. I guess Mr. Dodge had a Mexican father, very respected leader. This Mexican became adopted by the Navajos. They trusted him, an' he became one of their clan. No question about him; he was married to the Navajos. An' he was killed, an' this was the only boy that was his.

"An' that's where the leadership came on for Mr. Dodge, an' he was a chief all his life up to his death."

Annie Wauneka changed subjects and began to tell us about her own past. She told us how she had been taken from her real mother.

"Mr. Dodge was very fond of his other wife, Nonabah. She was very attractive an' a very smart woman. So my mother had to be pushed aside with an understandin' that 'whenever you deliver a child, I must pick this child up . . . with that understandin'.' That's my mother's story. So she said, 'When you were born an' about eight months old, here comes along Mr. Dodge an' says, "We're ready to pick up the baby." ' So there I go with a new family. My mother, I guess, have the very traditional home. I was born in a hogan, as I understan'. They were really traditional . . . pure dirt hogan life. But over here to my new home, they had a house, a stone house with wooden floor, nice stoves an' another big house with four bedroom an' kitchen. They're still standin'. An' I guess I went into a real modern, nice home—that's to be compared to the rest of the Navajos."

Annie Wauneka attended government schools, and at an early age was drawn into what would become a lifelong career of helping her people.

"So in 1918, or 1916, or somewhere in there, I was placed at Fort Defiance BIA school an' that terrible epidemic hit the whole country. Flu. An' I remember that little wooden hospital there at Fort Defiance, an' there were lot and lot of sick students. At first, one or two died; pretty soon they're just dyin' off like flies, an' I wonder what the devil is goin' on. I got sick myself, but not too much. There was a nurse there; she was the only nurse there an' she needed help. An' they used to put lanterns throughout the hall in the hospital. It wasn't a very big hospital; it was small an' before lights, you know, they use kerosene lanterns. I guess electricity wasn't as much as it should be then.

"So I was the only little helper around, an' I used to clean those lanterns for her. She would call me an' say, 'Will you wash these lanterns an' make them bright an' shiny? We'll place them in the hospital.' An' that was my job. An' I would see them sick before, just come into the hospital, an' some them just comin' an' dyin' right off the chair. They hemorrhaged, every one of them hemorrhaged, an' they were sick about a day or two; they were gone the next day. An' the hospital was packed an' the nurse, she says, 'Will you give water to the sick? Will you give food to the sick?' An' I would give food to these sick an' she said, 'Feed them,' an' I tried to feed them. It was terrible; they hemorrhaged.

"An' I remember, they used to put these bodies away, you know, for somebody to dress them. Even that they couldn't do. They'd just wrap them up in a sheet an' just pile them on top of each other . . . just pile them. An' corpses was sittin' in the hall, I remember it very clearly. An' there were horse-driven wagons, an' they used to just pile them up like a bunch of wood an' haul them away."

Annie noted that Chee Dodge's other children first were sent to Catholic schools. When trachoma broke out Annie was sent to St. Michael's Mission School, and then her father decided that she would be sent with her sister, Mary, to the Albuquerque Indian School.

"So we were hauled to Gallup in some big wagons, an' Mary was told to take care of her little sister. So we got on the train an' went on headin' for Albuquerque. It was just about evenin' when we got to Laguna an' Laguna children was to come on the train. An' we're all lookin' out of the window; everythin' was new. I was watchin' those Pueblos comin' on to the train; an' peoples is runnin' around me, you know, givin' the warnin', an' I didn't know what it was. I don't think any of us did. We just sat there lookin' through the window an' here, I guess, there was a train comin'. Somethin' happened to this train, an' we were asked to run just as far as we can into the cabins. So I was runnin', too, an' heard this great big locomotive. The head was plowed into the back of our train, derailed some of it, an' all of us just fell on top of each other. Some jumped from the windows an' broke their hips an' their arms an' all that. We just fell on top of each other in this big train.

"So we're asked to leave the train; so we got out. We sat up there under a tree. I didn't have any friends. Of course, my sister is there, an' the young, grown girls they like to get away. So I was asked to take care of the suitcases, an' I sat there under one big tree all night long until next mornin', until they fixed the train an' we went into Albuquerque the next day. So then came the Albuquerque Indian School, an' I went on until I'm in the eleventh grade.

"An' then, just as usual, like all other Navajos, my aunt, the one that raised me, says, 'Bring her back. She's got to herd sheep. She's got to do this; I'm all by myself.' So I had to. Every time I come home durin' the summer vacation all I did was sheepherdin'. Every time I come home there'd be a batch of sheep sittin'. The next mornin' I had to get goin'. Between my aunt an' my father they owned hundreds of head of sheep. So I was actually a family sheepherder, is what my brother, Tom Dodge, says, 'Oh, here's our family sheepherder.' "

Annie never got back to school and soon she married George Wauneka.

Her father had his sheep at Crystal, New Mexico, and he moved his cattle to Tanner Springs, the area where Annie still lives. The house was built in 1929. Soon Annie began to go with her father to attend meetings.

"He'd come to us an' say, 'I want you to go to the meetin' with me' meanin' George an' myself. There was a huge meetin' at Klagetoh. They had no chapter house, nothin'; it was under a big tree. He would be talkin' to these people just what the problems are an' he was a beautiful speaker. Navajos understood him; they respected him. An' Navajos would come up, 'Here's Mr. Dodge—meanin' the interpreter is comin', our great leader is comin'.' All the while he was speakin' an' they feel the way he jokes, the way he opens the meetin's. It's marvelous how he did it. So I just sit there watchin' him, you know, watched these people how they react to all of this. Just watched him how he releases the message, communication from the government to the Navajo people. An' he advises the Navajo people what to do an' what not to do, an' he talk about livestock improvement—he was so much for livestock improvement. He told them to get better rams, better bulls, better horses through education. He encouraged the Navajos to send their children to school.

"An' I remember he'd talk about the little community school at Klagetoh. He says, 'There's goin' to be a school built here; the government is goin' to build a school here for you.' Everybody rave [remembering the excitement, Annie clapped her hands]. There wasn't even a thing at Klagetoh then. An' Wide Ruins, Tuba, you know, all over he would just make tremendous reports. Just makin' reports an' then there was no Tribal Council. An' I would ask him, 'Why do you do these things, Daddy?'

" 'Well,' he says, 'these Navajos needs attention. They need care. They need to be educated. Now you go out to those hogans, see what you see.'

"I remember him sayin' that the over-grazin' by livestock was a tremendous battle he had to go through; an' when he talk to the Navajo people about it, he used to always relate back to the Long Walk. He would say, 'Now look, they round up an' took us to Bosque Redondo where we were supposed to be cleaned up an' killed by Comanches an' the youths. Somehow, somewhere the white people, the white government, decided that the Navajos are goin' to be destroyed. So the white man came in such a way an' took us to Fort Sumner, but he save our lives although we had hardship. It's the white man that took upon himself to save the Navajos.

" 'Now when we came back we had nothin' in our hands, came back to nothin'. The government gave us two ewe sheep to each family that returned from Bosque Redondo to make a livelihood, an' we were so successful in raisin' sheep that in a few years we had thousands and thousands of head of sheep, includin' myself. What did we do? We overgrazed our lands. No more feed, forage; no more water. Dust. Now the government comes back an' says save your land. Here is the white man again savin' the land for us, so let's get rid of the sheep.'

"An' I would think about what he said. When we go home, I says, 'Why did you say this thing? Most of them was opposin' you, but you said this. Why?'

"He says, 'That's the way it is, an' it's goin' be that whether they like it or not.'

"An' I would say, 'Are you part of the whole gang?'

"He says, 'I'm the Chief. I'm supposed to tell these Navajo people, my people, what to expect.'

" 'Do you think the white man is right?'

"He says, 'They're usually right.'

"I disagreed with him at times and he says, 'Now, listen, you sit down here. You're supposed to have learned how to listen. Don't be afraid to get up to speak on behalf of the Navajo people when that white person is not sayin' the right thing. You get up there an' say when he is sayin' the right thing.' "

Soon Annie Dodge Wauneka was standing up to speak for her people. She began as an interpreter and in that vein she got into the center of a dispute when a government agent came to Klagetoh to reduce the stock and ease the problem of overgrazing.

"I remember one time there was a big crowd at the horse pen. There was a poor old Navajo woman with a grandchild . . . had a horse, a palomino horse, real nice one with a colt. An' this poor old lady for whatever reason she was left out in gettin' a grazin' permit. You see, a lot of them didn't get their grazin' permit. An' here she brings this horse to the district supervisor, an' there I stood by the fence. She did everythin' she can to keep that one horse. She said, 'Could I keep that one horse? It's all I have. I drag in wood with that horse. I go to the store with that horse.'

"She did, she exhausted every effort, but what does the supervisor do? 'You got no business keepin' that horse, old lady.' He throws it into the pen for sale.

"That's when I got so mad. I used to be a good roper, so I went to the corral an' roped that palomino an' I got it out of the corral. An' there was the district supervisor just writin' away whose horse is this, you know . . . an' I give it back to the lady. An' I says, 'you take it home.'

"Just as she was startin' to pull that horse out, the man, I guess, was told what I've done, an' this white man come an' try to get the horse back. So both of us were holdin' the rope. He was holdin' one end, I was holdin' the other end, an' the poor old lady was standin' between us an' she says, 'Please let me have that horse.'

"So I was closer to the horse than him, so all of a sudden I jerk this rope out of his hand, an' I was whippin' the horse until it start runnin'. I said, 'O.K., gentleman, go get that horse.' And did we argue in front of those people. Everybody was on my side. That was a big battle for me there that one day. I said, 'That's just a little privilege for this poor old soul. Let her have that horse as long as she lives. She's not goin' to last very long.'

"That was back in 1945 or somethin' in that area. An' here she just died last winter. Here I says, 'She won't last very long. Let her have what she needs.' An' here she just died . . . 110 years old. That old lady! Amen."

Chee Dodge took ill with pneumonia, and the family was called to-gether. Annie related the day.

"We went up to see him. He seemed to be all right, but he says, 'I don't think I'll live very long.' An' he says, 'I want you to know that somebody has to carry on this leadership.' An' I just stand there lookin' at him. I thought he's not goin' to die.

"He says, 'It won't be long from now. Somebody has to take up the leadership.' The way he explains is, 'A rope or string that has been pulled real straight an' up an' high is the way this actual nation is. Don't let this rope drop to the ground. An' somebody sees it droppin' to the ground, somebody pick it up an' stretch it again.' "

It was Annie who picked up the rope. Mr. Dodge died January 7, 1948, the day he was supposed to have been inaugurated as Tribal vice-chairman [in 1938 the Navajo Tribal Council system with elections had been instituted]. Annie returned to her home and kept working with the tribal chapter at Klagetoh. She began to think about running for the Navajo Tribal Council.

"When the time came around I went to some Navajo women and medicine men. 'What do you think? Do you think I should run for Tribal Council?' They said, 'Sure, we're goin' to run you, we're goin' to run you.' An', of course, the elders say by tradition woman's supposed to stay home.

So some of the medicine men said, 'You stay home. You need to do your home chores. You got children to take care of.' An' the Navajo women would say, 'You really want to run?'

"I says, 'Sure, I'll run. If I don't do no good, it's only four years anyway.' I say this not knowin' that I would stay this long [she was still on the council at the time of this interview in 1976]. There's two men oppose me the first year; I beat both of them. The second term they had my husband against me. I did everythin' I can to get George out of the way, but he wouldn't. So he an' I, we oppose. It kind of bothered me. I thought he might beat me, but he had only eighteen votes against three hundred-some."

In the early 1950s the government sent out doctors to make a survey of illness on the reservation. First they found widespread hepatitis and then tuberculosis. They reported that tuberculosis was rampant, and the Congress appropriated the funds to fight the disease. Dr. Kirt Deuschele went to the Navajo Tribal Council and asked for help in the battle. The councilmen turned to their only woman member; Annie was voted into the job.

"I wasn't even asked my opinion. The vote went an' I was voted into the job. Well, I didn't know what TB was an' then, of course, I had to go back to my husband an' tell him what the council wanted me to do. 'Oh,' he said, 'nothin' doin'. You ain't goin' to work with tuberculosis. You're goin' to bring the disease home. We'll catch it, an' what are you goin' to do? Here we are livin' healthy, an' you're goin' to bring this disease.' He says, 'You stay off of that.'

"I agreed with him in certain ways, but I thought, 'Uh, uh, I've been voted in.' So I talk with Dr. Kirt Deuschele as to how I don't know nothin' about tuberculosis. I don't want to touch that thing until I know what it's all about."

For three months she studied under Dr. Deuschele. She talked with the tubercular patients at Fort Defiance.

"Instead of attendin' the council sessions, where was I? Runnin' around all over. Well, I had to sit by those Navajos in those sanitariums. I would announce what tuberculosis is, gave them the picture. I don't know if they were misinformed that this was a disease that the white man discovered, but it spread so badly they blamed the white people. I told them, 'No, this was a world disease; everybody has this disease.'

"An' they were away from home so I did all I can to convince them that they must stay, maybe six months, maybe two years. So my next job was to have everyone, one at a time, come down with me to the laboratory an' see their X-ray, see how bad they had this disease. So they understood, too, the people, an' many of them decided to stay."

After Annie reported back to the council she went on the radio every day, talking to mothers about tuberculosis and other diseases.

"I was on the radio every day talkin' about certain diseases, how to treat it, how to diagnose the symptoms. I used to go to squaw dances an' examine just where they haulin' their water from. If they were haulin' it from a pond I says, 'Throw that out. Get a windmill or some pump 'cause you're feedin' human bein's; you're not feedin' dogs.'

"I did a terrific health education. In the hogan they didn't have any dish cupboard; they just put dishes on the floor. I used to bring them orange crates for the dishes. An' bringin' soap, too, as though I was advertisin' this commercial, but I wasn't. I went out there an' told them how to wash dishes. An' I would inspect their water barrel outside, their water buckets an' tell them to put their dishes in the orange crates and cover with a cloth . . . an' so forth. I'd take their sack of flour off the floor an' used to bring around big cans, too. I'd say, 'Throw your ingredients in these cans; your sugar, your flour. Put them in the cans; they're safe.'

"Flies, that was another big problem. I told them, 'Put your screen doors on, your screen windows.'

"So I came back to the council after I found out what the problems were about, about the livin' conditions. I asked them for some money to have the Navajo hogans have a wooden floor 'cause dirt floor can create all kinds of problems, especially tuberculosis. I guess I asked for too much money; they turned me down. They said, 'You don't know what you're talkin' about. They'll just use it where they want it; they don't know anythin'.'

"I was so mad at my council members. So I went to the council members' relatives that were in the sanitariums. I went all the way around. So the next time they were meetin' and I had the floor, I says, 'Mr. So-an'-so, you have your nephews, wife, or so, at the sanitarium. They elected you. Now you put in some money for wooden floors. That's all I'm askin' for is wooden floors, screened windows.' I asked for lesser money this time; that passed.

"To this day look at those little boxes you see on the reservation; they go for more windows than just one little tight house. So we're far better ahead than we ever were before, but we still need to do a lot. There's still some families back there that are in destitutions. They still have to be taken care of. Well, part of it is their own fault.

"Then this old darn alcoholism shows up. Navajos listen beautifully before those days. I used to come to the chapter house when I hear of a meetin'. I don't care where it is; I spent my nights any place. They were good people. They offer you tea an' bread, if that's all they had."

Annie Wauneka fought to get the tubercular Navajos into the sanitoria for treatment. And she didn't care who stood in her way, even if it was a revered medicine man.

"I even went into an argument with one medicine man over tuberculosis way out at Rock Point on the reservations. I was lookin' for a patient that ran away from Fort Stanton sanitarium. So I went over there, an' there was a cattle sale that was goin' on at the tradin' post; an' I asked for this person. They say, 'She's out there.' So I went around the corral again. There she was standin' there so I call her aside an' I talk to her; an' here's this old big medicine man comin' up to me.

"He says, 'This is my granddaughter.'

"I says, 'Yes, I realize it's your granddaughter. She is sick.'

"An' he says, 'You made her sick.'

"I said, 'No, I didn't.' So I asked for his opinion. I said, 'What do you want us to do—treat your granddaughter in a hospital, or where should she be treated?'

"He says, 'I could treat this one.'

"I said, 'With what?'

"So he says, 'I know how to cure tuberculosis.'

"I says, 'Wonderful, I've been lookin' for a Navajo that knows how to cure tuberculosis all these years.' I says, 'You're here; why were you hidin'?'

"And all these people come around, an' they were 100 percent for him. Every time he speaks against me they roared an' clapped. So I didn't argue with him.

"He says, 'You're takin' these Navajos away to die, aren't you?'

"I says, 'No, I'm tryin' to give them treatment.'

"He says, 'Who is payin' you for doin' this?'

"I says, 'You. Navajo tribe is payin' me.'

"He says, 'I'm payin' you, an' then you take these people away to die?'

"I says, 'No. There's nobody's carin' for them. They're just sick here like your granddaughter. Who's carin' for your granddaughter right now?'

"An' he says, 'I do.'

"I said, 'In what way? Sure, you're her grandfather, but what are you doin' for her?'

"Then he says, 'What are you doin' for her?'

"I said, 'I'm here to get her back to the better treatment so she can be taken care of every day by the hour.'

"An' he says, 'No, you're not doin' that.'

" 'Yes, I am doin' that through other people.' There were Public Health nurses with me. I never went without Public Health nurses 'cause we have to have the record.

"So I said, 'Okay, here's the man that know how to treat tuberculosis.' I said, 'How wonderful, Grandpa, I wish you would come a long, long time ago.' I said, 'How do you treat tuberculosis?'

" 'Well,' he says, 'it has to be seen.'

"I said, 'Okay, that's wonderful. What do we do next? What medicine?'

"He says, 'This piñon pitch mixed with grease, sagebrush . . . medicine, boil bucketful to have them bathe in.'

"I said, 'Is that all?'

" 'No, get them sweat bath.'

"I says, 'That sounds pretty good. How about the medicine?'

"He says, 'Well, this piñon pitch or gum . . .'

"I says, 'How do you use it?'

"He says, 'Warm it up an' let 'em swallow it an' take them into a sweat bath.'

"I says, 'Doesn't this thing kick up in your throat?'

"He says, 'No, as long as you keep them warm, it goes down.'

"I says, 'Fine, then what?'

" 'That's about all.'

"I said, 'Oh.' So I told him the treatment in the white man's way. I said, 'They get good food, good beds, clean linen, clean this an' clean that. Let 'em sleep an' rest. How about you?'

"He says, 'They don't have to do that.'

"I says, 'Are you ready to go up against the competition?'

"He says, 'Yes.'

"I says, 'Fine. I'm with you today.' I says, 'I'm goin' to get rid of this Public Health nurse.' I said, 'I'm tired of her. I have to interpret for her. I have to chew her words.' I said, 'We'll get rid of them.'

"So I set up a date ten days. I said, 'You just get all the medicine that pertains to curin' tuberculosis, diarrhea, sores, what have you. Line them up. I'll come back an' pick you up with all these medicines an' your paraphernalia. An' then at Fort Defiance there'll be Dr. Kirt Deuschele, there'll be the other doctors, there'll be nurses. You know what they'll have? They'll have their needles full of medicine. They'll have their knives ready to cut people. You don't cut people. You're the best. They'll have theirs, an' you'll have ours. I'll be your interpreter. They can interpret for themselves.'

"He said, 'Yes.'

"I says, 'Fine. Don't forget it's goin' to be ten days. I'll be here about a day before to pick up all the things. Be ready.' I says, 'Let's beat those old darn doctors. I'm tired of them.'

"He says, 'Fine.'

"So we both agreed. Ready to go. An' I said, 'The government will have to make out a contract. These people have their contracts workin' on TB. They get lots of money for treatin' TB. This contract we can cancel, an' we'll contract with you. You're goin' to get the government money, an' you're goin' to have to treat this people right. Like these sweat houses . . . one is not goin' to do 'cause we have 2,000 patients in these sanitoriums. I'll see to it that a whole batch of them come through the sweat house. An' I think we'll have about . . . I don't know how many, maybe two dozens of sweat houses. An' you're goin' to have great big bottles of sterile peach gum.'

"An' I says, 'Your equipment has to be sterilized, Grandpa. You just cannot have it any other way—later on let your grandchildren play with it.'

"Well, he thinks along. He says, 'I could do it.'

"I says, 'Yes, you could do it. We could do it. I'll work for you. You want a woman to work?'

"He says, 'Uh, uh. There's a woman there? Nonsense! I don't need you to be sent to me.'

" 'Why somebody's got to cook a meal. This kind of food they eat in the sanitarium, what do you think they should eat?'

" 'Oh, just a piece of slapjack an' coffee.'

"I said, 'Uh, uh, Grandpa, you're goin' to get a contract. It's goin' to ask for better food, better nutrition. What are you goin' to do? You got to have a woman to work for you, to run the kitchen.'

"I guess I poured so much on him that he didn't know how to figure it out. I didn't know I had friends in this crowd. An' every time he spoke, people roared. Every time I spoke they all look at me so [Annie screwed up her face]. An' then two old ladies came forth. They says, 'Can we say somethin'?'

"I says, 'Good. Go ahead.'

"An' these two ladies say, 'You, Spider Wife, Medicine Man, you're nothin' but an alcoholic. We see you drunk most of the time. What are you goin' to do about that?'

"I says, 'Grandpa, do you drink liquor?'

"He looked at me an' he says, 'Everybody drinks.'

"I says, 'You. I'm talkin' about you. Here we're ready to agree to give you a contract. You're goin' to have to agree to quit drinkin', Grandpa, 'cause some of these will be your patients. Here's your granddaughter. You goin' to treat her? What if you get drunk on me? What do I do?'

"He just stood there an' he says, 'Oh, we'll get that.'

"I said, 'Okay, I'm goin' to be here. Now I want you to remember.' So I wrote a piece of letter. I put a date on it. I gave it to him. 'I'll be back a day before to take you to Fort Defiance. Let's win our battle.'

"So with that he left, an' people just jammed around him. An' I guess they were praisin' him that he could stand up against me an' so forth. I was talkin' to the Public Health nurse. I says, 'We can't take Elizabeth right now 'cause of this misunderstandin' with the medicine man. So we just come back next week to see if we can get hold of his granddaughter— her name was Elizabeth. Let's not bother right now 'cause of the commotion that's goin' on.'

"So while we were talkin' about that, here comes the old Grandpa again. I said, 'Look, here he comes.'

"So he comes over here, an' he looks at me an' he says, 'I want to tell you I cannot treat tuberculosis. I'm sorry I commit myself.'

"An' I got hold of his hand an' said, 'Grandpa, you can't deny that now. You an' I have made an agreement.'

" 'Well,' he says, 'I'm beginnin' to feel that I'm not competent in the treatment of tuberculosis.' He says, 'I do agree that there's a serious problem.'

"I says, 'Why did you tell me that I'm takin' these people away to die? An' here you just sit there an' watch these people die right in your yard. I'm the one that's tryin' to save them. Then you and your medicine bag an' everythin', just sit there an' let Elizabeth die. Is that your decision now?'

"He said, 'No, take her back to the sanitarium.'

" 'Well,' I said, 'Grandpa, you call these people back. Let's have another big meetin'. Make that announcement.'

"So his big voice says, 'Come on over here. Round up the gang. We're goin' to talk about some more disease.'

"So most of the people came back. I said, 'Okay, Grandpa, make that announcement.' So he was kind of hesitant, went about for a while.

"Then he says, 'I've decided I'm not goin' to treat tuberculosis.'

"I said, 'You didn't say the word—I decided. . . . You said you didn't know how.' So I questioned him some more. I says, 'Tell me, you know most of the medicine men better than I do. Can they treat tuberculosis?'

"An' he said, 'No.'

" 'So now you want me to go ahead an' work with the people?'

"He says, 'Yes, take Elizabeth.'

" 'Well,' I said, 'talk to her.'

"An' all those Navajo people just looked at him back, an' they says, 'Now tell 'em, you big liar.'

"So Elizabeth was brought over an' he talk to her very, very nice. He told her that 'we medicine men cannot cure this tuberculosis.'

"So I said, 'I agree with you. You cannot cure it.'

"So the next day Elizabeth was with us back to Fort Defiance, an' she's still alive today.

"When I see her she always comes up an' says, 'I remember you.'

"I says, 'I do, too.' "

Life on the Papagueria

FAR TO THE SOUTH of the state, four hundred miles from the lands of the Hopis and Navajos, is the Papagueria, the home of the Papago Indian Tribe. They are descendants of the ancient Hohokam who learned to tame the arid Arizona–Sonora Desert by building an intricate series of canals, an engineering feat it took many years for some Anglos to accept as the work of Indians.

It was through the Papago lands that the Spanish conquistadores and padres came to search for the riches of the Southwest. The Papagos were peaceful farmers, and they were quick to accept the ways of the intruders. Even today the influence of those early Spanish explorers can be seen in remnants of mission buildings.

For Enos Francisco, who lives in Sells, capitol of the Papago reservation, Christianity, the religion of the Padres, remains a part of his life. The sixty-seven-year-old former Papago Tribal Chairman lives in a modern home. In one corner of the living room a table is spread with religious objects of Christianity.

Francisco spoke in a faint voice, fainter than it should have been for a man his age. But he had had three heart attacks; those and other illnesses had enfeebled him. Even so he was eager to tell his story—the story of a youngster who could not go to school until he was ten years old and yet rose to the highest position of leadership in his tribe. He was one of the first Papagos to go to high school and then to go on to the University of Arizona. He would have earned a college degree if he had had even the slightest opportunity, but the days of the Great Depression were even more difficult for Indians than for many whites.

Nevertheless Enos Francisco went on to become vice-chairman of the Papago Tribal Council in 1953, and chairman six months later. He served

35

four years and later served another four-year term as chairman from 1960. One of his major accomplishments was to bring mining royalties to his tribe. Much of the work he did as tribal leader has brought not only income, but jobs to the Papagos, who are one of the poorest of Indian tribes in the United States.

THE FAITH OF A PAPAGO

Enos Francisco lowered his illness-racked body into the new vinyl armchair. He started his story with his birth in 1908 . . .

"I was born at Fresnal Canyon which is just north of Baboquivari, about six miles. I was born under a little bush 'cause there were no hospitals here in those days; the nearest town was in Tucson which was very far an' the roads were very bad. So we up there, we are born just at the best place as they can; some were born in the little houses an' some were were born just like I was, just under the little bush. The first thing after I was born my mother gave me coffee, 'cause she didn't have any breast milk, you know, after I was born. An' without any food, milk of any kind, she had me drink coffee for my milk until she had the breast milk. An' that's why I like coffee nowadays [Francisco laughed].

"We live in a little brush house padded with mud, a little round house. I was the second born baby. We had a brother, but he had died. I was the first from my real father an' mother; my other brother was half-brother. So anyway we were three in a room. But in the other houses you have the same kind of room with four or five members in the family. You know, it depends on how many in family you have. I had other brothers an' sisters; I had about four brothers an' about six sisters; they have all died, an' just my one brother an' two sisters left now.

"So we lived up there at Fresnal Canyon during the dry parts of the year, an' when the rains come we go to Topawa where our fields was for plantin'. An' when we through with our plantin' an' harvestin' our crop there, it's dry again so we had to go back to Fresnal Canyon. It happened on the season, plantin' time. Like we plant in the early spring watermelon, beans, pumpkin, corn an' other crops that are summer crops. We took care of them until we harvest them, an' we go back to Fresnal, an' then it is time for winter crops.

"In those days I have always said—an' I hear everybody say—that rains had come just on the right time. When its season comes for certain

A Papago woman sits before a typical home of brush and mud on the Papagueria. It was in this sort of home that Enos Francisco, who was to rise to the leadership of his tribe, lived as a small boy. ARIZONA STATE MUSEUM PHOTO BY P. LINDSAY

plantin' it always comes, an' we had that, an' nowadays I see that that has changed; it doesn't rain like it did in those days. It does not rain in summertime when it is supposed to rain for our plantin', an' it doesn't rain in winter just like it used to do in those days. So we don't hardly raise anythin' now, just a few things an' sometimes it dries up an' sometimes it matures a little bit, but not as much as it did in those days.

"We depended a lot on our plantin'. Sometimes we raise three sacks of beans an' other crop like pumpkins an' corn an' in the winter time the peas, an' we depend on it to take us almost all year 'round. My father was a poor man. He had only one or two cattle; not so many cattle as the people own today. My father was also a miner; they had mines, the Anglos, in Fresnal Canyon."

Now Enos Francisco moved to the edge of his chair and, with excitement in his voice, began the story his father told him of the Papago creation.

"What he told me, I compare to the stories that I hear now from the non-Indian stories; it just parallels to each other. He told me that his father told him about the creation. He said that in the beginnin' there was darkness an' the only thing that was floatin' around was Eagle Feather—just the only thing—which was later recognized as our Creator. 'Cause after the Eagle Feather that floats around became lonesome, an' He said He was goin' to create some other things so He wouldn't be alone; an' they'll be His creation, whatever He makes.

"So all He did was just say that there would be light, an' there was light. An' He said that there will be water an' there was the water. An' from water He made little people, like little dolls an' He breathed into them to become the human bein'. An' He did that for a few days, an' after He got all the people that He needed. An' He said that you will have to have a helper to take care of the people that He has made, so He appointed a person. He called him *E'etoi* [Elder Brother] an' *E'etoi* helped them; He put them on the ground that had been made the Earth.

"An' from there He put all several kinds of rules that we have to follow, that the people have to follow. The first thing He told them that they were these people an' they had to be very, very nice—good to each other, that they'd have to help each other an' be kind to each other. An' He put a rule that they should never kill anyone or kill each other—just to be livin' together happy all the time.

"An' He said, 'Don't ever waste anythin' foolishly. Don't destroy anythin' that you don't use—the grass or anythin' that grows on the ground. Just use it for your use 'cause what I will put in the ground is to grow for food an' for medicine—some of the medicines that you'll have to use when you get sick. An' if you don't do what I say, there will be problems. If you waste the trees that grow, then you'll have a problem of floodin' soil away, an' the soil won't be good as it is now if you waste any of the vegetation. An' if you don't do these things, the earth will have big arroyos. An' the rains won't come 'cause what vegetation you might destroy will not draw the water from above, which the Creator is layin'.

" 'An' another thing I will do is plant cactus an' every year when the cactus arrives, you go out an' get the fruit. They'll be fruit all the time from those vegetation that grow there; it will be always there. An' when cactus fruit comes, go out an' take it an' make syrup, jam an' make wine for your dancin'. That's all the wine is for; this wine is to celebrate with, an' no drunkenness, 'cause if you do, you'll be breakin' my rules of not usin' it right. When that comes, when the wine is ready to drink, then you can put on your dance . . . sing your rain songs an' pray. You know, it's just like prayin' when you are dancin'. Singin' is like prayin' for rain, so you'll have rains for your seasons. In that way you'll always have things to raise.'

"Then He says, 'When I put these rules there, they shall be called the law.' He says, 'They're my laws whatever I give you. If you break any of my laws there'll be trouble every time. An' there will be many, many laws that I will have to put down, an' one of the things is to be brave 'cause there will be some other people that will disturb you.' He was callin' that name what we thinks is the Apaches 'cause we had lot of trouble with the Apaches in those days.

"But He said, 'You have to be brave when those enemies come to you. Then that's the time you have to defend yourself an' you have to kill them. But never kill anybody for fun, or to get mad at. An' when your boys, your children, grow up, you must teach them to be brave an' protect your women an' your children an' your property. An' when your children grow up they will have to have endurance, you know, so as soon as they grow up, get 'em up early in the mornin'. Let them run for several miles before they come back an' eat. An' then they'll have to go out an' work an' gather up the food, but always be ready when somethin' comes up . . . to get together an' defend your women an' children an' property.

" 'But that's not all you're goin' to do. You'll be doin' lot of the work on your land, to protect your land. An' you have to protect your animals, your food; the animals that I create will be your food for need. But don't destroy them either; 'cause if you do, they'll be eliminated after a while. There won't be any, an' you won't have any meat for food.' "

Here Francisco paused, thinking over the story he had related, and then continued with this afterthought . . .

"But that has been done, an' now we don't have any, hardly any, wild animals 'cause that's what He said is goin' to happen. When the people started shootin' with the guns after a long time we don't have the wild animals an' we have to buy it, the meat. Now we have to raise the meat, an' we have to work hard for it."

We asked Francisco how it was that his people were called Papagos.

"When the Spanish came from the south they brought many things, an' they introduced, too, some of the things that we have, like beans, tepary beans. We are very fond of the tepary beans; we call them *bahwui*. They are white little beans. So we get to like them very, very much, an' so after the Spanish left, the Mexicans came an' saw us likin' these *bahwui* beans, so they just call us 'bean eaters.' They call us 'Papagos'— bean-eaters. Then the other people heard them an' they call us 'Papagos.' That's how we got our name. We call ourselves *O'otam* all the time before, so we supposed to be *O'otam* instead of Papagos."

We then asked Francisco to tell us how it was that he came to go to school.

"We were livin' at Fresnal Canyon, an' I had learned how to help my father; an' I helped with plantin' an' takin' care of the crop, an' my father began to feel that I was a very good help. Some children were goin' to school, but my father says, 'No, he's a good helper; I don't want him to go to school.' So I helped him an' everythin'; for ten years I didn't go to school. An' it happened that there were some prospectors that were goin' to Fresnal Canyon, an' they needed help. So I had a good chance to do some work for the prospectors an' also to help my father. An' I wanted to learn English to talk with them. So that's when I made up my mind that I should go to school an' learn like the other children do. An' I said to my father, 'Father, I must go to school. I want to learn somethin' so I can be more help to you, although I been doin' the best I can to help you. But that's all I'm goin' to be doin' all the time.'

"So he said, 'Okay, if you feel that way, it's okay with me.'

"So the next time the agent from Sells came around gettin' the names of the children to go to school, I put my name down. An' it was 1918, early part of 1918 in October when the man came an' said, 'We're takin' the children to Tucson to get a train to go to Phoenix Indian School.' He said to get ready, that he was comin' back again. So about a month afterwards, in November, he came an' put us in a wagon an' took us. We traveled two days to get to Tucson [about sixty-five miles from Topawa on the Papago reservation]. We traveled from here an' we camped at Pan Tak, which is northeast of Kitt Peak [the site today of a vast astronomical laboratory]. We camped there. Then in the mornin' we started again an' had our lunch at Robles Ranch, an' from there we went to Tucson an' got into Tucson in the evenin'."

Francisco recalled the fears he had of getting on the first train he had ever seen.

"I was scared. When the train came into the station, you know, how it used to do . . . it makes a lot of steam . . . shhhh, shhhh. I thought it must be very hot in the cars. I said, 'What am I goin' to do? Am I just goin' to burn up when I get in the car?' I didn't want to get in, but I was determined to go to school, so I said, 'I'm goin' in there.'

"We got in the train an' went, an' that was the most lonesome journey that I had. It seems like I was goin' away an' never come back again 'cause the train was goin' so fast. We got into Phoenix about midnight, an' at that time they didn't have cars for us; they just had flat wagons with teams of mules. The school was three miles away out in the open; now when you go to that school it's right in town, right in the middle of Phoenix."

Francisco stayed at the Phoenix Indian School for nine years, but then he decided, "I would like to involve a little bit more with other nationalities," *so he convinced his father to move from the reservation into Tucson, where he entered public high school.*

"I had a hard time. English was very hard for me 'cause we didn't have it that way in Indian School. An' the Depression was goin' on that time, an' it took a lot of money to go on to school. My father an' mother died in 1930, just one year after I was there so I had a hard time finishin' high school, just doin' the best I could. Durin' the Depression I used to go out an' work for some people to earn my breakfast—do just yard work. Noon I had the band boys—I played in the band at school—interested in me. So they had a little cafeteria there right at the school, an' those boys ask me into the lines an' they paid for it so I could have my lunch.

"An' after school I went lookin' for work again to earn my supper. An' the third year I stayed with some people to go to school, an' stayed with them an' do their chores—cuttin' grass, takin' care of the place an' stayin' while they were away. When I finished high school I was married. So I was a married man when I was goin' to the University of Arizona, an' I was workin' in agriculture-chemistry an' soils department, so I was takin' care of myself. But my first baby was born that year so that put a hardship on me—had to take care of the family an' first baby—an' the followin' year I had another baby. An' that took all my time just to work steady an' no school; that's why I didn't go any more."

For ten years Enos Francisco worked in Tucson, at the university and then in his own business as a landscaper. Then he was called back to the Papago reservation in 1952 and elected vice-chairman of the Tribal Council. When he became Tribal chairman, he started to fight for mineral rights for his people.

"At that time I learned about our mineral rights that we didn't have; everythin' that comes in goes off the reservation, an' we didn't have any income. An' before that Tommie Segundo who was chairman . . . he told me before he left, he said, 'Don't ever try to get the mineral rights for the Papagos. I tried. I have tried an' every time I try it seems like I just feel a stone wall. It will be worse if you try.' When he told me that, that just put more into me. I said, 'I'm goin' to try.' You know, I didn't say it to him, but in my mind, I said, 'I'll try. I'll try different words than you did.'

"So I learned that when he tries, he tells the small miners from town to leave an' don't come back 'cause this is our reservation an' you're intrudin'. An' then he tries to get the mineral rights, an' those small miners get together an' they form an organization that spoke bad against us. So every time Segundo tries to get the mineral rights, they fight back, these little men. The owners had their congressmen, you know, to back them up 'cause it would have to take congressional action to change that mineral right that Spain had in the beginnin' an' when the United States took over the land, it worked without givin' us our rights."

Enos Francisco hit on a plan. He talked to the Bureau of Indian Affairs, then he talked to the miners themselves, first in Tucson, then in Phoenix and finally he traveled to California to give his message.

"I started goin' to them an' tellin' them that we want our mineral rights. I say, 'I learned from my Creator when he said: "Work together, always work together an' you'll accomplish more." So now I come to you people to ask you to work together with us. If you will help me to get these mineral rights, we'll get some of the money to help ourselves. The people, the whole United States, have been payin' so much to take care of our people on the reservation. We'd like to learn to take care of ourselves; we make the money, an' we start doin' things ourselves. Maybe in time we'll be doin' everythin'. We'll educate our people an' I said, 'We'll still buy equipment from you, our supplies from you, and there will be employment from you to get us started. As it is we don't have any money to buy things; we always have to depend on the government to provide everythin' we have.'

"An' so they listened an' after the speeches that I made, everybody agreed, you know that it was good. An' I went to talk to the governors an' they listened an' said, 'Very good idea. We'll help you. We will form a governors' committee with other states, an' we'll have our congressmen to back you for your mineral rights.'

"It worked, too, 'cause I told them, 'We are very poor people. We don't have any money. We don't have fish like other reservations. We don't have any lumber like other Indians have. We don't have any coal that other people have on their reservations.'

"So everybody listened to me an' thought, 'Yeh, that's true. Those people, those poor people, they need money. They like to get ahead. They think real good, an' they're not selfish like we thought they were. They have good thinkin'. If we work together, we all benefit together.'

"An' it took from 1952 to 1955 when we finally got our mineral rights, when we finally got our rights back."

The Day I Stopped Hating the White Man

IN THE CENTRAL PART of Arizona are the White Mountains, a magnificent area combining lakes and streams, forests and mountains. This is where the White Mountain Apaches live. Their verdant areas stand in remarkable contrast to the desert lands of the Hopis and Navajos to the north and the Papagos to the south.

The White Mountain Apaches like to say, as you will see in the following interview, that they have always been in this land. But there is no historic record to back their view. Rather the Apaches are said to be nomads who came into the Southwest about A.D. 1200. These nomads were given the name "Apaches" by the tribes already in the area; Apaches means enemies. The Hopis called them that and so did the Papagos.

Apache tribes roamed throughout the Southwest, even extending, at one time, into Kansas. Some of the Apaches raided other tribes as custom, and when the white man came into the area he found a ferocious enemy. The Apaches were the last of the Indian tribes to be subdued. And when they were, several tribes were gathered together on the Fort Apache Indian Reservation by Executive Order on November 9, 1871.

Fort Apache still stands, not only as a museum relic, but as a headquarters for many of the operations of the White Mountain Apache Tribe. The White Mountain Apaches dominate 1.6 million acres of some of the greatest recreational area in the state. And the Apaches have taken a measure of revenge over their white captors. To fish, hunt or camp in this area, the whites today must purchase licenses and permits from the tribe. The Apaches also run a ski resort at Sunrise and operate a motel, stores and service stations. Generally, the Great White Father in Washington was more careful in selecting the lands for Indian reservations; rarely was such a "mistake" made as with the White Mountain Apaches.

44

It was at Fort Apache where we taped the words and stories of Nelson Lupe, Sr., a sixty-seven-year-old former Apache Tribal Chairman who at the time was involved in his own taping sessions. He was taping the songs and stories of other old Apaches so they would not be lost to the Apache people.

THE LIFE STRUGGLE OF AN APACHE

Nelson Lupe was at home in the log cabin at Fort Apache. Not so many years ago he would not have been welcome, for that building had been used by the colonel in charge of the Fort Apache headquarters. It was in this area, down at Whiteriver, where Lupe was born June 15, 1909. He was born on the reservation, but it had been this same area where his father and grandfather had roamed freely before the white man's conquest. As the taping began it was evident the bitterness of conquest had not yet fully disappeared.

"I was born in Whiteriver, an' I came to know that I was alive one day, I guess, when I was two years old, somethin' like that, when I had a new pair of shoes with the button on the side. My dad evidently bought them for me, an' I guess they put them on me in the mornin' when I got up. So out on the porch I was walkin' back an' forth an' I heard this squeak in my shoes, in the soles of my shoes. I loved that noise, walkin' back an' forth. That's when I came to know that I was alive.

"My dad was born in Cibecue an' my great-grandfather lived over by the Sierra Ancha Mountains, up there somewhere. My grandmother told me . . . the only thing that I can get from my grandmother is that we— the Apaches—live here all the time. They don't know where we came from, that we were here all the time. That may be true 'cause it seems there isn't any history where we derived an' where we came in from. But this mountain over here, between here an' Highway 60, they call it Silver Butte. That's a volcanic mountain; there's two—one big one, one little one shaped like a cone, an' they say that's an active volcano. There's a hot springs down below, down in the crease of the canyon. Way down below is the hot water, comes out of the ground there. So that indicates this mountain is a live volcano. An' accordin' to the Apaches they call that 'The Mountain That is Alive,' that's 'Comin' Out on Top.' An' that volcano has been there I don't know how many years it was active, but still my people have that name for it. So they think they have been in this area a long, long time. They think they were made here."

Lupe returned to talking about his own family, and he began with bitterness in his voice.

"My dad told me about his father, about the time he saw his father an' grandfather taken away. The police came to take them away. Somebody, some rancher, was killed in the Sierra Ancha Mountains, an' they blamed that on my granddad an' my great-grandfather an' two other relatives. You know, there's four people that went to Yuma Prison [the territorial prison] back in 1890 without any trial or fair investigation of any kind at all. . . . 'Those people killed that white man,' so they went an' pick up my grandfather an' my great-grandfather an' took them away. They were over there at that Yuma prison up to 1897, I believe. They both died in 1897. Yeh, died in prison . . . consumption, tuberculosis."

He turned to look at us directly, seeking a reaction as we shifted uncomfortably in our seats. We waited until he was ready to resume his story-telling. His eyes softened and he continued.

"Let me tell you about my clan. This history of my clan starts at Carrizo. Evidently they lived up about fifteen miles from that station—the police station—at Carrizo . . . way up the canyon. An' there was some people livin' there where the pine tree came off the mountain an' came down into the creek. An' these people were livin' there so these people were called 'The Pine Tree that Came Down off the Mountain of the Creek.' That's my clan, so we were recognized by this description of land that my ancestors live in.

"As time went on these people increase so they have to move to another place which is about two miles . . . three miles farther down where there's nothin' but oak trees growin', white oak. An' they were called White Oak people. An' as these, too, increase, as the new married people increase, they move a little further down which is about a mile down. An' there was a reed that grows in that place there that people make arrows out of, so they were called the people from 'The Field of Reeds.' So they were given this name.

"As we increased together, all of us, then the people moved again, out among the red hills. An' they were called *Dzilth Taden. Dzilth* is mountain, the hill; *taden* means that you live against the hill, the foot of the hill. They were given this name. So this is the history that my grandfather, my grandmother tells me, see? This is where we had the beginning as our clan.

"We were hunters an' farmers in the early days, particularly used to raise wheat, an' I remember when I was a little boy I've seen a flour mill over in Whiteriver. We have a wheat mill there . . . turn it into flour, wheat, corn an' everything'.

"According to the histories, I think, we were kind of a friendly tribe, a peaceful tribe. We kinda minded our own business. An' the other people, you know, like a bunch a young guys get together. They'd go out an' move around. They'd raid an' do the killin' an' pick things up, you know, clothes, horses, cows. . . ."

We asked him about the time the white man came into the area and forced the Apaches onto the reservation.

"Well, they realize that the white people were beginnin' to come through their land, an' my grandmother, she used to tell me, 'Never trust a white man. They're bad people,' she'd say. You know, I lived to grow up hatin' the white people. All in school I hate them. I never did like white people all during the time I was in school. I don't know why; the hatred was within the tribe for the white people. They said the white man did kill, kill the Indians for nothin' because they have the gun, they have the power. An' lot of times, they said, my people, they used to hide, you know, when the white people were comin' through. The white people, they just shoot 'em like animal."

Again the anger flashed in Lupe's eyes and he stopped talking. There was a long pause before he spoke.

"At Whiteriver my dad was a baker. Evidently he an' my mother got married while they were in school, while they were students. So his job was to help in the bakery shop durin' the time he was goin' to school at Whiteriver Boardin' School. So he became the baker an' I came to find that he was bakin' bread there for the school. An' we live in a house there right next to the bakery shop. The shop was in the back; we live in the front. But later on they just convert it into one whole shop. Then we moved back into the wickiup. An' I grew up in a wickiup—without floors, just the dirt—made out of bear grass an' poles.

"An' we just had to get used to the weather as it changes. They used to, you know, make me swim in the cold water, which I used to do, to get used to the cold weather—get down there an' swim in the cold water of the river. An' you did, too, golly, you get used to cold weather an' you never sat around the fire. You'd get out there an' keep yourself warm, keep yourself alive; move around, hunt."

Nelson Lupe is a collector of legends of the White Mountain Apache people; and here he related the days when he listened to the storytelling of the elder tribesmen.

"As I grew up, I used to listen to the oldtimers quite a bit. There used to be a lot of storytellin' at that time, which is quite an entertainment, you know, entertainment, or a pastime, like listenin' to a radio or TV, you know, when a man is tellin' stories. I used to take part in that. They used to say, 'There's a man tellin' stories. . . .' I'd go over an' listen . . . the old, old legends, stories for little kids. In the story is a hero who lived righteously; he was kind. There's one there all the time. So they said, 'Be like this one, the person here.' So that's how they used to tell the story. So this is our aim when we grow up; we want to be like him, like that hero there.

"An' we have to learn how to pray, the kids would learn how to pray. That is the reason the Great Spirit steps forward to help, to do the good things an' love people. An' He become a good provider for the people through the whole spirit. An' this they used to tell this to us.

"An' as I grew up I found Apaches to be very kind people. Wherever you go those early days people didn't have nothin' to eat. Most families didn't have anythin' to eat. There were long spells between the next good meal. An' whatever they had they used to share . . . give you a little piece, just a bit, an' that was enough. An' they learned to share. My grandmother lived off the land; she never came into town, even later, to buy flour an' stuff, coffee, you know. She used to make corn bread when I'd visit her . . . corn bread, an' then she used to have some jerky, an' make gravy from the deer meat, sometimes beef. An' she used to have mescal [a cactus native to the area], barbecued mescal. An' she would soak that an' we'd have somethin' like fruit juice. We'd drink that. An' lot of times they'd mix this mescal juice with the little red leaves. My grandmother used to pick a lot of them an' manzanita, too."

The conversation moved to Lupe's days in government schools.

"I went to Whiteriver School. My father had a great ambition for me so he decided he want me to go to public school. So I went to public schools an' I never did like white people. I never did like the whites. There was just me in that all-white school. You see, there were some other boys, he remembered, went off to school at an early age. The first bunch of boys that were picked up to go to school, their hair is about that long [Nelson demonstrated], wild, just like a wild animal; g-strings on, some had mocassins, some didn't have anythin' on. They took them to Carlisle Indian School an' they came back with professions. It seems to be like

The Apaches, who roamed over a wide area of the Southwest, lived in encampments such as this before, and even after they were put on reservations. ARIZONA STATE MUSEUM PHOTO BY HELGA TEIWES

ninety-nine percent of them had a good education. An' father wanted me to go to school an' be in some profession, like a teacher.

"You don't have ambition as a youngster, but my dad saw somethin' in the future for me so he sent me to the white school, public school. We had about a half-dozen kids in there an' one teacher. I went to school there for about two days, I guess. So one day I asked to go out—we used to have an outdoor privy those days. So I asked the teacher, 'May I go to the little house out there?' She says, 'You may be excused.' An' that was the excuse I got, an' I never went back to that school after that. I walked past that outdoor privy an' I never went back to that school.

"My father whipped me a whole lot, but I told him I didn't want to go back to school there. Later on he put me in boarding school at White-river. I couldn't live at home 'cause the school was so strict that every kid that goes to boardin' school has to live there. I just finished eighth grade an' that was the end of my school. I was waitin' for that day, too, 'cause I hated white people there—the disciplinarian, teachers, superintendent, all the employees. The discipline was real hard. At Whiteriver any kid that run off from school, miss a meal, miss a roll call, they put a ball an' chain on him. That kid was made to carry that ball around to dining room, to classroom for about a week. That's the kinda treatment we got, discipline. I had my share of the cat-o'-nine-tails a couple times."

Lupe now spoke about his early family life, and he credits his success in rising to the leadership of his tribe—despite so little formal schooling— to the training he received in his family and clan life.

"I still have respect for those relationships. There's an old man that used to live above me. He used to call me grandson, an' I called him granddad. An' one day when I got married, you know, when I got married, I couldn't find a place of ground anywhere to cultivate, to farm. An' one day I decided to go down to a *tulpie* party, drink some of that *tulpie* [a corn liquor] 'cause I was discouraged. An' that old man rode up to me. He says, 'Grandson, where ya goin'?' He says, 'I know where you're goin'. Do you think that's good for you?'

" 'Well, I don't know,' I says, 'but I'd like to drink some of that *tulpie*.'

"He says, 'Well, I don' think so. You're not goin' drink any of that stuff. You turn your horse right around an' ride back up to your house with me.' He says, 'You started somethin' an' you keep workin' on that. You drag some more posts, an' you dig that hole yourself, an' you set those posts yourself before you look for help. You do it.'

"So instead of ridin' down there to drink, I went up into the mountain, chopped some posts an' dragged down about a dozen posts an' laid 'em out the way I was goin' to set 'em up. An' this old man told me, he says, 'Now, you're my grandson. I'm talkin' to you like you are my son. Whatever you do, you are goin' to go up. You're goin' to go up.' He says, 'You're goin' to pass some people on your way up, but remember those people. Remember them. One of these days you're comin' back down. An' when you start comin' back down remember those families you passed. Just remember that.'

"An' that has stuck with me pretty well in my life. An' I grew up never to look down on anybody, any of my people—except the white man. You know, I hate them."

So Lupe started with a small farm and then through his lifetime he worked at many different jobs; he was never too proud to take the lowest of jobs. In 1938 when he was "about twenty-eight" he was elected to the Apache Tribal Council. After World War II when he was not serving on the council, his wife, stricken with arthritis, talked to him about returning to leadership.

"One day in the hospital she says, 'Nelson, come on, I want to talk to you. Nelson, you've been a good man, real good. I'm proud of you. What I want you to do is sign up for council. I want you to run for council. You said no, but I'm askin' you to do that for our children an' our people. I know how you love your people. I think you'll make a good man.'

"So I ran for the council an' got elected. That was in '46. An' when I was on the council in 1950 I told them, 'We're not gettin' anywhere meetin' once a month. There's no way we can carry out the work. We discuss it. We leave it . . . we give it to the superintendent; he forgets about it.' I say, 'We're not gettin' anywhere at all. Why don't you establish a chairman, a permanent job?' I became the chairman."

Although there were other part-time chairmen, Lupe was the first full-time chairman of the White Mountain Apache Tribe. Under his leadership many important projects were carried out on the reservation including the development of a sawmill, recreation enterprises, a fish hatchery and construction company. Lupe said through the years there had been many hurdles to get over.

"I remember one time I told my people, I says, 'From corner to corner of our reservation we can farm, we can develop cattle, make the people see we are usin' this land to make a livin' for our people.' So we developed the cattle an' we got all the white man's cattle off the reservation. I had a fight with one of those people in Show Low. He didn't want to remove his cattle from the reservation. He consider himself as a full-blooded Indian an' doesn't pay any contributions. But he wasn't a full-blooded Indian; he was a full-blooded gringo."

Lupe paused, realizing that once again he had lashed out at the white man.

"You know, one incident that changed my mind about white people is that job I had in the mine at Morenci. There was a superintendent, his name was McDaniel. An' I had a boy about three years old at that time, an' that boy got sick. An' evidently this superintendent was interested in the welfare of the employees. So he found out that my boy was real sick, an' evidently my doctor told him that 'this boy is not goin' to live.' So McDaniel says to me, 'Nelson, any time you need help, just let me know.' This changed my whole heart. This man that I hated he says, 'Nelson, just let me know.'

"When my boy died he gave me a truck, gave me a man to take the body back to Cibecue. That day I changed. . . ."

Nelson Lupe stopped talking. He turned his head from us. When he turned back, he was putting his glasses on again.

"From that . . . ," Lupe said softly, "from that day I loved the white man. I still love him today."

BOOK TWO
THE NEWCOMERS

*Arizona was the Indians' land for
countless millennia regardless of the
lack of any written ownership. It was
their land because they lived on it
in harmony with its nature, their lives
determined by its configurations. . . .
Then suddenly it was no longer theirs.
Their land was ours.*

LAWRENCE CLARK POWELL IN
Arizona, a Bicentennial History

Uncovering the Story of Man

THEY CAME, THOSE NEWCOMERS—first the Spanish, then the Mexicans and after them the "new" Americans—in search of gold and silver, to possess territory, to preach the word of their own God and some only to find a new and freer way of life.

They came to take over a land that did not belong to them, and in the end it was their guns—and their numbers—that won them the land and the domination over the Indian tribes. First, they came from the south out of Mexico, and then they began to pour in overland from the East and across the Colorado River from the West. The first settlers were subdued, and their pleadings most often were not heard; the newcomers were too busy in the conquest of the land, its people and resources to do more than shove the Indians aside.

It was, in fact, to be many years before a great respect would grow for the Indians and the way they had lived in harmony with this harsh land of the Southwest. It took many years of a new kind of exploration, a reverential digging into the past, to build that respect. The "diggers" were the archaeologists who uncovered stunning accomplishments of home-building, of engineering, of constructing in the desert vast systems of canals for irrigating farmlands.

One among the many great scientists who worked to unlock the stories of the past is Dr. Emil W. Haury. As a young man he was on digs with the most honored archaeologists, and as an established and honored scientist he was to uncover at Ventana Cave on the Papagueria evidence of 11,000 years of man's existence in the Southwest. He was to bring more understanding of the remarkable Hohokam who engineered those canals in the desert. In 1956 Haury was elected to the National Academy of Sciences, and four years later was named a fellow in the American Academy of Arts and Sciences. He has presided over the Society for American Archaeology and the American Anthropological Association.

Haury has been a teacher's teacher at the University of Arizona where he has been head of the anthropology department and the director of the Arizona State Museum. And in his research in the field he has been more to the Indians of the Southwest than a "digger"; he has been an understanding friend, advisor and respecter of ancient cultures and traditions.

THE CHALLENGE TO UNLOCK THE PAST

Emil W. Haury is a big man; he fills out a chair. Even at the age of seventy-two when this taping was made, he was fit enough to go into the field for an arduous dig. He was born in Newton, Kansas, May 2, 1904, the son of a professor. Haury began his story with the lures which drew him into a lifetime career of trying to unlock the past.

"When I was a boy growing up on the campus of a denominational school in central Kansas—Bethel College—I had an interest, a sort of undefined interest, in archaeology. And part of this was generated by the fact that my father and mother were in California in 1908, and on their way back they visited the Walnut Canyon ruins up near Flagstaff and brought home a potsherd or two. My father always had a cabinet in the parlor filled with curiosities—shells, I remember; seaweed, you know, kind of a stabilized seaweed; crystals, minerals and all that sort of thing; an Indian arrowhead or two, and a piece of pottery."

Then he recalled a visit to the California State Fair where he visited the Hall of Man in San Diego's Balboa Park.

"I remember there I saw a whole series of busts depicting the evolution of man, and that fed my interest further. And then on the return trip we came into New Mexico to see an aunt and uncle, and a cousin there who was several years my senior. He was an archaeological nut and had been prowling around in the Roswell area and made a collection of potsherds and arrowheads. So I had a chance to paw over some of that stuff. Well, all this sort of began to shape up in my mind, and I remember thinking, 'Well, Great Scott, there's nothing of Indian interest in Kansas. This is just an idle dream; nothing can ever happen.' "

But a set of circumstances brought him in contact with Dr. Byron Cummings, the University of Arizona's famed archaeologist, and the youngster was invited to go along on a dig at Cuicuilco, near Mexico City.

Haury recalled the adventure of the 1925 train ride from Newton, Kansas, into Mexico.

"I'll tell you, that was a long haul, all through Oklahoma, through Texas down to Laredo. By the time I got to Laredo, which took a couple of days, I was dirty, needed a shave, and tired. And then came the long haul from Laredo to Mexico City and that was a couple of days and a couple nights. And riding in a chair car, you didn't have the privilege of going to the diner; you had to buy food along the railroad track when the train stopped in those villages, and that stuff didn't look inviting to me. So I made do with candy bars, an apple or two, and things I could get from newsboys. Well, by the time I got to Mexico City I was pretty weak. Fortunately, Cummings met me at the railway station and took care of me.

"Well, it was there, there at Cuicuilco, that I decided that this was the way to go. You see, this inspired in me a deep curiosity about human history—in other words, what had happened through time to our forebears, Indian or whatever. I suppose the first thing that got to me were the romantic aspects of archaeology which is really what gets to most everybody—'Gee whiz! Here's something that is out of the past.' And there's a sense of excitement about it, and I'm sure that my early reactions were based on those very superficial, emotional kinds of things. But as time went on, and I could see that if you're talking about the removal of many feet of lava (which had locked in the Cuicuilco site), and this rests on many more feet of accumulated refuse, or evidence of human occupation, then here is the challenge: It is to unlock the story from that kind of material and to recreate, re-establish man's story. Speak for him, because he could no longer speak for himself."

In the fall of 1925 Haury enrolled at the University of Arizona, and his career in the field started swiftly and spectacularly.

"The first dig really on my own was in the summer of 1927 when Cummings gave me a little money, checked out an old Dodge truck from the university garage and said, 'Go to northeastern Arizona and find some Basketmaker material. We're short of Basketmaker material in the Arizona State Museum.' It was a wild assignment, and he was really a courageous man because I knew nothing about northeastern Arizona. I'd been around a bit, but I had never been challenged with the logistics, you see, of getting out into that wild country and going about the work myself.

"Fortunately, E. J. Hand, this hardrock miner from down in the Chiricahua Mountains who also had worked on the dig near Mexico City, was already in northeastern Arizona doing some work there for Cummings, and I was to join him. And I also had picked up Major L. F. Brady who ran a ranch school in Mesa, and he was a great one—he knew that country up there. With his absolutely essential assistance I was able to get up there and begin to go to work and try to pull something together. And Hand was an untutored individual, let's say, in an academic sense, but he had enormous common sense and related naturally to things in the ground.

"Travel was thoroughly different than it is today. Gasoline was hard to come by and very expensive, and food was not as varied and as readily accessible as it is today and, too, we had almost no equipment. We made our camp in the far northeast corner of Arizona, found the site we wanted to work in, called it 'Vandal Cave.' We just camped in the open. We had no tent. Just laid out the sleeping bags, and if it rained we climbed in under the truck. We also had a limited food supply, and we had a half-mile to the spring, a little drip spring which gave us about a bucketful of water a day. And four of us had to use that water to wash in, and cook, and drink. And that taught me something about the preciousness of water.

"But here we were in the Indian country, far back in the so-called wilderness. We didn't have contact for a couple weeks. The trading posts were some miles away so we made do. We'd get a Navajo goat and use that for fresh meat. We had a sack of flour and other staples with us; it was a relatively limited diet. I can remember when Hand and I got out of that place later in the summer and got to Ganado, we bought a dozen eggs and went up in a side canyon and cooked the whole dozen.

"But that's all beside the point. That experience taught me a lot both in the logistics that one had to surmount—the logistical problems of travel and also the logistics of work because there we had gotten into a site that had a dual occupation, a Basketmaker horizon and a Pueblo 3 horizon. We didn't call it that in those days, but here were early remains which we found deep, and some later occupation relating to later people, higher up. This factor of stratigraphy was the thing that got to me in Mexico, because that's where we had a good demonstration, you see, of the worth of the stratigraphic piling up of these archaeological remains. That was one problem.

"The second problem that was high on the list was how do you date these remains? Now, remember that this was 1927, and that's before the broad application of tree ring dating. Then two years later when the tree-ring thing really broke, we found out that the values were simply twice higher than they should have been. We had to slice everything in half."

Dr. A. E. Douglas, also of the University of Arizona, had opened the way to the scientific system of tree ring dating, and Haury worked closely with him. It was at Show Low in Arizona's White Mountains, the area of the Mogollon Indian culture, that Haury, working with Lynn Hargrave, was in on a momentous discovery.

"Hargrave and I went to Show Low where in 1929 we found the beam, let's say, the bridge that joined the historic sequence of tree rings and the prehistoric sequence built on the archaeological specimens from places like Mesa Verde, Chaco Canyon and the Aztec Ruins. That was the breakthrough; that was the big breakthrough.

"Douglas was there on the momentous evening of the day we found this log, and he looked it over and he began to develop some conclusions. We were in a hotel, which really was a home opened for tourists in Show Low, sitting around a sputtering gasoline lamp, and he was making these correlations. And then he finally said, 'If this is correct, and I think it is, then we can say the Chaco Canyon Ruins date in the 1000s or 1100s, that Mesa Verde dates in the 1200s. . . .' And this was the first moment that we really began to see where those ruins fitted into the Christian calendar."

The conversation moved to central Arizona and the study of the remarkable Hohokam civilization. There had been excavations at Snaketown and much probing of the irrigation canals the Hohokams had engineered. Maps had been made of the canals, but the canals themselves were not dug out until Haury took a team into the area.

"Nobody was paying much attention in the way of digging them out; there's nothing more backbreaking than digging out those irrigation ditches. It was a lot of hard work and put nothing on the museum shelves. So we did some testing in 1934 and 1935, and I think that was the first extensive—and actually even this was limited—testing of the canals, and we got some interesting information. But with that work we were only able to extend canal irrigation back to about A.D. 800. But we knew, we could say to ourselves, that if the dating of Snaketown as a village takes us back to the time of Christ, or before, 200 or 300 years before, those people had to have irrigation even though our evidence only carried us back to A.D. 800.

"So that became one of the goals of returning to Snaketown in 1964: Can we find the evidence for earlier irrigation systems? If you have a people living in that hot, arid environment, that they're living a stable village life, they could only be agricultural there if they practiced irrigation. Therefore since we had evidence of a stable village going back that far, there must have been irrigation. So we had to look for it, and we found it."

We asked if there were some who doubted the ability of those early Indians to accomplish such feats of engineering.

"The early archaeologists always said that these people were good engineers, that they knew something about the behavior of water. But I don't think that beyond the superficial observation—'Gee whiz, we've got tens of miles of canals here'—there was all that recognition. There were, and I think there still are people today, who are a little bit reluctant to accept the evidence that as long ago as the time of Christ, or one, or two, or three hundred years B.C. that we have these unwashed 'savages' here in this country with the capability of digging canals miles in length, leading water to the fields, cultivating the fields and growing domestic crops."

When Haury left Gila Pueblo at Globe as assistant director and came back to the University of Arizona in 1937 he began to turn his attention to the Papagueria. This started him on the way to his celebrated work at Ventana Cave on the Papago reservation. There were hurdles on the way to Ventana. On one dig where evidence of an Apache raid was found, Haury's students were stopped by a delegation of Papagos.

"They said, 'You must stop this work.'

"We asked, 'Why?'

" 'Well, your excavation is going to release the evil spirits of the Apache, and our children are going to fall sick. We don't want you to do it.'

"So we quit; and I spent the next week, or more, together with a helpful friend from Sells negotiating with the Big Field District Council, trying to get them to see what we were going to do, trying to get them to understand there wouldn't be any bad spin-off from our work, that it would help us and we would contribute to the knowledge of their culture. But they were absolutely unswerving. We sat there with nothing to do. We were stopped.

"One thing I've always tried to do is respect their wishes because we're guests on the reservation. We have to respect their wishes."

So the search began for another site. Haury was told about a place called Horn Lying near Ventana. That site did not work out, but en route a cave was pointed out and it was there, at Ventana Cave, that Haury went on to make yet another major discovery.

"Well, on the way back from Horn Lying we drove in to the area of the cave. It's about a mile off the road. We took this very rocky road in for a mile, climbed up to the cave. The cave has two parts, an upper part and a lower part. The lower part is more exposed; the upper part is somewhat more sheltered. As we walked over the cave I felt a springiness underfoot which is an indication of compact and organic material, and it just looked awfully good. And I said, 'Well, here's where we're going to work.' "

So the camp was set up and the work begun. The first excitement came when mummies were found. Haury worried about the reaction of the Papago workers on the dig.

"I still had to teach classes and all that, but I did have my field agents, and Bill Bailey was out there doing that work. The first day he worked there, he telephoned me. He said, 'We have found two objects today.'

"I knew that he had most likely found burials, or mummies. It turned out to be the case. He said, 'What are we going to do?'

"I said, 'Do you have any reaction on the part of the men who found them?'

"He said, 'Absolutely none.'

"Well, anyway I went out the next day, and we got this thing resolved. The Papago workers were not the slightest bit interested in the fact that we had encountered mummies. So they helped dig them out, and helped carry them off the hill; never gave us any trouble with them. They just hadn't related to the fact that these conceivably might be their ancestors.

"Well, the importance of the excavations was that as we went deeper, we progressively moved out of one cultural horizon into another. After we went down through the first meter or so of material, we got out of the dry zone where there were plant parts and pieces of sandals and baskets and wood objects and all that sort of thing. Then in the zone that had been moistened we also ran out of pottery, but we were still getting artifacts. As we kept probing we eventually got down five meters before we ran out of cultural material.

"At about three meters we got into hard material of a red color that produced artifacts. They lay on top of the gray material which contained charcoal, fossil bone and artifacts. So we knew we had a great time span; we had convinced ourselves that we really had a bonanza there."

After the first season of digging at Ventana Cave, Haury devised a more controlled system and the great discoveries were put together.

"We can say that the cave had essentially a continuous record. There are gaps in it, but it's about as continuous as you can ever find a record of human occupancy for something like 10,000 or 11,000 years in one spot. The gaps are occasioned by people moving out because of changing conditions. We know that in the earliest horizon the cave floor was moist. We knew that era was another period of time when materials were washing into the cave, but people still used the cave. And subsequent to that the occupation was more or less continuous.

"As far as the cultural material is concerned it seems to be continuous; there are no radical breaks. The only radical breaks would be between the bottom layer which contains the fossil animals at 11,000 years and the subsequent horizon which may have been a thousand and one years later; there was a break there. But this was the first time that we had that kind of a record in Arizona."

So Haury had established fossil animal life going back 11,000 years in Arizona and also had been able to put together a fascinating record of man's early life in this area. We asked him to give us an overview of those first settlers in this area.

"You have to put the people that you're studying in the context of living in the country without the benefit of all the things that we think are absolutely necessary today for human existence. They didn't have them; but they made a go of it, and they somehow hung on. So a sense of comparison develops within you and you ask: Why is it that we need all of these things today? Why do we feel that we have to have ready available clothes, or TV, or whatever? Couldn't we do better?

"Of course, these are rhetorical questions and questions that can't be answered in the present context. We don't do better because we're not willing to do better. We're not forced to, you see, because these things are available to us. Those people didn't have this availability, but they had the capability of adjusting to what nature provided for them.

"I won't say that it was any more unique here in the Southwest than it was anywhere else in the United States, or North America, or the world, for that matter. What it does tell you is that man has a tremendous capa-

The explorations at Ventana Cave on the Papagueria in southern Arizona produced evidence of 11,000 years of man's existence. ARIZONA STATE MUSEUM PHOTO BY HELGA TEIWES

city to adjust to whatever conditions are where he's living—all the way from the Arctic to the tropics. He's a highly adaptable individual or animal. He has that capacity, and he will make do as long as it's at all possible. Well, the Indians did it here and I think they did adapt beautifully to the arid environment.

"But we must remember that the oldest inhabitants here take us back to a period of time when they didn't have the aridity that we do today. It was somewhat different, and yet they had the capacity to change their ways as nature changed. But they stayed here. The changes didn't force them out. When you look at the remains of the oldtimers and you see that they did so much with so little, you can only develop a tremendous respect for them, not only as individuals, but for homo sapiens as a fellow who can get along even through great adversity."

MARIA URQUIDES

The Roots of the Newcomers

FROM THE SOUTH THEY CAME with their horses and crosses, their weapons of iron and their doubly directed zeal: to convert the "heathen" and to lift from the land its riches of gold and silver.

Their roots were in Spain, the country that had sent them to the New World to conquer. And even though they never fully succeeded in their conversions and they never found the riches of the Seven Cities of Cibola, the influence of their days and years of occupation have never left the Southwest. Today their names are on street markers, schools and public buildings . . . Coronado, Cabeza de Vaca, Fray Marcos de Niza, Father Eusebio Kino and Fray Francisco Garces. There is virtually no area of the Southwest that even now remains untouched by those men and the others who came from Spain and Mexico.

Maria Urquides is a descendant of those early adventurers. Her story is a remarkable one in the American tradition: she rose from the barrio— the Mexican-American neighborhood—of Tucson to become a national figure in the fight for education that would help her people rise. Education, you see, was not always on equal terms; in fact, there have been some schools in Arizona where Mexican-Americans have been segregated as recently as 1970.

For her parents and grandparents life was seldom easy, and Maria, too, had to battle all through her life. She was born December 9, 1908, in the *barrio libre* on the edge of downtown Tucson. She would never have dared dream of the world that was to be a reality for her, a world that she made by fighting prejudices to become one of the most honored of teachers and a leader in the national struggle to bring bilingualism to schools in the Southwest.

The "girl of the barrio" was to be sought by five presidents for assistance on national committees and commissions. She was accorded the highest of honors by her city, and by the University of Arizona. The National Education Association, the Arizona Education Association and the League of Mexican-American Women of Los Angeles presented her distinguished service awards. She spent almost half a century in education, beginning as a teacher in Tucson and ending her career as a high-level administrator in the same district. When this taping was made Maria Urquides was retired, living in a small, comfortable home only a few blocks from the campus of the University of Arizona. When she was a young girl, she could not attend the university; it was beyond the means of her family.

Instead she went to the State Teachers College at Tempe, now Arizona State University, and from there earned bachelors and masters degrees at the University of Arizona and followed with additional graduate work at the University of Mexico and the University of California at Berkeley.

GROWING UP MEXICAN AND AMERICAN

Considering the tremendous Spanish and Mexican influence on the Southwest, it is paradoxical that there even had to be a fight for bilingual education. The Maria Urquides story is one that bridges the gap between the Spanish, Mexican, and Anglo cultures, and the narration begins with her family's migration from the south.

"Both of my grandfathers came from Spain, and one of my grandmothers, my maternal grandmother, came from Alamos, Mexico. My father and mother were both born in Tucson. My father was born in 1854. He was born right outside the wall . . . the walled city of Tucson. And my mother was born in 1871 and she was born in a little house that later became the El Charro Restaurant [today that home is an historic site, saved from downtown urban renewal but ironically converted into a Greek restaurant in Tucson's La Placita development].

"Mother used to tell us how her father, Joaquin Legarra, bought a little home where Penney's Department Store is downtown now. And some people talked him into starting a meat market, so he mortgaged the little home in order to send money to Sonora, Mexico, to buy cattle and bring the meat to Tucson. Well, the cattle lost so much weight in bringing them through to here, that my grandfather had great difficulty and his venture failed. So he lost his home, bless his heart.

"The family was having a very hard time, and then he died when my mother was about, oh, she was about eight. So it was even more difficult and they used to make candles, they used to make starch, they used to make tortillas and sell them to the soldiers at Fort Lowell in order to pull through.

"On my father's side . . . he was left an orphan when he was fourteen, and the Lee family adopted him. The Lee family had one of the first flour mills; it was at the foot of 'A' Mountain. They were the ones that raised him after he was fourteen, and my father used to tell me the very interesting story about the Indians and how the Lees used to have him run up to the top of 'A' Mountain and see if there was any dust on the horizon. If there was dust on the horizon that meant the Indians would probably attack that night, and if there wasn't, why the family went to bed a little early. My father would tell me the Indians would come to—I don't want to use the word steal, but that's what it was—come to steal some flour. So if my father spotted the dust, they'd just take turns guarding whatever there was to steal."

We asked about the struggle in her own home to get along in those early days.

"You know, I never remember feeling poverty in my home; my father always managed to have a pantry. The first time that I am conscious of living in a home was the one we had on Convent Street which is right where the Tucson Community Center is; you know that little gate where you go into the center that is right where our home was. [The community center was part of the urban renewal of downtown Tucson that wiped out most of one of the oldest of the barrios.]

"And they built the home of adobes—beautiful adobes twenty-four inches by eight inches. It took a bulldozer to knock the thing down, I know. When they went through that downtown urban renewal project I just stood there across from my old home. I stood by the cathedral watching them tearing it down, and it really was with mixed feelings."

They call it "progress," this urban renewal which has wiped out many of the marks of earlier cultures. In Tucson this "progress" obliterated the adobe wall that once surrounded the Presidio de Tucson.

"Mother and dad had eight children. Three died; one was stillborn and the other two died in infancy. Five of us have survived, and we're still living. In that little house we had a pantry, and I can remember that my father always bought as much as he could, you know, wholesale . . . a bag of beans, a bag of flour . . . because he was a prospector and he used to have to leave that much food for us when he would go out prospecting for two or three months.

"Prospecting was very difficult, very difficult. My father did have some land near where the Twin Buttes mine is now south of Tucson. He homesteaded there so he did have some land there. After school was out we would go down there in the wagon for three months. My brothers' heads would be shaved, and I remember taking, you know, those little boxes of dried prunes and peaches which you could get for a song then, and beans and flour. And then away we'd go into the desert to my dad's land. And the first thing that we would do when we got there is butcher. I can still remember dad swinging the great big hammer and hitting the cow or steer that we were to butcher . . . to stun him and then slit the throat and we'd have a pail to catch the blood so we'd have blood pudding. The head was roasted. The kidneys and liver we used immediately, and we jerkied most of the meat so we'd have meat for the rest of the three months.

"This must have been about 1913, and we stayed out there in the desert while my father went around trying to find some minerals. Oh, yes, I remember eating rattlesnake. We would go out and search for a snake, and then my father would kill the rattlesnake and then he'd measure one hand from the head, another hand from the end of the rattlers, and the middle part is what we could eat. You see, towards the end of the three months we would run out of the food we had brought along so we had to make do. We would catch jackrabbits, too, and he'd make chorizo [Mexican sausage] out of the jackrabbit to make it a little more palatable. The cottontail rabbits we fried and they were good.

"And we would go out and hunt for *bellotas*. You know what *bellotas* are? Acorns. And we would bring them in, and we kids used to make our money that way 'cause we used to sell the *bellotas* when we came back into town. And we felt sort of badly, because we'd take the trade away from the Indians who used to bring the *bellotas* to town."

Maria began to talk of life in the barrio, the predominantly Mexican section just to the south of downtown Tucson.

"You know, I think the reason that we never felt all of this thing about discrimination is because we all needed each other so much. The Indian would come in with the wood, with the piñole, with the acorns and with the tortillas—the corn tortillas—and sell them. And the Chinese were

Dressed in their Sunday finery a Mexican-American family stands before an adobe hut in the barrio of Tucson in earlier days. ARIZONA HISTORICAL SOCIETY

responsible for the roving fresh vegetable carts. And we—my family—were lucky enough. Dad owned about four lots, and so there was a lot of vacant land around us. There were little stables there, and there would be about four Chinese vendors who would keep their wagons there to have an early start. And they would take their vegetables—and you know how artistic they are—they'd clean the carrots and the onions and the *calabacitas* [little squashes] and they'd arrange them on their wagons, cover them with gunny sacks and wet them. And this was in the evening, and I can often remember going to sleep with the sing-song of their chatter.

"They'd sprinkle the gunny sacks with water, and it was just like an evaporative cooler to keep the vegetables fresh overnight. And then they'd start early in the morning and come back at night with empty wagons. They were a terrific people. I had a very soft spot in my heart for the Chinese. Of course [here Maria smiled like a naughty child], we used to steal a little carrot every now and then from them."

We asked how it was that in a family who had to struggle so much for existence there was such impetus to pursue education.

"People have always asked me that. Father was just rabid on education. In fact, the only time that I really remember my dad and mother having an argument was one time when we got up too late to go to first Friday Mass, and so she kept us from school to go to the second Mass. My father came home and found that we had been kept from school that morning in order to go to Mass. And he said, 'If they missed Mass you punish them another way, but you don't make them stay home from school. They have to go to school.' And he took us by the hand and took us to school."

When did she first get the desire to become a teacher?

"When I was a junior in high school it was because of Mary Balch, one of my teachers, that I turned to education. Before my junior year I was more interested in baseball and basketball and that sort of thing. In fact, I made All-State forward, let's see, that was in 1924. I remember Mary Balch because she talked to me very seriously and said, 'Maria, what are you planning to do?'

"And I said, 'Well, you know I have a job at Steinfeld's Department Store and I just maybe will continue to work there.' Used to work there in the summer, and I also said, 'Sometimes I'd like to be a nurse.'

"And she says, 'What about an elementary school teacher?'

"And I looked at her, 'Are you kidding?'

"She says, 'No, I think you'd make a very good teacher.'

"And she also said, 'Now I know that your family can't afford it very well, but Tempe State Teachers College is a two-year college, and if we could get you in there and then in two years you'd be out earning your living.'

"So I told my family, and, of course, at that time *nice*—quote, unquote —Mexican girls didn't go away to school, and my older brother was very much against it. My mother cried, but my father made the decision, after Mary had gone to talk to him, that I should go. And so I went to State Teachers College. There it was that I felt discrimination for the first time. No, actually I felt it a little bit at Tucson High School because when I, the Mexican girl, got leading parts in operettas because I had a nice voice, I remember getting a nasty note.

"It was hard on me from then on, from when I became a leader . . . from then on I had to live in sort of a void. And that, I think, influenced me more than ever in what I tried to do in sponsoring bilingual, bicultural education."

We asked her what she meant by living in a void.

"When I started into the music field, you see, I was moving from the laboring class into the middle class, and both sides avoided me somewhat. The Mexican-American thought I was becoming a *gringada* [an uncomplimentary word for an Anglo], because, you see, I was the only Mexican that would get a leading part in the shows; the rest of the class was all 'gringo'—pardon me for using that word, but that's the word that was used at that time.

"So I lost the friendship of some of my Mexican-American friends, not because I wanted to, but because they believed I was shunning them. They were putting me aside, believing that I wanted it that way. And I couldn't visit the 'gringo' homes, the homes of the friends I went to school with, because that was taboo for a Mexican girl at that time.

"So I can remember sitting on the steps of Tucson High crying my eyes out because I didn't have a date for the prom. The 'gringo' would never think of taking *me* at that time, and the Mexican-American said, 'She is not interested in me.'

"But I think that what made me overcome that is the terrific love and security that I had at home, 'cause that's the only way I can explain my not being hurt more at that sort of thing."

And then when she went to Tempe to college. . . .

"When I went to Tempe I was the only Mexican-American except my cousin who was there, but she had come from an entirely different situation. She had come from Ray [now in the general area of Kearney, a mining district in southern Arizona]. Most of the Mexican-American workers up there lived in Sonora. Sonora was Mexican-American and Ray was *the* community. Well, my cousins lived in Ray. You see, my cousin's father was a superintendent of something in the mines, so they were elite. At college I roomed with her, and that is when I began to feel discrimination there. I asked for work and I was given the job of cleaning the bathrooms and the toilets, and that is the job I kept for the rest of the time until I found a job singing over at La Casa Vieja in Tempe which was Sally Hayden's place. She was the sister of Senator Carl Hayden. And that's the way—singing for the diners—I earned my living while I was in college."

When she graduated, she got her first teaching job in Tucson at Davis School, teaching ancient history, art and music.

"I graduated in '28, and I started teaching in September. My father passed away in November of '28. I had only given him two paychecks. You know, I had given him a little money from my paychecks.

"My dad was a terrific man. He had been street commissioner in Tucson for twenty-five, twenty-eight years and he had held the job under Republican and Democratic mayors. But we used to always have to pray that a Democrat would win, you know, because dad was a Democrat. But the Republicans would keep him on so my father used to tell us, 'Look, if you're hired for eight hours a day and you don't give as much as you can, that's just like stealing.' I guess that's why all of us have been pretty good workers.

"Well, my father died very happily with all of us surrounding him; he told my mother that."

There was a faint smile as Maria remembered an odd incident that followed her father's death.

"When he died, the newspapers came out that his father had come from Spain, that his mother, too, had come from Spain. Well, I got a call from the head of Mathews Hall where I had stayed up at State Teachers College in Tempe and he said, 'Maria, why in the world didn't you tell us you were Spanish?' I guess if I had, I would have gotten a job doing something besides cleaning toilets!

"Yes, that was in 1928, but I suppose the worst discrimination I felt came later when a group of girls went to Washington, D.C. We went visiting the National Gallery there, and then we went across into a little luncheonette and they gave the girls menus. They gave them menus but didn't give me a menu. At first I didn't think a thing about it. I thought, 'Well, maybe there are only two menus.' So then when it came time to order they asked the others what they wanted and ignored me. By that time I began to realize what was going on. So Chrissy, one of my girl friends who was a peppery little gal, said, 'Say, my friend wants to eat, too.' And the waiter said, 'But your friend can't eat here.' Right in the shadow of the Capitol!"

Maria then talked about her first teaching assignment in Tucson.

"Davis School was 99.9 percent Mexican and Yaqui Indians. We used to get the Yaquis late, and I didn't notice that at first. I wasn't conscious of their problems because I was busy teaching, and I loved it. My goal was to have those kids learn that first grade vocabulary so they could go into the second grade. But then I became conscious of the poverty, of the problems of the Mexican-Americans and the Indians, and the fact that they couldn't learn if their noses were running, if they needed tonsilectomies, if they hadn't had breakfast. So that's where my social work came in . . . in visiting families and seeing that they were in the best condition so their children could learn.

"I realized, too, that these children would come to school from one drab situation into another drab situation. At that time our schoolrooms were all painted in battle-gray or browns, you know, like they paint the ships in order to last. And it was very dreadful to teach so I kept asking the district to please paint my room: Would they paint it a nice green or a nice yellow, something bright? And they refused for three years. So one day, one weekend, I got some paint and I got some of my sixth grade boys, and we painted my room green.

"And I guess that was the first thing I did wrong as a teacher; I did something on my own.

"Well, then I decided we needed shade for the windows—it got pretty hot in those rooms for many months of the year—so I decided to put some shade trees down outside. To raise the money we sold hot dogs. I used to beg, borrow, steal; got day-old bread, and Swift Company was very nice, they'd give me the hot dogs. So we bought trees and planted them. When I came back the next summer, the trees were dead. And I asked the janitor, 'You lazy so-and-so, why did you let the trees die?' I really was getting after him and he said, 'Maria, I had orders not to water them.' "

The incident did not subdue her. She planted an oleander hedge to get shade. Shortly afterwards she was transferred out of the barrio area school and shipped across town to teach at Sam Hughes, then an Eastside Tucson school in a pure white district.

"Well, that was a revelation to me, going to Sam Hughes School to teach. It was the best thing that ever happened to me, by the way, because I really got to know the other side and those people got to know me. Of course, children were children to me, and I loved them, too, at Sam Hughes, and they loved me; and evidently I was successful there, too. At Sam Hughes I just marvelled at what I saw. Here there was grass on the ground and here were trees and library books. The difference in schools was not the fault of the district. If there was any fault with the district, it would be that they would let an affluent group of parents do things at one school that couldn't be done at a school where most of the parents were poor.

"And all this was going through my mind: What is it . . . just poverty that is making education of kids at Davis School different or is it methodology? What are we doing to these kids? So then when I went to Pueblo High School [on Tucson's south side], I realized what we were doing to them. Something struck me and I said, 'Here we are. We used to punish kids at Davis School. We told them they couldn't speak Spanish; that they had to learn English.' And then we turn around and give them Spanish in high school.

"And you see, by the time these kids got to high school, well they were so indoctrinated in speaking English and not Spanish that they were prostituting the pronunciation of their own names, anglicizing them, and, worse, they did not even know English properly."

Maria explained that the Mexican-American youngsters had anglicized their own names to avoid criticism. And she knew something had to be done to turn things around. She spoke to Spanish teachers at Pueblo and soon things were turned around in an experimental program that included an honors course in Spanish.

"It was a beautiful job those teachers did there. You could see what it was doing to the kids. They were going back to correctly pronouncing their names. They were holding their heads high. They knew for once in their lives who they were, and they were very happy with their language. And not only that, we noticed, too, the kids that were taking these courses in Spanish were getting higher grades in English, too."

And that was the beginning of Maria Urquides's battle to put bilingual education into the schools. As a representative to the National Education Association she had fought alongside black leaders in the desegregation fight. Mainly through her efforts, the Arizona delegation succeeded in the desegregation of local NEA associations. Then she turned to her own cause.

"So they were desegregated and the whole focus turned toward the black. That was the time of Watts, you know. After that I went to Monroe Sweetland, who was the NEA representative for the southwestern states and I said, 'Monroe, we have worked hard in the NEA for the black. Now I want the NEA to do something for the Mexican-American.' That was in 1965. So he said, 'What do you want?' I said, 'I want you, the NEA, to give us enough money for a group of teachers to go into the southwestern states and see what is happening to the Mexican-American student. I want to see if they're using any different methodology, because I think that we're doing the kid a disfavor when the only potential that he brings into the first grade that the Anglo does not have is his potential to become bilingual.

" 'And we're saying to him, "You can't use this language," and we're destroying him inside psychologically, and we're producing half of what he could be. We say they're bilingual; they're not bilingual. You're not bilingual until you can hear a language, you can write it, you can read it, and you can speak it. And these kids graduate not even bilingual, not even mono-lingual sometimes.' So I said, 'Please get me some money.' And we got the money, and we visited, I think it was fifty-eight different schools around thirteen districts in the state, and then we wrote the book, *The Invisible Minority*."

There were many meetings, symposiums and hearings in Washington, in Los Angeles, and in other cities. She pressed the leadership in Washington saying, 'Now, look, it's time you paid attention to the silent minority.' The big push toward federal funding of bilingual education came after a symposium of congressional leaders in Tucson. Bilingual education, although still not properly funded, became a reality and now Maria looked back. . . .

"They used to accuse us of being narrow, of believing that teaching Spanish to the Mexican-American child was a panacea, that it would solve all his problems. Absolutely not. It wouldn't solve all his problems, but neither would teaching him English and whipping him for speaking

Spanish solve all his problems. So neither is a panacea, but I think that being able to keep your own language, that means that you can keep your own culture and you're not ashamed of it.

"And you know what you are."

The Arrival of the "Anglos"

FOR MORE THAN TWO CENTURIES the desert and mountain regions of the Southwest were dominated by the Spanish. They had not completely subjugated the early settlers, the Indians. With some tribes they had made their peace; others they continued to pursue and fight until their final days.

And the final days for the Spaniards came not long after the turn into nineteenth century. In 1821 the Mexicans finally succeeded in ridding their land of the invaders, but Mexico was not to hold control of the Southwest, Texas or California for very long. The "Anglos," the Spanish name for those palefaces who came from the East, rapidly expanded into the Southwest, claiming more and more territory for the young United States of America.

They called them "Anglos," but those early pioneers were far from being all of Anglo-Saxon heritage. There were many who came from European countries like the Goldwaters, the grandparents of one of to-day's most prominent political figures, Senator Barry M. Goldwater. Those early "American" adventurers came for many of the same reasons as the Spanish conquistadores: for gold and silver, for acquisition of land, and, for many, to leave behind their problems for new lives in the Southwest.

And so it was that many of Arizona's most famous families trace back to pioneers who left Europe to begin again in the American Southwest. When Senator Goldwater is asked about his family, he starts with the flight of his grandfather from Poland. And with pride he explains that much of his independent spirit traces back to his people who fought for a foothold in Arizona Territory.

Barry Goldwater became a national figure when he was the Republi-

77

can nominee for president in 1964. He lost that race by a wide margin, but even then his strong voice, his independent views and his blunt honesty won him wide respect. Today he is a leader of Republican conservatives, a newspaper columnist, a photographer of the Southwest and a man in love with his state and his country.

THE STRENGTH OF THE EARLY PIONEERS

Senator Goldwater was at home for this taping. It was just a bit more than a month after the Republicans lost the presidency to Jimmy Carter and the senator had something to say about that, too. But he began with the early days, with the stories of his family. . . .

"Well, I guess you've got to start a little before Arizona, because I think Arizona became an accident of life with my grandfather. My grandfather was born in Poland and he was one of twenty-two children, and I've been trying since about 1930 to trace them. I found his brother, Joe, who was with him in Arizona, and another who was the mayor of Bulawayo, Rhodesia, and one in Australia and that's about as far as I got. Well, they left Poland, I guess, for the same reason all Polish Jews left— they wanted to be free from the Russians. So they went to France and then to England and in 1854 they came over to this country, my grandfather Mike and his brother Joe together. My grandmother, Sarah, came later with two children born in England, my Aunt Caroline and Uncle Morris. They came across the Isthmus of Panama; they were carried in baskets.

"The men came around the Horn, and they stopped briefly in San Francisco and then settled in Sonora, California, where my grandfather ran a saloon and pool hall and his wife was a seamstress. They never made it . . . never made any money up there. They went down to Los Angeles about '58, had a billiards hall and general notions store across the street from the present city hall. They weren't doing well. They heard of the gold strikes on the Colorado River so Mike, my grandfather, loaded up a wagon with merchandise and went to what was then Colorado City —the present site of Yuma. Mike didn't find any gold, but he found he could sell merchandise so he moved to the little town of La Paz as business partner of a friend from Los Angeles, Bernard Cohn.

"Now, La Paz was about six miles back from the normal course of the river, but sometimes the river would swing over and they could unload freight at La Paz. That partnership wasn't entirely satisfactory. Mike bought out Cohn's interest and sent to San Francisco for his brother Joe to come to Arizona. In the fall of 1866 my grandfather and my uncle— my Uncle Morris who was then a maturing fourteen—were traveling back from San Francisco and they found Herman Ehrenberg, who was probably one of the greatest of the early Arizona pioneers, shot to death near Indio. Ehrenberg was a German who fought in the Texas Revolution and made maps of Arizona in those days that are almost as accurate today as they were then.

"Well, about that time the river meandered away from La Paz, so they moved their warehouse downstream about six miles to a little settlement called Mineral City, which had a better river landing. Mike renamed it Ehrenberg in honor of his murdered friend [Joe Goldwater became postmaster of the city in 1869]. The river always cut into the bank, the east bank, so that freighters could always unload there. So you might say that my grandfather came to Arizona as an extension of why he came to the United States—to be free of political tyranny and to make some money. And he came to Arizona to make some money—but he never made a lot.

"After they established the store in Ehrenberg, my grandfather Mike expanded into other ventures. About the time he bought out Cohn, he and Cohn had stepped forward when the owners of the Vulture Mine near Wickenburg had rich ore but didn't have money for a mill. Mike and Cohn financed the mill, putting up $90,000 in the process. Mike left the business over at Ehrenberg in charge of Joe and Morris while he stayed at the mill until he'd collected the money to pay back the big loan he had arranged.

"He also went into a freighting business with a Dr. W. W. Jones, a Virginian whom he had known in Los Angeles, contracting to haul military equipment and troops to camps in Arizona and also to furnish the army troops with hay, grain, beans, corn and other necessities. The grain contracting business looked so promising Mike opened a store in Phoenix in 1872—at the northwest corner of First Street and Jefferson, where the Barrows Furniture downtown store is located—and placed Uncle Morris in charge when he had just reached his twentieth birthday. Things didn't work out well, so the Phoenix store was closed at a loss. Mike and Morris moved to Prescott, and that's more or less been the family home ever since. Morris became the central figure in that store; Mike sold out to his sons in 1880.

"My Uncle Henry and two younger brothers, Ben and Sam, were supposed to be partners with Morris in the firm that was known as M. Goldwater and Bros. Ben and Sam were more interested in gambling, and both unfortunately died young from tuberculosis. Henry was sort of a ne'er-do-well. You never saw him; he was always off looking for gold. He was always looking for a grubstake. Every time he came to see my father, he wanted money. Henry came back to Prescott from time to time, and his wife, a lovely and long-suffering lady, helped organize the first library in Prescott.

"Morris ran the store along until my father, Baron, finished his education and came out to Prescott to join Morris. Right from the start Baron Goldwater thought Phoenix was the market for expansion, because when the Santa Fe came into Phoenix it was no longer isolated from the world. In 1895, I think it was, my father wanted to move to Phoenix. My uncle didn't, so they played a hand of casino, and father won so he came to Phoenix. And down here we've been in the mercantile business until we sold to Associated Dry Goods about 1958 or 1959.

"My Uncle Morris lived to be eighty-seven, and he was one of the founders of the Democrat Party in the territory. He served in the Territorial House and the Territorial Senate, also the State Senate and was president of the senate, and was mayor of Prescott for twenty-two years. He also was vice-president of the Arizona Constitutional Convention, so he had a great background in politics. My grandfather, too, at one time was the mayor of Prescott.

"An interesting little story that Mo Udall and I tell about his grandfather, David King Udall, who was a polygamist, and, of course, the polygamists settled at Saint Johns and other faraway places for the purpose of keeping away from the federal officers, in a nation that never accepted the Mormons' idea of pluralistic marriage. Well, one weekend David King Udall had to go to Prescott on business, and as he rode into town the federals arrested him and put him in jail. That's when my grandfather was the mayor. That night he got a horse, got a key to the jail, went down and opened the jail. Told David King Udall to get on that horse 'and get your ass out of town and stay out.' So he never came back, and the Udalls and Goldwaters have been good friends ever since.

"Tragically I never knew my grandfather. He died six years before I was born. Nor did I know my granduncle Joe. My grandfather was a big man; he was sometimes called 'Miguel Grande' by his Mexican friends. That was unusual for a Goldwater because he was well over six feet and over 200 pounds. Most of the men in the family up until I came along were very short men. My father was about five-foot-four, my uncle was only about five-foot-one. They were little men, but my grandfather was a giant.

"One day they got shot at by the Indians in Mint Valley up near Prescott and two balls hit my granduncle. They rode on to a ranch and sent for a doctor who dug the balls out. Joe wore them on his watch fob and they were buried with him.

"I was very lucky to have been born at a time when a lot of our early greats were still alive. They weren't tough men as we see them in movies and on television today. I asked my father once, I said, 'Don't you own a gun?'

"He said, 'Yes, I have a pistol, but I've never shot it. I couldn't hit anything with it.'

"And he couldn't. I said, 'How did you get along in the younger days?'

"He said, 'Nobody ever carried a gun in Arizona except a cowboy who was riding the range, and he carried a gun to shoot animals or to get his meal. Very rarely did a man wear a gun into town.' He told me once, 'I think the only shooting I ever saw in Phoenix was when a couple drunks made a bet that they couldn't hit a watermelon across the street—and they didn't.'

"So these men, as I remember them, well, they were strong men intellectually and morally—and physically if they had to be. They were not the rough, tough, shoot-'em-up, bust-'em-up kind of people that we see on television and read about today.

"Uncle Morris boarded for years in the home of Mr. and Mrs. Fisher and stayed on after Mr. Fisher died. Twenty years later he said public opinion got the best of him. He said, 'I had to marry Aunt Sally.' He was fifty-five then. But she was a tough old gal. Some place in my library I have letters that she wrote describing a trip up the Colorado River on a boat and how the men were gentlemen. When they hit a sandbar, they'd get off and push; the women would stay on deck. And coming into Prescott through Chino Valley she tells of lying under the wagon, loading buckshot in the guns for her father and brothers to shoot the Indians. I have a hunch she probably shot a few herself."

Goldwater shifted in his chair, looked out through the picture windows of his hilltop home and surveyed the great spread of the city of Phoenix below him.

"Here, we're the sixth civilization to have lived in this valley and it was an oldtimer named Jack Swilling who came riding in from Wickenburg and noticed how rich the soil looked as his horse kicked it up. And Jack came down here and found the old canals the Indians had for centuries, and he built some more of those weir dams of brush and diverted the water and started what became the Salt River Project. The people that followed didn't have that challenge left, although they had the challenge of attracting industry. There was always this challenge. There was always something left to do. And today as I sit up here as I do every day when I am home in Phoenix and look out at my town, I can think of things that still have to be done. It won't be done by the older people like me. They'll be done by young people who will come in here and see things that we never saw."

When he paused again, we asked him about his attachment to Arizona and his closeness to its people. He smiled as he answered . . .

"Well, I think it was probably my mother that caused all of that. My mother came out here from Nebraska with three months to live—tuberculosis—and about $1,500 she'd saved nursing. She was the first registered nurse in the Territory of Arizona. She and another sick woman bought an old army tent, put it up where Sunnyslope is now. And she didn't die, and she kept getting better so she went back to work and she finally saved a little more money and bought Roosevelt and Central [a valuable corner in downtown Phoenix today] for $1,500. I kind of wish we still had it.

"Well, my mother, Josephine Williams Goldwater, lived to be ninety-six and never came close to dying of tuberculosis. I think she just finally died of having too much four o'clock bourbon.

"But when we were children the earliest things I can really remember would be her taking us out to the Indian School, for example, in a buggy to watch the flag come down. And we met Indian children there. We played with them. Of course, the Maricopa Indians used to come into town every Saturday and sell their wares, and we'd go down and talk with them. And with the advent of the automobile—I think we got our first car about 1914—then she used to take us camping. She'd drive us to California, and I remember night after night sleeping out on the ground, and she'd be lying there with a rifle by her side in case coyotes were around. I remember one trip to California took us five days and now you can drive it in six and one-half hours.

"We'd go up to the Indian country. The first time I went up to the Hopi country I was seven. We'd go to the Navajo Reservation; and then she took us to see everything in the state you could think of. And then, of course, having been born when I was, I had the opportunity of hearing about things. Every night on Central Avenue—and I was born about where the Westward Ho is—every house would have the front door open. The door was open; the whiskey was on the sideboard. They'd come in, have a drink. If anyone was there they'd talk; if not, they'd go off to the next house."

This took us to Goldwater's love affair with politics and he related how it all began for him.

"Well, I had been interested in politics naturally all my life. I remember driving a Model-T Ford with my uncle who was then running for the senate in Yavapai County. In the back seat with him was his Republican opponent. And I remember going into a town like Jerome; and I had a big bell, and I'd get out on the corner and ring that darned thing and talk about a speech. And these two guys would get out and just raise hell with each other. Oh, it was terrible what they'd say to each other. Then they'd get back in the car, get a bottle out and have a drink, and were real good friends. That was my first real exposure to politics. And I became a precinct committeeman; my mother and I were the only Republicans in my family.

"Well, when I came back from World War II we'd had a pretty fair city government in Phoenix, but it was never quite what we wanted. So they organized the Charter Government Committee and my best friend, Harry Rosenzweig . . . well, they made Rosie and me the committee to collect candidates. So we got candidates, and I went off fishing. Harry called me one day and said, 'Say, we're short two candidates.'

"I said, 'What the hell are you going to do about it?'

"He said, 'You and I are going to run.'

"I said, 'Christ, we couldn't get elected dog catcher.'

" 'Well,' he said, 'we're going to run.'

"So we ran and we led the ticket, and I became vice-mayor and he was a councilman. And then in '50—'49 or '50—we wanted to run a Republican for governor. We hadn't had a Republican governor since . . . for twenty-two years. So we talked Howard Pyle into running, and I told him I'd manage his campaign. I didn't know anything about managing a campaign, but I had an airplane. So we just started out to go all over the state, and we got old Howard elected. He was running against Ana Frohmiller who was about the best vote-getter we had in the state then, but somehow or other Howard squeaked through by a couple thousand votes. And the next time around—'52—he reminded me that I had talked him into running, now I had to repay him by running against McFarland [Senator Ernest W. McFarland].

" 'Well,' I said, 'Howard, you're out of your goddamned head.' I said, 'Nobody is going to beat Ernie McFarland.'

"Funny thing, about then I was in Mac's office in Washington on a water matter and he said, 'What do you think of me becoming Senate Majority Leader?'

" 'Well,' I said, 'Harry Truman's the president and that's quite a load for you to carry. And if you do take the senate leadership, someone's going to beat you.' I said that never thinking that I would be running against him. Sure enough, that was one thing we beat him with . . . well, that and Eisenhower running for president. I should never have beaten McFarland. If he had come home and acted like a candidate, I'd still be selling pants.

"But he didn't and I got elected to the Senate and then got re-elected. And they started in '63 wanting me to run for president. I said, 'No, I don't want to run for president, don't want any part of it.'

"Well, I finally said I would run because it would be running against Jack Kennedy, and I talked to Jack about it and we planned sort of a whistle-stop campaign where we would really debate and he'd get up and say his piece and I would say my piece. None of this prepared crap that the press had to use . . . just get out and talk about the country. Well, when Jack was assassinated, I just said that's the end of it.

"But then I got so much pressure from so many young people to run, I finally—right in this room—said, 'Well, all right.' But I didn't want to do it.

"We knew we couldn't beat Johnson, but we knew we could keep the Republican Party from falling into the hands of Rockefeller and the Eastern Gang, as we called them, which we did and which allowed Nixon to run the next time. And the organization we put together was so good it was still working, and it is still working. It got Nixon elected. And I ran

For Senator Barry M. Goldwater (third from right) politics began with a seat on the Phoenix City Council in 1949. Second from the right is Harry Rosenzweig, the senator's lifelong friend. ARIZONA HISTORICAL SOCIETY

in '69 for the Senate and got re-elected and got re-elected once again. So that's where I am."

We asked Goldwater about his afterthoughts when Lyndon B. Johnson swamped him in the 1964 presidential race, whether he had any regrets.

"No. I remember the day I was putting my finishing touches to my acceptance speech. I'll never forget it, sitting up in the Mark Hopkins [the hotel in San Francisco where the Republican Convention was being held] and over in the corner is a guy from Opinion Research with a flip chart, and he was showing me the percentages—twenty for me, eighty for Johnson. And I turned to the group and I said, 'Look, fellows, just for the hell of it, let's tear this acceptance speech up and write one and tell them to go to hell, that we don't want it.'

"We knew we couldn't win. There was no way in the world that this country would have elected a new president which would have been three presidents in two-and-one-half years. That was one thing. Another thing was we were at war, and Johnson wasn't exactly truthful about it. He said he would not enlarge the war and Goldwater was a 'hit-the-red-button, kill-'em, bomb-'em candidate,' and I got beat.

"I never regretted it. As I told Jerry Ford the other day [the taping was done not long after Ford lost to Carter in November of 1976], I said, 'You know, the mistake you made was not losing like I did. The way you lost, all your life you're going to wake up and say, "Jesus, what did I do? I wore my tie wrong. I didn't have my hair combed." ' I said, 'I don't even worry about it.'

"People have asked me the question, 'What would you do differently?' There wasn't a thing that we could have done differently. I think, had the election gone another week we would have gotten up to that magic perimeter of 55–45 percent because we did pick up tremendously on Johnson in the last month. But we would never have won it."

We asked just one more question about the presidential race: Did he believe now that his campaign had made some solid contributions?

"Oh, yes, I think so. Unfortunately most of the things I said would happen, have happened. We've had bad inflation. We've had a depreciation in the value of our money. We've had fighting in the streets—in Watts and Detroit, at least. We lost a war. We've lost our place in the world.

"I think if I'd been president we would have prevented all those things. But we did give the conservative mind a place to rest and give the young people something to think about when they were offered the choice between liberal and conservative, even though today there's still a great misunderstanding. But people today are more interested in retaining more of the money they make. They're very concerned about the diminishing power of this country. So I think it did some good. I think it made people think, and that's what politics is all about."

It was time to turn from politics and back to Arizona, and Goldwater reminisced about his boyhood days in Phoenix.

"I remember we didn't even have paved streets. We had dirt sidewalks, ditches along the streets. Well, we had the Center Street Gang and that was Harry Rosenzweig and his brother [prominent Phoenix jewellers] and my family. And there was the Third Avenue Gang and the First Street Gang. And we used to just get together and fight. And we all learned to box from the man who was the father of John Henry Lewis of Phoenix, who later became light-heavyweight champion of the world. I still have a few bones missing in my nose.

"And we would have mudball fights and rock fights and fist fights. We played football and basketball. As young men—I say young men up to high school age—we really didn't have much idea what we wanted to do. I think it's gotten worse today. I think young people get much older than we were.

"I wanted to go to West Point, and I wanted to be an army officer. I was put up for West Point, but my father died, and I didn't go. I always kicked myself for not doing it. I would not have ended up being a merchant. I liked being a merchant, but I always liked the military."

Goldwater began to discuss his views of Arizona.

"This is the land of '*mañana.*' I remember, in fact, when they took siestas in the state. You don't have to break your butt to get it done today; wait till tomorrow and get it done. This is a charm of the state. I always said that Arizona is a 114,000-square-mile piece of heaven which just fell.

"I think we've taken from the Mexican, we've taken from the Spaniard, we've taken from the Indian. The culture hasn't needed any improvement. It was perfect when we got it, and it's still perfect. And let me add something more about the strength of the people who pioneered this territory.

"I knew of some very big business deals made in Phoenix that were made with a handshake. The last lease that I executed for Goldwaters was in 1929, and I made it over the telephone. It was a twenty-year lease amounting to a lot of money, and I got a call the next day from the own-er's lawyer who said, 'Don't you think you should have this more formal?' And I said, 'What do you mean?' He said, 'Let's put it in a letter.' So a twenty-year lease was finally placed in a three-paragraph letter.

"The next lease that I signed required two years to write, covered thirty-six pages and was so cleverly written that I'm sure either side could have broken it.

"I think that honor among those early men and women probably was one of the great unlooked-for, but certainly accepted, facets of their lives that caused Arizona to be what it is today. As I think of what our pioneers have accomplished, I have to say they were—and are—men of honor."

The Americanization of the Old Pueblo

TUCSON, THE OLD PUEBLO, sits in a "teacup" valley surrounded by the lofty peaks of the Santa Catalinas, Santa Ritas and Rincons and the low, craggy silhouettes of the Tucson mountains. It is at the head of the Santa Cruz Valley, only an hour's drive—by modern highway standards—from the Mexican border.

For centuries waters that flowed through these valleys nurtured Indian tribes. And for the Spanish conquistadores and padres this was fertile, if desert, territory. It was in this area that the padres strived to convert the "savages" and it was here, too, that the "savages" labored to build missions to honor the Spaniards' God.

In 1775 the Spanish established the Presidio de Tucson and it was not until December 16, 1846, that the first American flag was hoisted over the adobe-walled village. A United States Army unit, the Mormon Battalion, en route to California under Lieutenant-Colonel P. St. George Cooke, took Tucson without firing a shot. They ousted the Mexicans who had replaced the Spanish when they were finally driven out of Mexico in 1821.

From that point, even though the Mormon Battalion stayed in Tucson only two days, the Americanization of the Old Pueblo was rapid. Earlier in the 1800s there had been trappers, fur traders and mountain men coursing the territory that would become Arizona, and Tucson soon became a main stop on the east-west route. It was through Tucson that the Butterfield Overland Mail Company ran its stage coaches, and when the Southern Pacific Railroad came to the Old Pueblo the growth of the city was assured.

For this interview Roy Drachman sat in an office high up in a downtown building. He could look out at the valley where his family came to settle. To the south he could see the area where his father operated Elysian

Grove, a recreation center for early Tucsonians, and to the north he could look at the modern shopping centers he helped develop.

There were many families who helped develop Tucson, and the Drachmans played important roles just as the Goldwaters did in the Yuma, Phoenix and Prescott areas along with other early pioneers. And as it is with other stories of Arizona's early days, there is an intertwining of those early families as you will see in the opening paragraphs of this taping with Roy Drachman.

THE GROWTH OF AN AMERICAN FAMILY

The Tucson story is a personal story to Roy Drachman. His entire family life was wrapped up in the development of the Old Pueblo; there is a school and street in Tucson bearing the family name but even those honors do not tell the depth of the family's contributions to this desert city.

"My grandfather Phillip came to this country from Poland. There he lived in a little town called Petrograv, and he was one of several children. In those days the Russians were in control of Poland and any youngster, after he reached the age of fourteen, was conscripted into the army, taken away from his family and never seen again. And my great-grandparents realized that Phillip was getting of that age, and they started digging a hole under the floor of their house. They would take pots of dirt out at night, and they built a place under the floor for my grandfather to hide. When the Russians came by they said that the boy had run off and they didn't know where he was. But he lived with them a couple of years under those conditions, and finally they wanted to get him out of that country. And apparently he contracted some lung problems during that time, and he was probably one of the first persons that came to Arizona for his health.

"I know that my grandfather and the Goldwaters were very close friends. As I understand it, he went from Poland to England and then to the United States on the same boat with Barry Goldwater's grandfather and great uncle. The three of them landed in New York. My grandfather went to Philadelphia, and the Goldwaters went around the Horn to California. And they kept in touch because later my grandfather went the same route and joined the Goldwaters in California. In the meantime my grandfather's brother, Sam, came over to this country and also went to

California. And Phillip and Sam came to Arizona together. They went to La Paz first and then on to Tucson. My grandfather came into Tucson sometime in the mid-1850s. He stayed here several years and established a home. Then he went back to New York City to get married. I think it was one of those old arranged marriages; I don't know for sure. But he did go to New York and married my grandmother whose name was Rosa Katzenstein.

"Anyhow they went by boat to the Isthmus of Panama and then got on another ship to go to California. They stayed in Los Angeles for a while, and then they came to Tucson. The railroad at that time, which was about 1867 or '68, went only from Los Angeles to San Bernardino. From there they took a wagon across the desert to Tucson. My grandmother told me about that trip. She said it took twenty days, and today we can fly that distance in forty minutes.

"Sam Drachman came to Tucson and married a woman from a family of Spanish derivation, and they had four children. My grandmother and grandfather—Phillip Drachman—had ten children and all were born in Tucson except Mose. Mose was born in San Francisco while my grandparents were there on a trip. There were four boys: there was Mose, Albert, Harry, and my father, Emanuel. My Uncle Harry's middle name was Arizona. I don't know whether he was given that name or adopted it, but he was known as Harry A. Drachman and his middle name was Arizona.

"And then the youngest of my aunts was Phyllis; she died at the age of eighty-seven in California in 1976. Only three of those ten children born to my grandparents stayed in Tucson, and between the three of them —Harry, Mose and Emanuel—they had eleven children. And most of that eleven left Tucson. I guess one of the most famous was Rosemary, Moses's daughter; she lived here most of her life and wrote *Chicken Every Sunday* and quite a few other books.

"I didn't know my grandfather at all; he died in 1889 and I was born here July 31, 1906. But I knew my grandmother very well, and she used to tell me about the early life. She lived most of her life in Tucson in homes with dirt floors, as most of the homes had. But she said they had a lot of social activity, and everybody knew everybody else. There were a lot of parties, in the homes and at the old Orndorff Hotel. And the Elysian Grove and Carrillo's Gardens were gathering places in the early days.

"My grandfather had some freight wagons and they'd haul from Yuma to Tucson and then on to Lordsburg, back and forth. And then he had a carriage business, hauling people from the railroad station, like a taxi service today. My grandfather also did contracting for the government in hay—cutting hay—and there were large areas out in the San Pedro Valley, and they'd go out there and harvest the native grass, for horses of the cavalry troops stationed here then. And one time there were six Mexican men working for my grandfather who were out there harvesting. The Indians attacked, burned the wagons and killed one of the workers.

"My father, Emanuel Drachman, as a youngster worked for my grandfather taking care of the horses. And I remember one of the old teachers telling how my dad was kept after school one time; he had done something wrong. And he cried that he had to go home to feed horses, that if she kept him too late the horses wouldn't get anything to eat.

"My dad was born in 1872, so he was just a youngster when he was doing that. But in those days there were no jobs here for young men. Harry Drachman went to work for the Albert Steinfeld Company—Uncle Albert, they called him. He was the benefactor for a lot of people here. He was the richest man in town, so they looked to him. Mose worked for him, too, until he became an agent for a coffee company. Then my dad went to work at the Southern Pacific Railroad shops—in the blacksmith shop. He became a very strong man, and everybody said he was the strongest man in town. He weighed about 205 pounds, stood five-nine and was all muscle and man. I heard many oldtimers tell how my dad loved to fight. He always was getting involved in fist fights. He was apparently a tough guy.

"They used to tell about the time Tucson was playing the Cananea, Sonora, baseball team here. My dad was captain and manager of the Tucson team. He had been a pitcher, but as he got older he just played catcher. The Cananea team had some big leaguers, including a man by the name of Bert Whaling, who later played with the Boston Braves. He was a big man, about 220 or 230 pounds. Cananea had beaten Tucson pretty badly in the first game. Tucson won the second, and in the final game Whaling came running down the line from third base, and my dad was the catcher and he knew he had the Cananea runner out by tagging the plate. So he just flipped the ball to Whaling who wasn't looking. The ball hit him in the face and he came over to my dad and slapped him. My dad shook a finger in his face and told him he'd take care of the matter after the game. Well, the people in the stands roared; they knew what was going on.

"Well, as it happened my dad was the last man at bat in the ninth inning; and when he struck out, he threw the bat and reached over and pulled the catcher's mask off Whaling, and they started going at each other. They tell me my dad just drove him right back towards the crowd, knocked him out, and Whaling just fell in a clump in front of the grandstand. Tucson had lost the game and the series to Cananea, but they'd won the fight and that was the most important thing. The Tucson fans picked my dad up on their shoulders and carried him all the way to the beer garden in the old Elysian Grove, and they had a big celebration."

Elysian Grove was an important family recreation spot in the early days in Tucson, and Roy's dad staged many events there, bringing many firsts to the city, including the first airplane flight.

"My dad owned Elysian Grove. I guess it had the first swimming pool in Tucson. It was located south of where Carrillo School is now. The school is built just where the pavillion had been. The pavillion had a wood floor, and they used it for roller skating and for dances and on occasions they'd have speakers in. I remember as a youngster when Teddy Roosevelt came through here, my dad took me down and said, 'I want you to remember this.' I guess I was about three or four at that time, but I think I remember it.

"My dad brought the first motion picture machine to the state of Arizona, and he was the first motion picture exhibitor here, putting on movies down at Elysian Grove. And he'd also bring in entertainers, live shows, companies from Mexico and so forth. He got to be quite a weatherman because he'd open in May—usually *Cinco de Mayo* was the beginning of the season—and lots of times in May there was cold weather; we still have that in May sometimes. And that cold weather would just knock him out of the box. He would start out in debt every year, and he barely made a living.

"When we were kids we were poor as the devil. I remember we used to take our shoes and put playing cards inside them when they wore out. That kept our bare feet off the ground . . . we found out that cards were for something else besides playing. But we always ate, and we never really suffered much. My dad, I remember, used to give my mother fifteen dollars a week, and for that she bought the food and paid for any help she had, like 'Uncle José,' a Papago Indian who used to come and clean the garden and cut wood. Our old home was at the corner of Main and McCormick and that's just about where the Tucson Community Center is today."

Roy Drachman smiled as he continued.

"My dad had this beer garden, saloon, down there at Elysian Grove, and I remember we used to go down there, me and my brother Frank, and my dad used to say: 'Well, you can have a tall lemonade or a little shot-glass full of beer.' We always took that little shot-glass of beer, and my brother and I thought we were big shots. In back of the bar there was the usual picture of Custer being massacred by the Indians. We'd stand there at the bar and look at that picture and, of course, it was a very exciting thing for kids to do.

"When prohibition came in my dad closed the Elysian Grove, and a man by the name of Ben Goldsmith came along from Mexico. He had a handlebar mustache, and I remember he was a very short little fellow, a wonderful man. About 1915 Goldsmith and my dad built the Broadway Theatre at the southwest corner of Broadway and Stone. There was no air conditioning in those days, and it could get very hot in the summer time. They had a lot of those sixteen-inch oscillating fans, and the sides of the theatre were built so they could be opened up, pulled up by ropes. And my dad put a pipe along the ridge of the roof with sprinklers on it. He'd turn the water on as soon as the sun would go down, and it would cool the roof. I guess that was one of the first cooling systems around here."

Emanuel Drachman continued in the movie business, but disaster struck the family in 1918.

"I remember the day very well. It was May 23, 1918, and Douglas Fairbanks had come to Tucson and made a picture—the first movie that was made here. It was called *Heading South*, and that May 23 was the opening night. I was sitting up front watching the movie at the Opera House. The movie had just started when the film stuck and we saw the flames break out. They first started up in the booth. Everyone got out of the theatre. There was no panic. But the theatre burned to the ground, and my dad had no insurance.

"It was a rough time. My mother came down and was standing there watching the building burn. She had tears running down her cheeks. Of course, as a youngster I knew it was bad, but I didn't know how bad. We went home, and my dad came in the back door through the screen porch. And I said, 'Is there anything left, Pop?' And he said, 'Yeh, you can have

PHOTOS TAKEN BY GODFREY SYKES
RESEARCH MEMBER OF CARNEGIE INSTITUTE
TUCSON

VIEWS SHOW FIRST FLIGHTS IN TUCSON
MADE ON FEBRUARY 20,1910 BY CHAS. K.
HAMILTON. FLIGHTS WERE MADE FROM
OLD ELYSION GROVE, AN EARLY AMUSE-
MENT PARK EXISTING WEST OF MAIN ST.
AND EAST OF SANTA CRUZ RIVER.

The first airplane flight in Tucson was made in 1910 from the old Elysian Grove, where Roy Drachman's father provided family entertainment for early Tucsonians.
PHOTO BY GODFREY SYKES

it.' And he threw me a great big padlock. He said, 'This is what's left.' "

But that disaster didn't stop the Drachman family. The theatre was rebuilt and operated by Emanuel Drachman and his partner. At fifteen Roy ran the Opera House during the summer, and at nineteen he managed the Rialto Theatre, which still stands in downtown Tucson, but is only a faded image of its old glory. Roy went on to become one of Tucson's leading businessmen; brother Frank was advertising director of Tucson Newspapers, Incorporated, until the time of his death. We asked Roy why he thought his family persevered through all the difficult times.

"Well, I don't know. I know when my grandfather died in '89, Harry Drachman, my father's brother, was nineteen and the oldest boy, so he became head of the household. And I remember his sisters saying how tough he was on them, how he acted like the father. He sat at the head of the table and saw that they were properly washed up when they came to the dinner table.

"And I had tremendous respect for my grandmother. She had ten children, the youngest a year old, and there she was left without a husband. All the boys, including my father, pitched in and supported her in those days. And we were all taught the same thing in our home. When I started to work ushering in the theater and making five dollars a week, I had to give my mother two dollars a week for my room and board. When I made more, I paid more. As long as I lived at home it was that way, and it was the same for my brother.

"My dad just made us realize there wasn't any free lunch, you know, and I think that came from the training he got when he grew up.

"I've thought about what it was that helped them make a go of it in those early days. I think they must have had a great spirit, all of them. If they hadn't had spirit, they wouldn't have come to this country in the first place. And knowing that they were coming to what you might call, looking back, wild country, primitive country, they were prepared to accept the privations and hardships, and I think they responded to them.

"You know, today when I go to Europe I talk to a lot of people, and they talk about coming to America to own a home, to own some land. Most of them can't do it over there. And that's the way it was back there; my grandparents came for the opportunity of this country, to be able to be free, to own a home, to own some land.

"And they had a great spirit. They were adventurous, ready to do things. Here, look up there on the wall. See that picture? That's the picture of the first airplane flying in Tucson. It was brought to Tucson on a flatcar and assembled here. They took it out to Elysian Grove—my dad's place—and got it up in the air. I remember watching it fly. I was only a little one then, but I remember it. No one really believed it would get up in the air. But it did. It flew. It took spirit to try those things those days, and those people had it. That is what made them great."

Trader to the Indians

NORTHERN ARIZONA, even in modest terms, is a country of contrasts. It has the 12,000-foot San Francisco Peaks and the vast and awesome depths of the Grand Canyon. It has high, arid desert—the land of the Navajos and Hopis, and it also has lush, green forests and meadows—1.6 million acres of it on the White Mountain Apache Reservation, and the private lands are in the hands of the "New Settlers."

The Locketts came into northern Arizona in the late 1800s, and they ran sheep on the land, the green meadow land. It was in Flagstaff in 1906 that Clay Lockett was born. He came from a family who ran sheep, but he was to gain an early fascination with the "First Settlers." He earned degrees in archaeology at the University of Arizona, and by 1932, he was out in the field studying the lives and ways of American Indians.

For a period he worked in government service with the Indians, and then he turned to trading. As a trader, Clay Lockett exerted a major influence on the development of Indian artists. He helped many of them to get started, and he also worked to raise the quality of their art work.

Clay Lockett's summer home is in the pine-studded valley that sweeps north from Flagstaff up to the majestic heights of the San Francisco Peaks. At the age of seventy, Lockett demonstrated much of the strong independence of the West's early settlers. His views are uncompromising and backed by a lifetime of experiences in the field.

TAKE WASHINGTON OUT OF THE RESERVATIONS

Clay Lockett was at home in the natural beauty that surrounded him—the gorgeous mountains and forests outside his Flagstaff home and the magnificent paintings and sketches that hung on the walls throughout his home. He is a casual man and he talked easily about the early days of the Locketts. . . .

"Dad came from, well, originally he came from Missouri and he arrived in 1880 in Flagstaff. It took him three years to get here . . . drove horses across the plains of Kansas. He didn't say the *'state* of Kansas'; he always said, the *'plains* of Kansas.' And when he came the buffaloes were all gone, but the buffalo bones were there. These big buffalo hunters would kill all the buffalo, took the hides and left the bones. So you could make a buck or two by picking up buffalo bones and taking them to the railway. I don't know what the hell they did with the buffalo bones . . . buttons, or fertilizer, or something. . . .

"My dad was able to get two wagons. He had a crippled brother that had 'total' disability from the Civil War—fourteen bucks a month—and he could drive one team of horses. Anyway the two of them started west and when they got to Flagstaff, the railroad was coming through and dad, with his two teams of horses, got a contract to haul railroad ties."

He liked the country so much he never left. He was in the sheep business from then on. Living in the Flagstaff area, the Locketts often were hosts to noted scientists who would come out from the Smithsonian Institution and universities to open archaeological sites. And young Clay Lockett often would go with the scientists on those early digs; his interest in archaeology has never left him.

"I went down to the University of Arizona where I met Dr. Cummings [the celebrated archaeologist, Dr. Byron Cummings] and we got along fine, and I got in the department and ended up with two degrees in archaeology. When I got out of college I was offered a job as head of the Arizona State Museum for a thousand bucks a year. Even in 1932 that was not much money. I'm not going to give you my whole life's history, but I was principal of the Pearce High School [in southeast Arizona] for one year, and then I got into the Indian Service. I was in the Indian Service for eight years on the Navajo Reservation because of my sheep background which I supposedly knew something about; I didn't know a hell of a lot. And my anthropological background . . . I got a job with the Indian Service. After eight years, I decided that I was much more interested in live Indians than dead ones.

"While I was there the Commissioner of Indian Affairs was John Collier, who was, in my estimation, one of the most able, most understanding commissioners we've ever had. He was the little guy that was such a thorn in the flesh of the Department of the Interior and the Bureau of Indian Affairs for so many years that Franklin Roosevelt finally said to him, 'Now, look, John, I'll admit that we've done wrong for the last hundred years with the Indians. So you are now the commissioner and you straighten it up.' And he tried.

"On the Navajo Reservation the big deal when I was there was the problem of soil erosion. The land was so overgrazed it was just pitiful. So after a big survey it was decided that a big stock reduction, or stock adjustment was needed. And the Indians were very much against it, naturally. It was their living. I'd have to say, 'Well, you've got 400 sheep. You can only run 200. But 200 good ones will bring you as much as 400 poor ones.'

"I was always more interested in their arts and crafts than anything else. So I finally made a break and said, 'This is it, Uncle.' I had gotten a little disgusted with government red tape and figured I'd quit before I got fired. So when I left the Indian Service I went to Tucson and opened my store down there. You know, all Indian stores for many years in Arizona and New Mexico were called curio shops. I objected to that right off the bat: 'I don't want to be under curio shops in the Yellow Pages.' 'Well, what do you want to be under?' 'Indian Arts and Crafts.' 'Well, you'll be the only one in there.' So I was under curios so those people would know what the hell we were talking about.

"When I was up there in the Indian Service there was no particular incentive for the Navajos to weave. The price was down on the stuff. The wool was so bad you couldn't hardly weave it. The government had improved the Navajo sheep so they weighed more and got more wool per sheep. But the wool was greasy and kinky. So the thing that I was interested in while I was up there then—although it wasn't my business—was to develop, to help develop, wool weaving, and the people who were interested in good weaving, interested in reviving the good old designs in rugs, in going back to the vegetable dyes and improving the quality of the weaving and the price. This was also the time of the beginning of the Indian Arts and Crafts Board, somewhere, I would say, around 1935.

"Up to that time most Indian traders said that any kind of a rug that's going to sell to anybody had to be black, white, gray and red. That's it. It has to have the fanciest design that you can get, and it has to have a border. And the fancier the rug, the more you're going to pay for it. But some of those old rugs, the years before, had been very simple—stripes and very subdued colors.

"And then some young guys who were not old-style traders moved in, and they wanted simple designs in good taste; no borders and all vegetable dyes. All the other traders thought that they were crazy until these guys, these kids, took all the prizes at the Gallup [New Mexico] Ceremonial and sold all the rugs. This really started a new trend.

"In the thirties, I'd say, the weaving and silversmithing was pretty bad really. It was getting too commercial. The Indians were trying to make something that would look very Indian, like putting thunderbirds and swastikas, rain gods and all kinds of junk on their work. And they were manufacturing a lot of jewelery. A silversmith is going to make what will sell. If a trader says, 'I want ten bracelets like so and so, more or less like this, put less silver in them, make 'em a little fancier, put this kind of stone in them, well, I'll give you X number of bucks,' why the silversmith is going to make 'em that way, see?

"So when the Indian Arts and Crafts Board came along and traders, and dealers like me, for instance, liked the better stuff, all I had to do is go to the trader—you always dealt with the trading post, not directly with the artisan—and say, 'Look, make 'em heavier, make 'em simple. Put the best stone you can put in 'em, and I'll pay you for 'em.' Up to then silversmithing, weaving were kind of at a low. The world was saturated with bad Navajo rugs and bad jewelry like it is today; we're getting an awful, awful lot of bad jewelry on the market today.

"There's going to be a point where you get rid of all the bad jewelry—and all the hotshots that are making it today are not Indians. When the bubble breaks on this then we'll go back to the good stuff again."

Clay Lockett turned now to give an inside picture of the artisans and their dealings with the traders. We had asked if there was a period when the Indians had been badly ripped off by the traders.

"Well, yes, and no. In a place where . . . in an area where there was an Indian trader who didn't like rugs, for instance, had no feel for 'em . . . well, like it was in Lupton [on the Navajo Reservation] in the old days when I was up there. There was this trader there, this old boy, who said to the Indians, 'Well, I'll give you a dollar a pound for the rugs and that's it. I don't give a damn what you do with them.'

"As a consequence the people who were around there who really weren't very ambitious, they'd just weave a rug with as much sand in it as they could, and no design, and they'd card it very little, and spin it very little. And they'd put it together into a saddle blanket that would weigh ten pounds. They'd roll it up and bring it in with a string tied around, and he'd put it on the counter and say, 'Ten pounds, ten bucks.' That was it. Well, that's the worst thing you could do for Navajo weaving.

"Gradually over the last thirty, forty years a Navajo woman really doesn't have to weave any more. For many years Navajo women had the sheep and they raised the kids and in their spare time they wove the rugs. And the men, they took care of the religious life of the family, and a few of 'em would do silversmithing, but not all by any means. They took care of the gossiping, and they traveled around—politics and that kind of stuff. But the women owned everything. When the woman did weave a rug, she'd take it in to the trader, and she was very much dependent upon his likes and dislikes and what kind of price he'd pay.

"Now two or three things have happened. Today everybody's got a pick-up truck or knows somebody that's got one. And the weaver, the good weavers, are still weaving and they're making better rugs and they're getting a lot more for them because they don't have to take 'em to the one trading post near them. They can take 'em over to one place after another. They can go any place. So the better weavers are making better rugs and demanding more money, and the bad weavers are just not weaving; they can get a job picking tomatoes or pulling up carrots, or something else down around Phoenix and make a lot more money than they can weaving a bad rug."

Lockett spent a lifetime among American Indians, and we asked him to turn "philosophical" about their condition.

"You say, what about the Indians? That's a tough one because from tribe to tribe they're different. In the state of Arizona there's, I don't know, fourteen tribes, something like that. Some of 'em are wealthy, some poor. They're all getting more education and are more aware of their own problems. They're not desperate any more, most of 'em. And really most of 'em have a pretty bright future I would think, if they're willing to work for it a little bit.

"Now the Navajos got tons of money, they've got tons of money from their mines and so forth. But they're always bitching because Uncle Sam won't help them more. But by the same token they want to get out from under everything. They want to start a state of Navajo and be the fifty-first state, or something.

"The only tribe that's really rabid on the old ways are the Hopis. The Hopis were here . . . well, we don't know whether they were the first In-

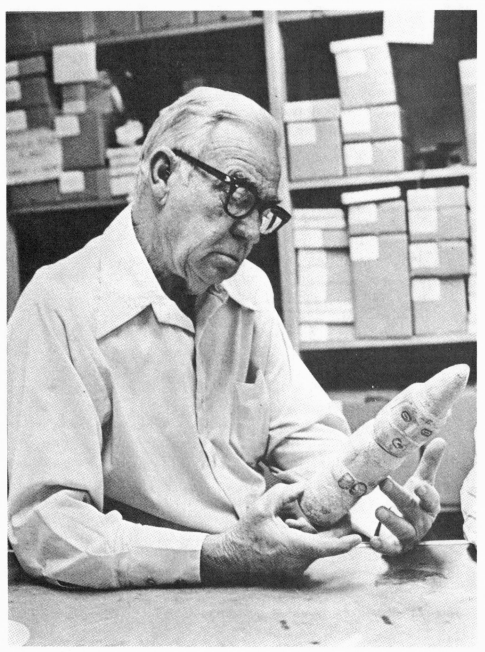

Clay Lockett, whose knowledge of Indian art and artifacts is nationally respected, here appraises a piece donated to the Museum of Northern Arizona in Flagstaff.
MARC GAEDE

dians up here, but they were undoubtedly descendants of the prehistoric Indians, so they've been here a long time. And there are two factions, like Republicans and Democrats, up there—the conservatives, you know, and the moderns. Many of them don't want to change. And the Hopis are tough little guys who can make it, but the old guys are going to have to die off before the new guys can carry on. The old ones, they don't want any sewers put on the reservation; they don't want this stuff in the ground —'our ancestors are underground. If you want to have this, go out in the open some place and let the sun dry that stuff up; we don't want sewers underground.' "

Lockett viewed the problem of change, of holding on to the old ways and still moving ahead with the new ways.

"Of course, I have mixed emotions. The wonderful days of the Navajo medicine man, you know, when they had the sings and the sand painting —all that was great from an anthropological standpoint—to be able to look at those things. There are still sings some places on the reservation. But the Navajos weren't dumb; they knew what to take.

"When we insisted on having hospitals; at first they didn't want to go. We had to drag them in almost, because the medicine man said, 'You'll die if you go in that hospital.' But it wasn't very long that the women— the Navajo women—when they had babies would go in to the hospitals. And then they would say, 'We have baby and it lives. We have one on the reservation, about every third one lives.' So the women got smart; it didn't take too long to educate the Indians. I mean they educated themselves; you don't push anything down the throat of a Navajo. But if he sees something that's good, he's going to take it.

"What I'm trying to say is that I don't think that we can, that Uncle Sam can, stand over them all the time and say, 'You can't do this and you can't do that.' My thought is that just as quick as possible we must let the Indian become just another citizen and forget about him being an Indian.

"I'd like to see the BIA out of existence, ban the thing. Let the Indians run their own affairs and say to 'em, 'All right, here's your reservation; there's your land.' It would be kind of tough; a lot of 'em would go out of existence. But say, 'You're going to vote, you're going to pay taxes. You're going to be just like anybody else.'

"It's kind of stupid to say, 'You're an Indian, so you're different.' "

The Days and Nights at a Trading Post

TRADING POSTS dotted the Indian reservations almost as quickly as the Indians were herded behind the boundaries set by Washington. Even today there are many such posts, some still serving the Indians and many catering to tourists seeking Indian art and craft work. The oldest, continuously operated establishment on the Navajo Reservation is the Hubbell Trading Post.

The Hubbell Trading Post was established in 1876, and it has survived the naturally destructive ways of the white man. It has been preserved in such a perfect state that in 1967 it was made a National Historical Site. If you are speeding along Interstate 40 across northern Arizona, you can, by easing up, turning off at Chambers and heading north on State Highway 63, make a detour into the early days of the frontier.

There in Ganado on the Navajo Reservation is where Don Lorenzo Hubbell came to build a name for himself as an Indian trader and friend to the Indian. His home and trading post stand today almost as they were when Dorothy Smith arrived in 1920 to tutor Don Lorenzo's grandchildren. A Hoosier, Dorothy Smith had been lured by the adventure of going west. It turned out to be more than just another adventure. She was to fall in love with and marry Roman Hubbell, son of Don Lorenzo. And she was to be more than a teacher, too; for many years she and her husband managed and ran tours out of Gallup, operated mail and passenger routes across the reservations and also ran Hubbell Trading Post.

In the late 1950s when her husband fell ill, she took up the management of the trading post.

In Sun City, a retirement community west of Phoenix, we found Dorothy Hubbell living quietly. At seventy-seven, her posture perfect and her white hair stunning, she had not forgotten her great adventure. She remembered the details with clarity, as if the many years had not really passed.

THE TRADER WHO WAS FRIEND TO THE NAVAJOS

Dorothy Smith Hubbell had a difficult decision to make as a young woman. She could stay at home with her family in Indiana and face a comfortable life or she could answer the lure of the West and make the long trip to the Navajo country of Arizona. In 1920 that kind of a trip was still quite an adventure.

"Soon after World War I teachers were scarce, so when my name went out of the Albert Teachers Agency listing service, I began to get letters from different parts of the country. And among the letters which I received was one from Mrs. Barbara Goodman, the widowed daughter of J. L. Hubbell at Ganado. She told me about the children in the family and that they needed a private teacher for the four youngsters. Well, it sounded very exciting to me. But my family was not very happy because it was far away. Finally they agreed, and so I sent a wire saying I was available.

"But that very day we had word from my sister that she was ill. She was a student at John Herron Art Institute in Indianapolis. And my mother said, 'Now look, I can go see her. That isn't so far away. But if you should be ill in Arizona, I never in the wide world could get out there.' She said, 'No, you can't go.'

"So I had to send a wire that I was sorry but my plans were changed and that a letter would follow. I went down to talk to an aunt of mine with whom I felt very close, whose age was more nearly mine and she said, 'What's the matter with you? You're young, you don't ever get sick. Why don't you go anyway?'

"I went home all enthusiastic and maybe out of disgust, I don't know, my parents finally said, 'Well, try it for a year.'

"Not until I got to Ganado did I find that all three of my wires arrived on the same mail. Can you imagine what they must have thought? My, what an awful start that was, but what could be done? The mail to Ganado arrived only once a week at that time."

Dorothy Smith was met at the train station in Gallup by Don Lorenzo Hubbell and was taken to Ganado by Roman, whom she was later to marry. She recalls her first impression of the Hubbell house. . . .

Above: *The interior of the Hubbell Trading Post, now a national historical site, shows some of the array of merchandise used for trading. The post is located at Ganado, Arizona, on the Navajo Reservation.* Below: *Roman Hubbell, late husband of Dorothy Hubbell, negotiates with a Navajo woman for the purchase of a rug at the Hubbell Trading Post.* DOROTHY HUBBELL COLLECTION

"I didn't know anything about an adobe house. I just never knew about adobes, and this house—it's adobe and rock, and the walls are very thick. When I arrived there for the first time it was just at dusk. It was before dinner, and it wasn't quite dark enough for lights. When they lit the lamps—they had two gasoline lamps in the hall—and that made a pretty bright light. The hall that I entered that night was very much as you'd see it if you visited Hubbell's today. The pictures were on the wall, the baskets were hung from the ceiling and the floors were covered with Navajo rugs.

"That first night I was at dinner I was surprised because there were guests at the table. One was Earl Morris, the archaeologist who had been working on a dig in Canyon del Muerto. And the dinner conversation intrigued me no end because I didn't know anything about archaeology. I just remember their telling that they had found fifty-two mummies in this one cave and feather pieces or ropes and handmade rope shoes or moccasins. And, of course, it was very exciting, but I soon found out that was not unusual, that we had guests almost every night. There was no place for anybody to stay in that area; there was no place there but Mr. Hubbell's.

"So anybody who came through, whether they were writers, or painters, or geologists, or government workers, why, we had them. They were there for dinner and overnight. Mr. Hubbell would not charge anything; he would not permit anyone to pay, and they were welcome if they would take what we had. And oh my, there were so many famous people who stayed with us—Teddy Roosevelt, Leopold Stokowsky and his wife, the Mexican composer Carlos Chavez, and Irvin S. Cobb, and Will Rogers and his son, just to name a few. They were wonderful nights at Hubbell's.

"I remember that first dinner I had there. The two girls who waited on the table, they were Hopi Indians; they also did the housework. And the cook was a Navajo man, Loco, who worked for the family about twenty-five years, and the baker was a man from Mexico. If you visit the trading post even today you can see the oven outside there. We baked bread for the trading post and for ourselves, and we baked twice a week. We could bake 200 loaves at a time. And, of course, we had our own cows —two milk cows—and we had chickens and peacocks. We had sixty-six horses and mules there because the Hubbells did all their freighting by wagons and horses and mules. I remember sometimes during the winter we had to count on ten days for the freight wagons to leave loaded with skins, or rugs, or whatever we sent, and then to be reloaded at the destination with our supplies and get back to us."

Don Lorenzo Hubbell stands as one of the great personalities of the history of northeastern Arizona and Dorothy Hubbell now talked about the man who was to be her father-in-law.

"He was a very interesting man to know, and I'm very glad I knew him the last ten years of his life. Don Lorenzo's father had come out in 1848 and he freighted for a while, so the records say. He had a train of forty-eight wagons with oxen—four oxen to each wagon. In New Mexico he married a woman in Pajarito. Her name was Julietta Gutierrez. The records say her father was one of the territorial governors there; that was before, of course, New Mexico belonged to the United States. Don Lorenzo's father was named James Lawrence Hubbell, so you can see where Lorenzo's name came from.

"When Don Lorenzo arrived in Ganado, in Arizona, he must have been twenty-two or twenty-three, and all that was there was a little building, which he purchased. Before that he started in a little place about three miles north of the present trading post. He homesteaded a quarter-section, and then in time he built a dam about three miles north of us with three miles of ditches and flumes to carry the water down to irrigate his land. And he cleared 100 acres, put in mainly alfalfa which he then baled and sold. And he also built a reservoir in his own place and had laterals which went to each one of the fields for irrigation."

Don Lorenzo had worked hard to build up the area, but later he had to go to Washington to fight to retain his land. Only by special act of the Congress was he given a patent to the land. Now Mrs. Hubbell related some of the other difficulties Don Lorenzo had settling the land.

"He told me one time of the precautions they had to take. He was in the trading post alone one time and a group of Indians came in to rob the store. He was by himself, and they dragged him out and tied him to a wheel of a wagon, he said. And just at that time Many Horses, a Navajo he knew, came by on horseback, and he said to these men, 'What's the matter with you? You are harming the only person who has come into this area to give you any help at all.' And Many Horses and Don Lorenzo became very good friends after that. They made an agreement later that whichever died first, the other would see that he was buried up on what is called Hubbell's Hill. So Many Horses, the first one to die, is buried up there, and five of my family are buried up there, too.

"Don Lorenzo was gentle but very firm, and he was firm when work had to be done. For instance, when that bell rang at six-thirty in the morning, that let everybody know it was thirty minutes till breakfast time. We'd have breakfast at seven and then everybody got to work. At noon we had fifteen minutes between bells to know that we'd have lunch. But at night it was delightful because we could take time at the table. We'd have interesting guests usually, and we'd sit in front of the fireplace afterwards and have coffee. It was very stimulating. I think that is one of the very nicest memories I have. . . .

"But, you know, I learned more from old Indians who talked to me after my husband died. Sometimes the old Indians would come in and talk to me and they'd say, 'I remember when I was a little boy, when I was a certain age, I remember that this happened, or I remember that that happened.' And one told me, 'I remember when we had smallpox—a regular epidemic—and Mr. Hubbell was the only one who came by from hogan to hogan and brought us medicine.'

"And, of course, they thought it was miraculous that he could go from hogan to hogan with all his medicine, and yet he didn't get the smallpox. Of course, he had had smallpox as a young man and he was immune, but they didn't know that, and they just thought that he was marvelous.

"And one of them told me also that one time when they had heavy snows and they couldn't get at the wood to bring in—the firewood for cooking and warming—that he told them that they could come and help themselves from his woodpile and if necessary he'd tear down his fence-posts to help them."

We asked Mrs. Hubbell to talk about her early days of teaching the Hubbell youngsters.

"Well, we all had to have breakfast at the same time, and then we started at eight o'clock. We had a regular school bell and we'd have a twenty-minute recess in the morning. And in the afternoon we'd start at one o'clock, and we closed at three-thirty. Sometimes we'd have school on Saturday because if there was some kind of sing—you know, a ceremonial —out there on the reservation that we wanted to go to, the children would ask if they could go and make up school the next day.

"It was very exciting for me really. The family was wonderful to me, I must say. They just did everything they could to give me the help I needed, and I didn't have any difficulty with the children at all. I remember that first week in school I heard a very high sing-song outside, and I didn't know what it was. But the children knew. They just picked up their ears and the oldest one, LeCharles, asked if she might go to the kitchen a minute. She said the visitors were *Yeis* [dancers representing gods of the Navajos]. And I let her go, and she came back with a loaf of bread and also food so each child in class would have something to give to the *Yeis*.

"When we opened the door, there were three *Yeis* standing there. I didn't think I was in the United States. They had come from the dance, and they had leather masks which completely covered their heads. Their bodies were painted white—two of them, their bodies were painted white with gypsum and they wore short ceremonial skirts and carried rattles. And the third one had his body painted white, too, but he just wore a g-string and had a buckskin over one shoulder. And he was the one that held out the sack and the children set the food into the sack.

"All the time they kept singing. When they left they just nodded their thanks and went on. And I remember I said, 'Well, they didn't even say thank you.' And one of the children spoke up and said, 'Well, they couldn't because at the moment they represent gods and they can't talk English. They're not permitted to talk.' "

Mrs. Hubbell gave an insight to the Navajo way that clashes with the white man and his scheduled world.

"They wanted to work, but many times they didn't show up in the morning, and it was a long time before I understood why. I thought they just wouldn't work, but that was not it. They are very prone to stick to a clan, their own clan. And if someone in their own clan is ill and is to have a sing, or if he happens maybe to be an apprentice, or a chanter, and the medicine man says there must be a sing, then they'll go to that sing no matter what their job is.

"They have that strong feeling that they must go. When you understand that part of it, you can understand it all. But that doesn't help when you're busy in the trading post and you need help and you have nobody there. And it happens with the girls, too, with the girls that work in the house. Yes, they may not show up either, simply because someone in their family is having a ceremony and they must go. They must be there.

"It took time for me to learn this and so many other things in my years with the Hubbell family. It was a most interesting place, and that is why I wanted to see it preserved. A representative of the Park Service approached me about making it a National Historical Site. They asked me if I would be interested because the Park Service didn't have anything in their system to represent the early pioneering trader who had done so much in the West.

"Most of the old trading posts had either been abandoned or changed into supermarkets. But Hubbell's had not changed. Even today everything is just the same. Even the counters in the store are the same. It is so much like it was in those early days—those days when I first came west to the Hubbell family."

BOOK THREE

THE GENESIS
OF A FRONTIER TOWN

*When the Territory of Arizona was
created officially in 1863, it had no
schools, no churches, no newspapers,
no libraries, and no real cities. . . . it had
changed little from the time Coronado
and other Spanish conquistadores first
entered it. But between 1863 and 1912,
when it became a state, Arizona changed
dramatically. In those short forty-nine
years, it acquired the trappings of
civilization, of culture, of polite society.*

ODIE B. FAULK IN
Arizona, a Short History

How El Vadito Became Saint Johns

IN NORTHEASTERN ARIZONA's rolling ranchland the city of Saint Johns stands today as a monument to the waves of change in the Southwest. When the conquistadores came into the area they found it quiet and untroubled, and where they crossed the Little Colorado River they named it El Vadito (the little crossing).

It was here that Solomon Barth, a Jewish immigrant who accompanied the Mormons westward, came in the 1870s. There was water and grazing land in abundance, and Barth, a man of vision, saw its possibilities; it was perfect for growing the grain crops he needed to keep his freight lines running across the territory. It is said that Barth changed the name of El Vadito to San Juan in honor of a Mexican woman living in the area, Sra. Maria San Juan Baca de Padilla.

Almost a decade later Barth sold his land and water interests to a group of Mormons who had come south from Utah to settle the verdant valleys of Arizona. A pioneer son recalls a 1914 headline in the Saint Johns *Observer*, the town's weekly newspaper, that read, "St. Johns Population 1400 and Growing Fast."

Only in recent years, with the construction of a nearby power plant, has Saint Johns grown much. It is estimated the city had 2,000 residents in 1976. It is, and has been always, a small, neighborly country town. And from this historic town has come a United States Secretary of the Interior, a candidate for the Democratic presidential nomination, and at one time descendants of Saint Johns's first Mormon bishop held four judgeships in the state of Arizona.

Northeastern Arizona, wrote an early historian in the late 1800s, "is ruled over by King Solomon and Lorenzo the Magnificent." He was referring to Don Lorenzo Hubbell of the famed Hubbell's Trading Post and to Solomon Barth. The story of Sol Barth was recalled by Jacob Barth, born April 26, 1894, and at the time of this taping an active resident and leader in Saint Johns.

"My Uncle Jacob Barth came to the United States first, about 1853, from Poland, and then when my father, Solomon Barth, became of age, thirteen or thirteen-and-a-half, he wanted to come over, too. So he came and he went to Grand Rapids, Michigan, where Uncle Jacob was in the lumber business. Father started peddling and got down to Illinois where he met the Mormons who were moving west to Salt Lake. So he got him a cart and pushed it along with the Mormons to Salt Lake .

"I guess it was about 1855 when he got out there with the Mormons. And then he went down to San Bernardino, California, because he had some distant relatives there. He got to Los Angeles but didn't like it there, and then he went to work with the Goldwaters in San Francisco. I think he was a bouncer up there, but he was too little to bounce anybody. You see, he stood only about five-one and weighed about 140 pounds.

"Well, then in 1862 he came over to La Paz and worked for the Goldwaters. And later he had a mail contract to Albuquerque and at one time to Tucson. And I guess he was freighting all the way from the Colorado River to Fort Dodge, Kansas. He said it would take six months to make the round trip. And that is how my father became acquainted with the country around Saint Johns.

"He went through here and needed hay for his teams, and there was plenty of wild hay here and water from the Little Colorado. And then he could raise his grain, too. He put his drivers—the drivers of the ox trains —to farming in this area, but they didn't turn out to be very good farmers. So that's how he happened to sell the land to the Mormons when they came in. They were better farmers."

But when Solomon Barth came there were no Mormons, only a few Mexican families and the Indian tribes. Barth was a foreigner, but in 1864, as the Great Register of Apache County shows, he became a naturalized American citizen. Three years later he was in Cubero, New Mexico.

"Cubero was sort of a headquarters for him at that time, and one time in '68 father had quite a scrape with the Indians. He was captured when he went to trade with the Apaches down near where McNary is today in the White Mountains. Father had four or five men and a pack train full of trading goods. Well, the Apaches took everything they had—all the trading goods, their pack train animals and their clothes, too. I think it was a band of Apaches under Cochise. Pedro, who was the chief there, wasn't home when that happened, but he got back in time to save the lives of father and his men.

"The men were stripped of their clothes, except for their shoes, and turned loose. There was a French woman up there at the time, a captive, and she handed father some underwear. I think it was long underwear, and he was the only one that had any clothes at all. It was November when this happened and the nights were cold.

"Well, they made it out of there. It took them about three days to get to a Zuñi Indian village. The other men never got over the fact that my father was the only one who had any clothes—that long underwear—and so they called him 'The King' from then on. They called him '*El Rey*.'"

In 1870 Solomon Barth brought his brothers, Morris and Nathan, to America and they joined him in his southwestern business ventures. In '74 in Cubero, Solomon married Refugia Landavazo, and the expanded family settled in the village near the Little Colorado.

"There weren't many people in the area at that time, some Spanish families, I guess. Father built what we still call the hotel building, and Nathan and Morris both built houses. Those old buildings are all still here in Saint Johns. And later father brought my grandfather to Saint Johns. My mother, even though she was from a Mexican family, would cook Jewish dishes for my grandfather because he was a 'rabbi,' and there were a lot of things he wouldn't eat. I can remember that they would always have matzo and limburger cheese for him, too. I have no idea where they got those matzos for him."

Turning back to the sale of the land to the Mormons, Barth continued.

"Well, father sold his land and water rights to the Mormons, and I've still got a copy of that deed. The Mormons had come down under the leadership of David King Udall and Ammon Tenney. I guess it was Tenney who was the main one Father dealt with, and the deed I have shows the Mormons paid him with 770 American cows and $2,000 in other personal property.

"And the Mormons were good farmers, and they did well here in this area.

"You know, there were many Indians around this area, but we never had any trouble. This was sort of a neutral zone, a peaceful area for about fifteen miles around Saint Johns. When the Indians wanted to trade, they'd come around and build fires out there on the hills. Well, father would see the smoke and knew that somebody out there wanted to trade, and they'd get together that way.

"Later on they'd come into our store, and I remember one time when I was a kid I kind of got smart with an Indian and father told me, 'Now just because they can't speak English, don't think that they're not smart.' Father dealt with the Navajos and Apaches and the Zuñis, and he always treated them with respect.

"That was quite a store we had in Saint Johns. We worked long hours. We'd be open all day, and we'd stay open at night, too, you know. They had a coal oil lamp hanging out there, and the townspeople would come in to do all the gossiping, to get all the news. Father, for a long time, got the only newspaper in town, so the townspeople would gather around and he would read them the news.

"We handled all sorts of things at the store. One time we even sold coffins. Many people came through the store, and father, you know, he'd credit everybody. People he'd never seen would come by and they were short of feed, or something. Well, he'd let them have it, and I never heard him claim that he ever lost anything.

"Father was a very strong person, physically as well as in his character. He was small, but very wiry. I heard him say that he could ride a mule—he had a mule by the name of Pike that he thought very much of —a hundred miles a day. The thing about that mule was that there were always people on the road who would lose their horses, and they would want to borrow Pike to round them up. Father would say, 'All right, take him.' But Pike wouldn't let anyone else ride him. That mule just wouldn't stand for it."

Had the Barths, as Jews, encountered religious prejudice? When Solomon Barth got into politics and served twice in the territorial legislature, the Arizona Miner, *a newspaper published in Prescott, carried this sarcastic note in an 1878 edition: "[In Apache County the] Mexican Sheriff and the Mexican Supervisor are under the absolute control of the great and good rabbi."*

The old Barth Hotel in Saint Johns was a gathering place for many celebrities and pioneer families through the years. This picture was taken in 1914. JACOB BARTH COLLECTION

Arizona's first statehood governor, George W. P. Hunt (left), visited Solomon Barth in Saint Johns in 1916 when this photo was taken. JACOB BARTH COLLECTION

"Father never had any difficulty. No, I don't think they took to religion like they do now. No, I don't think there were any difficulties. You know, I never thought when I met anybody, 'Well, he's a Jew, or he's a Mormon,' or anything like that. You just didn't think about it.

"But I guess, they, the Mormons, did call father a 'gentile,' but it wasn't out of any meanness. He had some good friends among the Mormons, and he helped a lot of them, too."

Those were rugged days and King Solomon had his troubles and his critics. But when he died, the Eighth Arizona Legislature passed a resolution to be forwarded to his wife and seven children. It read, in part:

"At the time of his death November 30, 1928, Solomon Barth was the oldest white man, in point of years of residence, within the state, and at the age of eighty-six years passed peacefully from the land he loved surrounded by the loving members of his family.

"Therefore be it resolved . . . that a permanent record of the life and public service of one of [Arizona's] most illustrious citizens is justly merited. . . ."

From Saint Johns to Washington

MORRIS KING (MO) UDALL, the last challenger to Jimmy Carter for the Democratic nomination for president, is a century away from his pioneer family that settled in Saint Johns in 1880. But he has been a pioneer in his own right, plowing many new fields and often going against the odds. The odds were lopsided against him when he announced his presidential candidacy. When he came out early against the war in Vietnam, the experts forecast Udall's days in the House of Representatives were numbered. And who ever believed that a one-eyed youngster could develop into a collegiate and professional basketball star?

But Mo Udall is very much like his father, Levi, and his grandfather, David King; he is a pathfinder and a ground-breaker, as they were in their days. When Mo campaigned across the United States, writers and commentators were quick to pick up on his "homespun humor," his "Lincolnesque" appearance. He spoke out on what he believed was good for the nation, warning about misuse of the land and its resources. He was a pioneer battler against the immorality of the Vietnam War as well as the rape of the land.

And if he had worn a different set of clothing, how different would Morris King Udall have been from the Udalls who went before him to settle a frontier of the Southwest?

GROWING UP IN A COUNTRY TOWN

Morris Udall began with his earliest recollections of Saint Johns.

"It was a little town and life was simple—outdoor plumbing and everybody knew everybody. I have so many memories about that little town. We had no crime as such. If somebody did something, why they were always given a suspended sentence, and you had a thousand pair of eyes watching all the time. You were really put on probation, and the whole community was your parole officer and that is what it really amounted to. But you were close to nature; the old swimming hole was a reality.

"The big open field behind the high school next to my house was a baseball diamond in the summer and a football field in the fall. We had basketball hoops in front of my house where everybody gathered in the community. The schools were really good. You knew the teachers; you knew the families. It was a close relationship. On those lousy salaries they paid in those days you really had a tremendous caliber of teachers who taught you intellectual discipline. I learned . . . I've seen so many students who had college degrees and didn't have any command of the English language. Well, I got command of the English language from two good teachers and learned some really fundamental things about writing that stood me in good stead both in law and in politics.

"I learned something very early that I thought of in the presidential campaign: Most all of the national leaders come from little towns. You get something in those little towns from the standpoint of leadership. In high school I was quarterback on the football team and captain of the basketball team, and had the lead in the school play. I edited the school paper, and wrote a political column for the weekly paper in the city, and had my own dance band. And I was a debater, too. So you got a smattering of everything, and it was really very good preparation.

"Dad believed, like the old Mormons, that work is the best cure for all your problems, and he deliberately kept a farm. He was a lawyer and judge, but he wanted his boys to learn to farm. So Stew and I, from the time we were in high school, really, ran Dad's farm. It was about 300 acres, and we'd have to irrigate at night when it came our turn in the community to use water out of the ditch. You'd use it solidly for three days, and you'd have to take a blanket and sleep out there and change the water over every three or four hours from one field to the next. And we'd get together a baler crew and bring in the hay. You learned how to bring in the hay and repair harnesses and mowing machines and simple farm equipment. And it was a very exciting life, a very satisfying life."

Udall talked of the activities of a Mormon community.

"The Mormons believed in keeping you busy, you know. On Sunday you'd go to Sunday school in the morning and church services at night.

On Tuesday it's the young people's organization with dances and classes in self-improvement and everything else. Wednesday the relief society meets, and there's other church activities on Thursday and Friday. They keep you busy all the time. Stew and I were very active and kind of leaders in the young set. Dad was a judge, and we'd go up to the courthouse and watch trials. So we set up the kids' court and had elections for prosecutor and defense attorney, and we actually had trials where one of the Greer boys had stolen two dollars from his brother's bank.

"We put him on trial, had a defense counsel and empanelled a jury. Out in our garage we'd have all these little kids sitting in the jury box, and we'd be arguing to them. Well, we'd have those trials and convict some kid and then confine him in the chicken coop for three hours with the 'sheriff' standing guard to see the sentence was carried out.

"Stew and I always put on a kids' rodeo every year where we'd round-up everybody's calves and have roping . . . roping the calves, bulldog them, have cow-milking contests and different kinds of things like that. And when the fall came, all the attention turned to football. In December we'd turn to basketball. There were things going all the time. And we had movies in town and that was a family affair. You'd go on the average of once or twice a week to the movies. Radio came along in our area when I was a kid, and that was a contact to the outside world. But it was a big deal to go somewhere, even off to Holbrook about sixty miles away."

We asked Mo about his family and his parents' influence. His father had risen to become one of Arizona's most distinguished jurists, and his mother's close feeling for people resulted in her writing together with a Hopi woman a warm and personable book on the Indian way of life.

"Mother and dad were two entirely different people. They had an extremely harmonious marriage; they were very, very close. Dad was the judge, and while he had a lively sense of humor—I think I got some of that—he was more staid and stolid and had many of the old rugged, reliable virtues. He was kind of the patriarch of the church in that whole area. And our relationship . . . well, you know, we were never close pals, that sort of thing, but we knew our father was somebody big in the community and he was there and he would talk to you. He was not a stern disciplinarian. I don't think I ever got spanked or whacked, or anything like that. He taught more by example and exhortation and that kind of thing.

"In connection with his closeness to the soil, we farmed, Stewart and

I, and we always had cows to milk and take care of. We'd always have at least one and sometimes five, and it got to be an awful drag. You had to get up in the morning and milk the cows before you went to school. And when you came home from football practice, you had to do it again. Stew and I always had hassles. He would have something on, and I would have to do the milking.

"We always had pigs, and we would feed the garbage to them. And Conrad Overson was the old slaughter-man in town, and twice a year he'd come by and slaughter the pigs. And you'd help him clean them and hang them up on a hook. And everybody would have bacon, and then you'd make sausage and that sort of thing. And we also had chickens, and Dad took an interest in all these things. I learned a lot from him about how you handle animals and the rhythm and cycle of nature.

"Mother was a much more lively person. She had been a school teacher and had a great sense of humor. I think a lot of my humor . . . that much more of my humor came from mother than from dad. You know, the Mormon women are viewed by many as not liberated. My mother was extremely liberated in a very real sense; she was an independent person. She'd argue politics and things with my father. She had strong views. She was always buying good books for the kids to read. She wrote little pageants and plays. She had a mind that could translate Mormon history for the kids. When we had to write something—I was valedictorian in the eighth grade—she helped us, she helped me write the speech and, in fact, typed it out. She had a good feel for words and for writing.

"And she liked to dance and sing. We had a piano in the front room, and she was great for getting the family around singing songs together. The house had no central heat, just an old wood stove in the dining room, a wood stove in the kitchen and a fireplace in the living room. And in order to keep warm the family was together in the evenings—either huddled around the fireplace or doing homework in the dining room around the stove.

"And all the family had chores, and Mother would see that they got done. One of my jobs was to bring in the wood; snow, or sleet, or rain, you always had to have a stack of wood on the porch. And it wasn't just to have a fireplace to look at. You just weren't going to have anything to heat with and you weren't going to be warm if you didn't get the wood. There was no heat in the bedrooms at all, so when you got ready to go to bed you'd dash for the bedroom and dive under the blankets."

*When Mo ran for the presidential nomination many stories were writ-
ten about the boyhood accident that took one of his eyes. But in this taping
he tells the full story of the accident and how close he came to being
totally blind.*

"It happened, I guess, when I was six. It was in the summer before I
was to start school and my closest friend, Fenton Overson, who later became an All-State basketball player, lived down the street. And one of the
things we'd play was to imitate the grownups with horses, and we would
take Coke bottles and make harnesses with little ropes around the collar
and harness this back to little logs and things we'd drag along and smooth
out the land, or hook up a toy plow of some kind. And we were hooking
up some horses, and there was a little piece of twine . . . rope about the
size of my little finger. He had an old rusty knife, and I held up the rope
for him to cut.

"He began sawing away with this old rusty knife, and it slipped and
went up and into my right eye. There was some pain, and it felt like stuff
was running out of my eye. He got scared and ran home. My mother took
me to an old doctor there in Saint Johns. I guess we were lucky in those
days we had a doctor, but he was drunk most of the time and not a very
good doctor when he was sober. He advised putting hot compresses on
the eye.

"Mother watched it and worried about it, and then we made a trip or
two to Phoenix to have doctors look at it and they questioned whether it
was a permanent injury or whether the sight would come back. That summer we went down to Safford—that was mother's old home country—and
we went by way of Globe where there was an eye specialist. Mother had
been worried about the color of the eye; the eye had changed and it was
looking strange. Well, the doctor said that the optical nerve was infected
and if that eye wasn't taken out immediately I would lose the sight of the
other eye.

"So we drove through the night to Phoenix, got a good eye man there,
and the eye was taken out the next day. The doctor there said it would
have been only a matter of days that I would have been blinded in both
eyes."

*We asked Mo to talk of his political development, and he started with
a discussion of his father's leadership and how his branch of the Udall
family became liberal Democrats.*

"Dad was fascinated by politics. He was a small-town guy, but he read a lot of history. His father had been a community leader and had been in the Arizona State Legislature. And Dad also was a community leader. I didn't realize until later, but when I was a little kid and the governor or any political candidate came to Saint Johns, he always met with Levi, my dad. And I think I became interested in politics even as early as elementary school when I ran for president of my class.

"You know, David King Udall, my old grandfather, was a rock-ribbed McKinley Republican. He was a Republican in the state legislature, and the family was Republican. The roots of the Mormons tend to be conservative Republican. Dad was switched by Woodrow Wilson, the burst of idealism, the League of Nations and the Fourteen Points. As far as myself, Roosevelt was a big influence on me in the '30s as I was in high school growing up. And then I think the real turning point in my life was World War II. When I went off to war my horizons were broadened. So I think Stew and I, both out of the war and the New Deal and the Roosevelt experience, became Democrats.

"As far as my own political ambitions, I guess they started at the University of Arizona when I became student body president. I don't think there are many college student body presidents who don't have further political dreams. I guess the thing that I wanted more than anything else was to go to Congress."

Udall's political career began when a reform candidate, Bob Morrison, became Pima County Attorney and named Mo as his deputy.

"He'd been elected on a reform ticket to clean up Tucson. The town was wide open then in 1949 when I came out of law school at the University of Arizona. There were houses of prostitution, gambling everywhere and alleged payoffs. He made me chief deputy in 1952–53, and I handled most of the burden of those major prosecutions, fresh out of law school. Morrison was extremely ambitious and he wanted to be state attorney general, and I was the obvious guy to succeed him as Pima County Attorney. Pima County was still Democratic, and I won fairly handsomely in my first political try for office. I put in two years. I was ambitious; I always wanted to go to Congress. As my term was coming to an end, Porque Patten [U.S. Representative Harold Patten], to the surprise of everyone, decided he wanted to quit. And I was the logical guy—county attorney of the biggest county in the district, and I had run well and I had all those prosecutions.

"I wanted to run but my wife thought I was too young, and she was terribly opposed to going to Washington. I let her talk me out of it; I always regretted it. So instead, Stew ran and made it. Since I couldn't go to Congress there was a new court post opening and I filed for the seat. But I got beat in the primary because of the placement of my name on the voting machine. Even one of my friends, a lawyer and election judge, couldn't find my name on the ballot. So I knew I'd had it. When the returns came I carried the precincts with paper ballots two to one, but I lost every single machine precinct.

"That was one of the crushing blows of my life. I suppose I'd still be on the bench in Tucson if I'd won. In a way it was probably a good thing I lost. You know, my whole life has been one of ironies. I've learned to take things as they come. Fate has a way of working things out. Here was my brother in Congress. That door was closed. Stew was doing well and apparently in a permanent career in the House. I thought, well, I'm going to be a judge. At that time Dad was preparing to retire, and he told me that he wanted me to take his seat on the Arizona State Supreme Court. It looked like an enticing position.

"But then Levi drops dead in May of 1960 from a massive stroke. And Paul Fannin was the Republican governor; the Republicans had never had a Supreme Court seat, and they were looking around for somebody he could appoint. They lighted on my Uncle Jesse, who was a Goldwater supporter, a good Republican, and appointed him. So here I was: couldn't go to Congress, my brother's blocking the way; couldn't be a judge, my uncle's blocking the way. It looked like I was through. So I accepted it, a rather bitter pill.

"I accepted it, and within ten months I'm in Congress! What happened was that Kennedy won the presidency and put Stew in the cabinet. And there was a special election, and off I went to Congress. So I found things have a way of working out."

Things worked out politically, but not personally, and Mo talked frankly about his family problems.

"My marriage had been rocky and shaky all through the '50s. Pat was a very spirited person. She was intensely interested in all kinds of things, but was sort of unsteady, and went from one interest to another. She didn't really much want to go to Washington anyway. She'd blocked me in '54, and she figured she couldn't do it this time. She was a good sport about it. But her interest began diverging. She didn't like Washington and any of the obligations back there. She was spending more and more of her time out here in Tucson, and she finally decided she wanted to make a break. And she told me, well, in the summer of '65, she came west with the children and she told me that she didn't know whether she was coming back or not; she'd wait till the fall.

"I got out to Tucson in September, and she said she wanted a divorce; she'd decided to stay out here. It was quite a blow, but I had seen that it was bad on the kids and bad on me; it was a strain for both of us, so I didn't argue with her very much. In fact, I think we're good friends to this day, and we've got a great relationship with the kids and she has a great relationship with Ella [Mo's second wife].

"Everybody's probably a lot better off because we went through it, but it was traumatic at the time. My relationship with the kids was a little bit in doubt for a year or so, but we developed a good, strong, loyal relationship ever since.

"I was single from January of 1965 when the divorce was—'66 when the divorce was actually signed—agreed to, until December of '68. Almost three years I was single, and then Ella and I got married. I had met her on Capitol Hill after Pat had gone, more or less."

Meanwhile on Capitol Hill, Mo Udall, that tall, one-eyed, ambitious youngster from little Saint Johns, had made his mark as a leader.

"You know, half the state legislators have dreams of going to the Congress and the U.S. Senate and then some day being drafted for president. It's like the guy who's made his college baseball team. He figures some day he's going to be in the World Series and be the Most Valuable Player. It doesn't happen that way very often, but it's the thing that dreams are made of and whatever you're in, I think, you go as far as your talents will take you.

"And you always build admirers and friends. I had a few people in the House when I became the leader of the 'Young Turks' who would say to me, 'Great things ahead for you.' When I ran for House majority leader in 1971, I had it very clearly in my mind that I was going to break this tradition of old leaders in the House and Senate. I was going to be a young, active guy and when the party's looking around for a vice-presidential candidate to balance the ticket, or somebody to run for president, when there's an open year, well, I'd be ready.

"Well in December of 1973 after the McGovern disaster—a year after, when all the jostling was going on—two Wisconsin congressmen, Henry Reuss and Dave Obey, both of them said, 'Each of us had the same idea independently this morning while sitting around thinking how in the hell are we going to win in '76. It's an open race. We ought to get fresh faces. Who in the House? And we both agreed independently, Mo, you were the guy. Why don't you run for president?' "

And that was the start of Mo Udall's run for the presidential nomination. A petition calling on him to run was signed by forty-five members of the House, and soon he began his two-year campaign. At first there were yawns, then chuckles about this "unknown" from that little state of Arizona.

"There were times at the beginning of the campaign when I wondered, too, what I was doing there. You'd go to a town and they'd butcher your name. 'You're running for what? President of what?' Unless you're a national figure to begin with, you have to go through that sort of thing, and there were times when you'd think, 'What the hell am I doing here?' You call a press conference and nobody shows, or in a little town in Iowa, ten people turn out to hear you speak.

"Even Iowa started out looking pretty good for me, but Jimmy Carter moved in and just pre-empted it. He had no job. At the same time I was trying to get a strip mine bill through the Congress, trying to get a land-use bill, trying to protect my voting record, trying to get home to Arizona once in a while. And Carter had nothing else to do except keep this rigid, tight little schedule he had fixed. He's a very organized, tenacious, indefatigable little guy. He couldn't be humiliated, shamed or slowed down. Everywhere you'd go there he was. I couldn't believe it. It took me a long time to believe he really was serious. It was kind of a joke, and I went through stages and phases where it looked good and bad.

"But the Iowa caucus was a low point; I came in fourth. I thought, 'What the hell, this is all going to be over pretty soon.' And many times leading up to those primaries I'd think, 'God, if I'm going to lose let me get clobbered and let me get out of this thing instead of hanging on.'

"The night I knew I was in the ball game was in New Hampshire. The polls were showing a week before that it was down to Carter and Udall. When I beat Birch Bayh and Fred Harris badly and came in a good strong second, I knew I was in the ball game and was going to be in the finals. A week later in Massachusetts I came in second to Senator Henry Jackson. Carter came in fourth which then confirmed my own feeling that Carter was weak and couldn't hack it. By the time we got to Wisconsin, which was my next big primary, all the others had fallen aside. It was clear that Sargent Shriver was no factor; Bayh had pulled out after the humiliation of coming in sixth in Massachusetts. It was clearly down to Carter and me, maybe with Jackson still in the picture.

"Crowds were getting big and the networks had assigned full-time television crews. I knew that all I had to do was to win one or two big ones and the momentum was going to roll, and Wisconsin was the first chance to do it. And if I had had one more percentage point in Wisconsin, I probably would have been the party nominee, and I think I could have beaten Ford easier than Carter beat him."

Udall paused and talked about the pressures that built up for him to pull out and leave the race to Jimmy Carter.

"At that point the die had been cast, and I was carrying the banner for the whole progressive wing of the Democratic Party. There was no way I could pull out even if I wanted to—and I didn't want to. I still thought we had a good chance to do the job. I didn't take the detractors and jokers all that seriously for we were still getting support and moving up in the polls. They used to say about me: 'How can a guy who's from a little state—the only Democrat from a little state—and a guy who's one-eyed, a divorced Mormon, possibly be elected?'

"They used to say that, but it didn't have any particular impact on me. I'd come that far by then. I knew I was very much in it then."

Had the two-year effort been worth it?

"Oh, yeah. It had been kind of an emotional period the last two months, but looking back there were two points that made it all worthwhile. One was that night in New York when I spoke to the Democratic National Convention. I had anguished over whether I should go before the convention, for it was unprecedented that a candidate should go to the convention hall. I talked to Carter about it. I knew going before the convention could be bad news. It could look like an ego trip.

"But I also knew that if I handled it right it could be an important occasion. I knew that my followers who were intensely devoted to me in ways that Carter's followers never were, had to have a kind of catharsis to be able to say our campaign had meant something, this is a good man who stood for our ideals, and so on.

"And looking back on the convention, most writers agree that my appearance, my speech, was the one moment of real emotion. Carter couldn't stir the convention. None of the other candidates did. Barbara Jordan [the representative from Texas] gave a good speech. But you look

Two famous products of an upbringing in the small Mormon community of Saint Johns—Congressman Morris K. Udall (left) and his brother, Stewart L. Udall, who served as Secretary of the Interior under the Kennedy and Johnson administrations.

back and ask what she said; there wasn't much she said. It was the fact that a woman, a black woman, speaking in those clipped Oxford accents, could come this far to be keynoting the Democratic Convention.

"So that night, that night at the convention was one of the two things that made it all worthwhile for me. And the other came when in October I made a series of swings for Carter back to the places that I had done well. I was in Milwaukee, Madison, Ann Arbor, Lansing, went to Ohio and New Hampshire, and people cried and brought out their Mo buttons and signs for 1980. And it suddenly dumped on me like a ton that I had built an intensely loyal national following, that I was somebody to these people. I was the symbol of their ideals and the progressive things that they had fought for and believed in, that I stood for these things.

"We turned out about 3,000 people at the University of Michigan. It was a Mo Udall crowd—people roaring and yelling like the campaign was still on. And it was a very sobering, yet rewarding thing to think that all out there over the country there's an army of people who believe in you and that you stand for something.

"Was it all worthwhile that two years of campaigning? Yeah, those things made it all worthwhile."

BOOK FOUR

THE CHANGING FRONTIER

*... a majority of Arizona's towns and
cities had been established before 1900,
so rapid was the influx after the end
of the Civil War. Mining accelerated in
the sixties and seventies. The eighties
were marked by an upward swing in the
rate of Anglo-American settlement. In
these years practically all of Arizona's
Indians were placed on reservations.
Somewhat as a consequence of this, the
cattle industry was rapidly expanded....*

Arizona Its People and Resources
UNIVERSITY OF ARIZONA PRESS

Birth of a Copper Colossus

IT WAS THE LURE OF RICHES that drew the conquistadores across the seas from Spain to search the hills and mountains of the Southwest. The Spaniards had heard of villages with streets paved with gold, and they came looking for the Seven Cities of Cibola.

Of that quest Lawrence Clark Powell, in *Arizona, a Bicentennial History*, wrote, "The Spaniards came for glory, God, and gold, and were disappointed in their desires." They did convert some Indians to their God, and there was some gold and silver to take to the Old World, but in the end Spain lost all of its foothold in the Southwest, and in the New World as well.

The failure of the conquistadores to strip the Southwest of its mineral wealth left the lure for thousands of others to come. Mining developed into one of Arizona's major industries, and its production of copper ore is today of world importance. It was mining that brought the name Arizona to the territory and state. In the mid-1700s ore was taken out of the Baboquivari Mountains in southern Arizona and sent across the international boundary to a place called Arizonac. From there the Spaniards shipped the ore to Mexico City. Arizonac is derived from the Papago words for little spring, *ali shonak*.

Arizona's copper lured a Canadian, James Douglas, who was to make the major strike at Bisbee with the Copper Queen Mine. The Douglas story is the story of mining in Arizona as well as service to the state and nation through, at this writing, four generations. It is the great-grandson of James who told the Douglas family story for this taping. James Stuart Douglas, chairman of the executive committee of the First National Bank of Arizona, narrated the story of one of Arizona's most remarkable families, beginning with his great-grandfather's mining discoveries and then moving ahead to the days of his father, Lewis Douglas. Lewis Douglas served in the Arizona Legislature, in Congress, as Director of the Budget for Franklin Delano Roosevelt and then as ambassador to the Court of Saint James.

TO THE COURT OF SAINT JAMES

James Stuart Douglas has followed his family's devotion to public service. The plaques and certificates on the wall of his Tucson office attest to that. His family pride showed as he began to talk.

"My great-grandfather was a Canadian by birth and by citizenship, and his father, George Douglas, was a doctor in Montreal. In any event because of his enormous intellectual capacity my great-grandfather became a very, very skilled metallurgist and geologist and invented a certain system for smelting copper. During the course of his life he ran into Colonel Dodge in New York, and Dodge asked him to come to Arizona and look at some properties he'd heard about in and around the Bisbee area. And to that extent he did come out here, and after much travail and unproductive leads he discovered the great Copper Queen Mine at Bisbee.

"That was long before the turn of the century . . . 1878 sticks in my mind. In any event he did discover this tremendous copper lode, and that was the introduction of Phelps Dodge into the copper industry. Dr. James Douglas, my great-grandfather, became chairman of the board of Phelps Dodge. He also founded the town of Douglas to produce a smelter, and the town was named in his honor. He also built a number of railroads to shipping points in southern Arizona. Later he retired to a farm in New York and died there. His son, James Douglas, who was my grandfather, after a variety of experiences in running copper mines for several companies, had founded the United Verde Extension Mine in Jerome and built the smelter in Clarkdale. My grandfather also founded the Bank of Douglas, the Bank of Bisbee, also owned the Bank of Warren which he finally merged into the Bank of Douglas. He and Billy Brophy started those banks, and then my grandfather sold his interest to Billy's son, Frank Brophy. Frank in turn sold it to the Valley Bank pension fund. The Justice Department made Valley divest the fund, and it is now known as the Arizona Bank.

"My father, Lewis Douglas, was born in Bisbee, but he attended school and college in the East. He graduated from Amherst with the highest honors in metallurgy and geology. He taught at Amherst after he graduated from MIT. Then he came west to work for his father in the United Verde Extension Mine as a mucker. My grandfather was a very, very powerful man, as was my father, and although there was a very strong bond of affection between them, their personalities, well, I won't say clashed, but didn't lead to harmony.

"So my father moved to Phoenix where he took up citrus farming with Frank Brophy and in due course ran for the state legislature and, of course, for Congress of the United States at the time when the state had only one representative. During the course of his second term in Congress, he was selected by Franklin Roosevelt to be Director of the Budget. My father was a conservative; he believed in not spending more than you earned. And in due course those philosophies conflicted with the pump-priming philosophies of Roosevelt, and my father resigned. Then, I believe, he became a vice-president of American Cyanamid and was asked to be vice-chancellor of McGill University in Montreal which is the same as being president. He served at McGill almost three years when the war broke out."

Lewis Douglas returned to the States to go into private business, but soon was serving the government again. He administered the Lend-Lease program to Britain, and was a deputy war shipping administrator before again returning to the private sector.

"In 1947, I believe, George Catlett Marshall became Secretary of State under President Truman, and I remember we were at dinner when a telephone call came through from Marshall asking my father if he'd serve as ambassador to the Court of Saint James, United States Ambassador to England. Well, he had served his country since he was twenty-nine years old, and he must have been fiftyish when he was asked to serve as ambassador and, while he was never one not to answer the call of his country, he had thought that he had perhaps given as much as he could possibly give, because you don't get rich working for the government.

"But he was persuaded to accept the job and did, and I'll let history speak to this, but from all accounts that I can hear from this side of the water he was one of the most distinguished ambassadors that the United States ever sent overseas perhaps with the exception of Ben Franklin.

"But at any event he did serve as ambassador during the very, very dark years directly after the war. He also assisted Lucius Clay in redesigning the plan for the rehabilitation of Germany. And curiously enough, coincidentally, when he was ambassador, his brother-in-law, John Mc-Cloy, became high commissioner to Germany. So between the two of them and Marshall, the Morgenthau plan was scuttled, and the Marshall Plan began to emerge. And my father, George Marshall, John McCloy and the Congress of the United States were leading movers to rehabilitate Europe. Europe was a vacuum; there was nothing left. It was bled dry so this is what prompted the Marshall Plan.

"It was over there that my father lost his eye in a fishing accident, and I believe it was approaching 1952 when he asked to be relieved as ambassador and he returned to Arizona. But that didn't stop his public service; he was always on call to presidents and secretaries of state throughout his life.

"I was never, of course, privy to decision-making, but many times I would have dinner with my father and many of the great figures. I remember dinners with Churchill, Eisenhower, Lucius Clay and many others who have now passed. I can recall the discussions as to the attitudes of the Communist world and the dangers that confronted the free world and how best to meet those challenges and so forth and so on. They spread over enormous geographical and intellectual horizons, as you can well imagine.

"The dropping of the Iron Curtain, the emergence of atomic energy and later hydrogen—all of these things put these men, these leaders of our country under tremendous pressures. And their conversations, I remember, would revolve around those things that best resolved the problems to avoid, you know, a holocaust that would destroy the world."

We asked Douglas to explain the problems his father had as a wealthy man, a conservative, but yet a Democrat and a party leader working under the liberal FDR.

"There really wasn't any great discomfort for my father, only in terms of policy. It didn't bother my father one whit to vote Republican if he felt that was the way, that that was best for the country. John Garner apparently took him to task on the floor of the House of Representatives as to what his loyalties were, and my father's response was that his first loyalty was to his country, his second was to his state, his third to his community and his last loyalty was to his party. And he more or less followed that all of his life.

"Still my father had a very high regard for Roosevelt. He didn't disagree with him always. I don't think he fundamentally disagreed with

Lewis Douglas, the Arizonan who rose to international prominence, is pictured here in England during his appointment as American Ambassador to the Court of Saint James. Left to right are Ambassador Douglas, his daughter Sharman, Mrs. George C. Marshall, Winston Churchill and Lord Profumo. James Stuart Douglas, who narrates his family's story, stands behind Mrs. Marshall. LEWIS DOUGLAS MEMORIAL LIBRARY

pump-priming at that time as an immediate dosage of medicine to our country, but what he was fearful of was that it might prolong its life, which is what happened. And I believe in 1934 he gave a series of lectures at Harvard which were later published in a book, *The Liberal Tradition*, and the subheading was 'Balance the Budget or Inflation.' Well, we still have inflation.

"Of course, that was provoked by financing one great war with a 2½ percent interest rate—with which he disagreed—and financing two other great wars—Korea and Vietnam—without appropriate taxation. But on top of that the old concept of fiscal and monetary responsibility more or less disappeared. So today we're reaping the results of inflation, and they're going to be with us a long, long time."

Douglas recalled some of his father's impressions of some of the great leaders of that time.

"He was an enormous admirer of Winston Churchill and a very good friend as well. Once he was having dinner at Chartwell, and he admired one of Churchill's paintings of three elephants under the arc lights of a circus. My father kept looking at it, and Sir Winston asked, 'You admire that painting, Lew?' And he said, 'Yes, I do, very much.' And when my father resigned as ambassador, Winston Churchill remembered and gave him that painting.

"Truman? My father said he was a remarkable man. He said he wasn't the smoothest man that ever lived, and he wasn't the smartest man that ever lived, but that Truman by and large was a man embued with a deep sense of loyalty to this country and great integrity. He said Truman never backed away from anything—ever.

"My father was an enormous admirer of Cordell Hull, and he supported most of the Secretary of State's policies. He was not an isolationist, nor was Cordell Hull, but pressures then were brought to bear on Hull that came fundamentally from the executive office. Neither Cordell Hull nor my father believed in tariffs. They thought that the imposition of tariffs led to autarchy, if you will, or to isolationism, and that isolation would eventually lead to war."

The conversation turned to another Secretary of State, Dean Acheson.

"My father was a supporter of Dean's, but he said one very curious thing about him. My father was in the hospital, and Dean came to visit him. And Dean Acheson had made a policy statement that the United States had no interest in anything south of the Thirty-eighth Parallel in

Korea. Well, father said, 'Dean, I'm not disagreeing with you that that should be our position. But what I am saying to you is don't tell the Russians this, because it's like playing poker and laying your hand down before you start betting.'

"Well, sure enough, in the spring of that year the thirty-eighth parallel was invaded by the North Koreans, and we were in the Korean War."

How does a son look back at a father who was a powerful international figure?

"His greatest attribute was that he was a great father. He never, at any time that I knew of, never did not have the time to speak to anybody, no matter who it was, or to help some one, no matter who he was.

"I guess the English newspapers described him when he left England as a very beautiful, gentle and perfect knight. And I guess that's it.

"With all this, my father never forgot his attachments to Arizona. He was born here, and he loved the state; the genesis of the Douglas family was in Arizona. There's something about Arizona that only Arizonans can feel, and it's very difficult to describe. My father never forgot his love for Arizona. Even at the Court of Saint James he was registered as a voter in the little township of Sonoita in the county of Santa Cruz, in the state of Arizona."

No Time Out for Revolutions

PROVIDING THE SUPPLIES and materials for the development of the Frontier West was left to enterprising merchants who came into Arizona from all directions. They headed for the mining camps, but even before that they had set up shop near military bases and forts. And as villages became towns and then cities, some of those merchants prospered and became the business leaders of the state.

It was just after the turn of the century that the Levy family moved into the territory to open the Red Star General Store at Douglas. The Red Star catered to miners, ranchers and farmers and as well did a flourishing business with Mexicans who came across the border at Agua Prieta. In those earlier days border businessmen had some unusual moments when revolutions broke loose across the line. In the following tape Leon Levy, a second-generation member of that pioneer family, tells of some of the lighter moments with Mexican revolutionaries.

Leon Levy tells of the strength of those early merchandisers and what they have meant to the progress of the territory and state. Leon came through the Douglas school system, continued on to the University of Arizona to became a student and athletic leader. He went on to become a civic leader, serving as president of the Arizona Board of Regents to bring his association with the university full circle.

From the little Red Star General Store in Douglas, Tucson's Levy's became one of the West's major department stores. At this taping Leon Levy was an acting consultant to Federated Department Stores, the nationwide organization which purchased Levy's in 1960, and also honorary board chairman of First National Bank of Arizona.

The Red Star General Store, started in 1903 in Douglas, offered a wide array of merchandise that often attracted revolutionaries from across the border in Mexico. Jacob Levy wears the bowler hat.

A MERCHANT PIONEER ON THE BORDER

Leon Levy sat in the office of the downtown Tucson bank building located only a few blocks from Congress Street. It was there that Levy's store was started in Tucson, but it was 125 miles away in Douglas that the first Levy store was opened. The family story, however, opens thousands of miles away from the territory of Arizona.

"My father's father came from Europe and settled in Peoria, Illinois, and that's where my father was born. At a very young age my grandfather died, and I think my father went through the sixth grade in school and then had to go to work to support his mother and brother, his younger brother, Ben, who was five years younger. The family first went to New York where my father worked in some clothing factories, and then they migrated to Texas, and my father opened a little store at a very, very young age in Floresville. Through mutual friends in San Antonio my father met my mother. She had been brought over from Europe at the age of three by her older brother. You can see, I'm quite a mixture; I'm a mixture of Polish, Russian, German and Austrian. And of the family that remained in Europe all of them were destroyed except one nephew; he was the only one to get out of Hitler's holocaust.

"Well, my father had this business in Floresville, Texas, but then they heard about this beautiful town, Douglas, which was started by the grandfather of our former ambassador to England, Lewis Douglas. This was right after my father and mother were married, and they decided that that was the land of opportunity, and they came west in February of 1903.

"When my mother arrived in Douglas she was pregnant with my brother Aaron who passed away in 1959. My father had $500; that was his worldly goods. And he started the Red Star General Store in Douglas which was 25 by 100 feet. My mother and father lived in the rear 25 feet of the store. Well, it seems my father needed an additional $50 to take care of the birth of my brother, and he went into the First National Bank of Douglas which later was absorbed into the Valley Bank system.

"The head of that bank at the time was a man by the name of Packard, later known as Daddy Packard. My father went to the cashier's window and said he wanted to borrow $50. The man said, 'Do you have anybody to sign your note?' My father said, 'No, I just came to Douglas, and I need this money, but I'm not going to ask anybody to sign it. I'm good for it, but I can understand.' With that he started to walk out of the bank. Daddy Packard overheard the conversation between his employee and my father. He walked over and he said, 'Levy, here's the $50.' My father said, 'Don't you want me to sign anything?' He said, 'No, you'll pay; you're all right.'

"And that was the start of a great relationship, and Daddy Packard always claimed that he paid for Aaron. Later my dad ended up on the board of the bank.

"Well, the Red Star General Store was started in 1903. My uncle came out to Arizona and helped build the El Paso and Southwestern Railroad; he was in charge of a bull gang on the railroad and lived in Brewery Gulch over in Bisbee. Then it was my mother and father and his brother, Ben, there in Douglas. Ben joined them in the store in 1906. My mother was a very strong person and she did everything, worked in the store, raised a family. There wasn't much that bothered her. For example, on one side of the store was a saloon and on the other side was a restaurant. And the saloon would close up about four o'clock in the morning, and the restaurant would open about five o'clock in the morning.

"And the walls were like paper so every time they'd have a fight or a shooting in the saloon, the bullets would go right through the wall. And this is why my mother feared nobody, no man or woman.

"I was born June 15, 1913, and my mother and father always said I was the lucky omen because things really took off for them after my birth. My mother had a very tough time giving birth to both Aaron and myself because in those days they didn't control the size of babies. As you can see I'm a pretty big man, and when I was born I think I weighed eleven pounds.

"My mother went through an awful lot. At the time of Pancho Villa's uprising in 1915 my brother went down to see what was going on and got caught in the crossfire between Villa and the Federales, and they had a tough time getting him out of there. We only lived ten blocks from the border and after Pancho Villa's raid at Columbus, New Mexico, they moved troops into Douglas and we actually had cannon by our house.

"In those days Douglas and the other border cities were the active business communities in the state. Tucson was a sleepy village, and Phoenix was really sleepy. Phoenix wasn't even on the main line of the railroad those days. There was a lot of activity on the border and a lot of interesting things took place. My father and uncle were as honorable people as I've ever known, and they developed the trust of the Mexican people. Many times Mexican people would come into the store and insist that my father keep their money for them. It wasn't that there was any question about the banks; they just had that much confidence in my father.

"Some of those people would come up from Mexico every six or twelve months because it was very hard going then . . . practically no roads and the railroad only went as far south as Nacozari. Many times the *novias* or brides-to-be would come up and in those days—and I still think it's a Mexican custom—the man paid for everything. So they would buy all the necessary things for the wedding; they would also buy a layette because they knew they weren't going to be back for a year, and they knew they were going to have a baby.

"One time around 1919 or 1920 one of the revolutionaries—and most of the Mexican revolutions were fomented in Sonora—came to my father and uncle with a million dollars in cash. They wanted to be supplied with blankets, equipment and so forth for the revolution. All the merchandise was to be delivered on the American side. Well, the million dollars were put in escrow in the Bank of Douglas, and my father got on the train to go to New York to buy the merchandise. By the time he got to Kansas City, the government had fallen and the revolution was called off. My uncle wired my father to come back and he did. He released the escrow, and the officials came in and gave my dad and uncle $10,000 for their trouble. And that was a lot of money in those days.

"Pancho Villa was a customer in our store in Douglas, and many of the great families of Mexico became friendly with my family. In later years when my mother was living in Tucson they used to come visit her. She was friendly with Obregon, Calles and Ruiz, just to name a few."

Leon Levy now talked about his school days in Douglas and what it meant to grow up in a border town.

"Well, it was a great life growing up there. My father, in those days, wasn't wealthy, but he was comfortable and had been successful. So I really never wanted for worldly goods, but I was well trained. My father impressed upon me that I was being raised with a cross-section of the world, with Mexican youths and all the others who made up the Douglas community in those days. My father would say to me, 'Leon, if you're with a group of boys and you want to go to a movie, but the rest of them can't afford it, don't go to the movie. Don't have those boys obligated to you. You live as part of this community and grow up in that way.' I never forgot that, and I tried to impart that to my children.

"My father and mother always impressed on us our religious background. Formal religion we didn't have because in the whole city of Douglas there were maybe seven or eight Jewish families. And my grandfather, who was a religious man to some degree, my step-grandfather, really, used to go around at the High Holidays to Safford, Bisbee and the other nearby cities and round up enough people to have services. They were orthodox services, and you have to have a *minyan* of ten men. So if somebody had to go to the washroom, they sometimes would stop the services.

"My father was a very soft person. My uncle was a bit different. He had the background of having to exist by his toughness and his wits. He had the habit generally of hitting and then finding out what the details were. My uncle weighed about 155 pounds and stood about five-nine, and there was a man in Douglas who made a mistake in sizing him up. This man was pretty close to six feet and weighed about 195. One day in front of the store this man made a derogatory remark about the faith of my uncle. That was a serious mistake because the next thing that man knew he was in the middle of G Avenue. One punch was all my uncle needed.

"My father and uncle would drive home from work every day in a panel truck that the store used for deliveries. And they'd drive all the way home talking to each other but never looking at each other. My father used to drive up Ninth Street, make the turn and then come down Tenth Street to drop my uncle off and then come a couple blocks further to our house. One time in making the turn, the door opened on my uncle's side. My uncle flew out of the car. My father drove up in front of my uncle's house and said, 'Okay, Ben.' And, of course, my uncle wasn't there. Pretty soon here came my uncle walking down the street just mad as hell.

"It's funny, but those are the little things in life that you remember."

Aaron, the elder brother, went to the University of Arizona where he saw the business opportunities in Tucson. It was Aaron who convinced the family to expand to Tucson. Aaron had been a football player, but injuries limited his college career to serving as trainer. Leon became a standout center for the Wildcats. In his senior year he, too, suffered an injury. He had planned to get a law degree, but things turned out differently.

"I got so involved in our store in Tucson I never went back to the university. The store was at Congress and Scott, and the business grew and prospered, even though when I entered the business in '35 it was in the midst of the Depression and it wasn't easy. Along about 1938, '39, Aaron and I began to think about expansion, and we purchased the property at Scott and Pennington."

World War II came on and delayed the move. Leon went off to serve with the United States Navy in the Pacific. In 1950 the new Levy's opened in downtown Tucson.

"I remember one prominent businessman who heard we were going to move to Pennington said to me one day, 'Are you out of your mind? You've got a good business here on Congress Street.' I told him, 'It's up to us to grow with the city.'

"And you know the same thing was said to me in 1959 after Aaron had passed away and I'd made arrangements to open our store at El Con on Broadway. And everything was moving right along even though in my mind I knew that the day of the independent, unfortunately, was over. I say unfortunately because this country was really built by small businesses."

In 1960 a representative of Federated Department Stores approached Leon Levy. Soon a deal was made and although Leon stayed on to direct the store's monumental growth until 1973, the change had been made. In Federated's Levy's of Tucson store today you can see the old pictures of the Red Star General Store in Douglas. Some days Leon Levy pauses in front of those pictures. He stares at the old photos and he can almost hear the shouting from the bar next door to the Red Star. Can it really be almost three-quarters of a century since the Red Star opened its doors in Douglas?

Life in Arizona's First Capital City

THE BIRTHPLACE OF GOVERNMENT in Arizona lies only a short distance off one of the state's most-traveled highways, but its monument remains almost totally obscured.

If you stop your car at Navajo on I-40 in northeastern Arizona, you can get to the site where the Arizona Territorial Government was organized on December 29, 1863. There is a monument to that historic occasion, but getting to it is something else. The monument is in the middle of a stock pen on the Spurlock Ranch, less than a mile from the freeway. There, John N. Goodwin took the oath of office as territorial governor.

How did the governor select that spot? Well, his party, along with military escort, had ridden west for the historic occasion. The party crossed the line of New Mexico December 27, but there were some doubts because a snowstorm had obscured markers and landmarks. To be safe the party moved on to Navajo Springs (now the roadside stop of Navajo off I-40) which was well within the Arizona boundary.

So the territory of Arizona became an official entity, and Governor Goodwin decided that Fort Whipple would be the seat of his government. It wasn't long before a city began to rise nearby; it was named Prescott after William Hickling Prescott, a New England historian who had written books about the Aztecs. Arizona's Territorial Capital was moved to Tucson in 1867 but was returned to Prescott a decade later. In 1889 the territorial capital was shifted to Phoenix.

Prescott has been called the Cowboy Capital of the World, and even now it claims to have staged the first rodeo on the Fourth of July, 1888.

Lester W. "Budge" Ruffner, director of a Prescott funeral home that came to the family through a winning hand at cards, is a lecturer and writer on the history of Arizona.

It was in an attic office atop the Ruffner Funeral Home in Prescott where Lester (Budge) Ruffner began talking about how his family had come to Arizona.

"Well, I don't know that we're any different than a lot of families that came west at that period of time. The Civil War was kind of a breaking point and destroyed a lot of roots for a lot of families. Morris Andrew Ruffner was a great-uncle of mine who was a Virginia farmer and was in the Confederate Army. He went back to his farm near Charlottesville, Virginia, after surviving the Civil War and there wasn't anything left. It was gone, burned up, destroyed; there weren't any animals, crops, equipment or anything. So he just decided to hell with it and pushed off for the West.

"As far as we can tell he walked most of the way, or rode whatever animals became available, and he came into the Verde Valley of Arizona in 1867. He settled there on the Verde River at a place that the maps still show as Ruffner's Crossing. It's about a mile and a half downriver from Tuzigoot National Monument. He started to prospect in that area, and he and a partner by the name of Angus McKinnon staked out Cleopatra Hill as a claim—which was quite an accomplishment. That hill later became Jerome. In 1876 they sold their claim on Cleopatra Hill for the astronomical amount of $15,000. Now that mine has produced, I've heard, anywhere from $600 million to $900 million worth of ore. But you can't be too critical; in 1876 that $15,000 was a lot of money, and they owed some money. They took that money and ran."

Budge Ruffner's great-uncle went to Phoenix to work and then convinced a nephew to come west. But that nephew, George Ruffner, liked cattle and horses, and he went to Prescott to work as a cowpuncher. Later he brought his brothers, Walter, Lester and Ed, to Prescott. Lester was the father of Budge Ruffner.

"Well, they were in several enterprises, among them a livery stable. They started a freighting business, freighting to the mines outside of Prescott. And it wasn't long before George Ruffner got into politics. He'd been a deputy sheriff, and in 1898 he succeeded the famous Buckey O'Neill as sheriff of Yavapai County. And he served from that time almost continually and died in office in 1933.

"Now I say almost continually because George Ruffner was not what

Left: *This was the reward poster for Fleming Parker, arrested for a train robbery, escape from the Prescott jail and for killing, during that escape, the deputy district attorney.* BUDGE RUFFNER COLLECTION

Below: *The hanging of Fleming Parker in Prescott in 1898 was a popular attraction for the citizens. The hanging was under the supervision of Sheriff George Ruffner.* BUDGE RUFFNER COLLECTION

you'd call a disciplined man, and frequently would go on a bender; he would go on monumental benders. And the first time he was defeated for re-election was right after he'd hung Jim Parker, who was an old cowboy friend of his who had robbed a train and then compounded that by killing the district attorney. And ultimately he had to be hung. He was sentenced to death, but in those days, of course, there was no provision for hanging to be done in a penitentiary. It had to be done by the county sheriff or under his supervision. So Jim Parker was hung in Prescott.

"Well not long after that George Ruffner went over to Camp Verde for a political rally. He was pretty drunk so they kept putting off calling him up to the platform to speak. Finally the chairman felt compelled to call on him. So George stood up and he said that he thought he'd done a good job as sheriff—he was wavering as he spoke—and said that he would like to have the office again. But then he said he didn't give a damn whether they voted for him or not. He made that statement. The result, of course, was disastrous, and he was defeated.

"That was his first defeat. He was later defeated sometime in the twenties, but he would always recover and go back and win again. He didn't believe in prohibition so he was a little lax in his enforcement of it. He would raid a still only when he absolutely had to, and when the public pressure got so it practically demanded it. I remember one time I was walking with my uncle, the sheriff of Yavapai County. I was a great admirer of his. He was my hero in spite of the fact that he was somewhat uncut in many ways. But I remember that day he was going across the street, and there was this cowboy coming across the other way. It was between the Saint Michael Hotel and what they used to call the Owl Drug Store, over at the end of Whiskey Row.

"And this cowboy was walking toward my uncle with great difficulty —straddle-legged and apparently in great pain; uncomfortable, to say the least. My uncle stopped him and says, 'Harry, was she pretty?' And this cowboy says, 'George, she was a gorgeous son of a bitch.' That was the total conversation."

Budge Ruffner pushed back in his chair and laughed. Then he had another story to tell about his uncle, the sheriff of Yavapai.

"The circumstance of our getting into the funeral business was a little unorthodox. In those days, I think it was 1903, they used to have high stake poker games in cloistered rooms in the Old Palace Bar on Whiskey Row. And my uncle was in a game with a chap by the name of Nevins who was the town undertaker. Well, he already owed a considerable bill to the Ruffner Livery Stable; he'd rent wagons and carriages, you see, for the funerals.

"Well, as the game went on everybody had dropped out on this one pot, a rather enticing pot, except Nevins and Ruffner. Nevins said he hadn't enough money for the pot, and he suggested they play double or nothing. He said, 'You just mark my livery bill paid.' And my uncle said, 'Fine, and if you lose, you just give me the undertaking parlor.' 'Fine,' said Nevins, 'that sounds reasonable.' And the game went on. Ruffner happened to win the hand and acquired the undertaking parlor. That's how the family got into that business."

In many ways Prescott was, and remains, a unique city in Arizona. It was a rough town, a cowboy town, as Ruffner explained, but New England families settling in Prescott gave it a genteel society as well.

"We didn't all see the same side of Prescott. There were those of us who didn't see the society side of it. We went into the jails, for example. We went to the Chinese josh houses to see 'em smoke the opium. We went along Granite Creek where all the cribs were and saw the action there. Prescott, you know, was known as the Cowboy Capital of the World then.

"You know, Fiorello La Guardia, the former Mayor of New York, used to come back here to visit because he'd grown up here as a boy and had gone to school here; his father was a bandmaster at Fort Whipple. And he used to talk about his boyhood experiences in Prescott. He'd grown the same roots that I had . . . had been up and down Granite Creek which was where the action was.

"But let me tell you this, Prescott has a character, and I don't give a damn what you say. Everybody says that about his own town, but I'm saying Prescott is different, totally different. The values are different. The things that some people think are progressive, or symbols of progress, don't impress the people of Prescott nearly as much as they do in other communities. I think here we are doing a pretty good job of holding on to our heritage. Yes, this town has character; it always had character.

"I think my father would have gone bananas if he had seen some of the changes, however. He died when he was eighty-two or eighty-three, and I think that some of his remarks were classic. Shortly before his death we were discussing the trends and he said, 'I really think that civilization began to collapse when we started cooking outside and going to the bathroom inside.'"

The Men Who Rode the Ranges

THE SPANIARDS BROUGHT CATTLE and sheep into the Southwest; four hundred years later livestock remains an important industry of the area. Ranching, however, did not become an important part of the area's economy until after marauding Indian tribes had been subdued following the Civil War; the Indians had found cattle raids a strong deterrent to many Mexican and Anglo settlers and, as well, an excellent source of food supply.

But when the Indians had been herded onto reservations, ranching began to flourish in the 1870s and the 1880s. The big spreads were formed in the territory in those years, and the cowboy became an important part of its development.

The cowboy of territorial and statehood days in Arizona was no kin of the Hollywood cowboy—as you will see in this taping of an old vaquero who rode the ranges along the border of Mexico. The cowboy was a laborer willing to work long hours—often starting the day before sun-up and turning in long after sundown—and satisfied with wages that would never make him rich. The clothes he wore were not designed to be flamboyant enough to attract a Hollywood producer; his duds were practical, aimed at combatting the elements of sun, wind and dust, and protecting the skin from cactus and chaparral.

The cowboy who carried a gun was not looking for desperados; he carried it to protect himself against wild animals or to kill for his meals.

The long days and nights on the range made the cowboy appreciate a couple of nights "on the town" and he spent freely for his entertainment and pleasure. But he was soon back on the cattle ranch, back to his role of a hard-working, often lonely, laboring man of the Old West.

Luis Romero, a rangehand along the Arizona-Mexican border, seldom had time to go to town to pose for a photo, but these cowboys of northwestern Arizona put on their fancy duds for this old studio shot. Second from the left is one of the many black cowboys who worked the ranges in the Southwest in early days. ARIZONA HIS-TORICAL SOCIETY

THE LIFE AND TIMES OF A VAQUERO

Luis Romero is a vaquero of days gone by. At eighty-five, he lives quietly in a mobile home on the same rangeland of southern Arizona where he rode and roped as a young man. His speech is heavily accented, his memory sharp and clear.

"I was born in Sonora State in Mexico I think late in '92. Live in Caborca and come in '98 across the border. My daddy worked in Ruby; he was miner. We live in Arivaca and we were poor. There's four sisters and three brothers and we live with the beans and tortillas. Sometime you eat straight beans.

"Once in a while I go to school. My daddy don't let me go always 'cause somethin' to do; you know, I need to help my daddy. I'm the oldest one of the crew and I need to help my daddy. And it's too far to the school; ride the donkey, you know, to go to the school four or five miles. You go one day and the next day you needed at house. I go one day a week and then I go one week a month; in that way I go to the school maybe five, six years. I don't know nothin'.

"I start to work, oh, about 1909, 1910, when I was seventeen, eighteen. I start to work for a Doctor Ball who had a ranch. He gave me a job to water his cattle. He pay me ten dollars a month and he give me rations—just a little coffee and a little sugar and that way I started to work. Lots of difficult workin' those days. You know, those bosses make you work in everythin'. You know, one day you ride the horse, next day you dig holes, next day you stretch some wire. That's the way you workin' those days.

"When we go out on the roundup, oh, just get up about three o'clock an' start to make a drive, round up the cattle, round up the calves. Put in sometimes all day. No dinner till sometime eight, nine o'clock at night. Sometime in those big outfits, sometime you start to round up in March—no, in April—and through late in May. Take two months. You sleep outside in the wagon.

"An' they come lots of people from all the places, lots of cowboys to pick 'em up his cattle. An' people come from the other side, from Sonora, to come for his cows on this side."

We asked how the Mexican cowboys, the vaqueros, were treated.

"Pretty good. They treat you pretty good. You know, old man own the outfit, he's a white man, but the cowboy, you know, he's all Mexican.

When I quit Dr. Ball, I go to work for Jarilla's outfit. He pay me twenty dollars to start. Twenty dollars room and board.

"And then I work for Ramon Ahumada. He's my boss for too many years. A rough man. He give you work day and night. He give you all to do this and that today, not tomorrow. We work all day from three o'clock in the morning till eight, nine, ten at night. An' he use the moon for work. At sundown he's about six, seven miles from the ranch, he use the moon to bring a bunch of cattle to the pen in the pasture, or where they're goin' to be put.

"I remember one time one new man come an' ask Ramon for job. All the time he got a job so Ramon, he say, 'Yeah, I got job. You go ahead rest today. Start tomorrow.' Next mornin' Ramon send that cowboy to bring in horses; he got fifteen, twenty horses—bad, bucking horses—in a pasture. An' you ride, three, four horses, an' if they don't throw you off, you got a job. Then Ramon, he send you to the mountain, see if you rope the calf, see if you rope one wild animal. If you ride good first, an' then catch one wild animal, then you have job."

Cowboying was a hard life, filled with danger. Luis Romero recounted some of the accidents and injuries.

"One day I'm goin' to catch a few horses for the roundup an' our boss, Jack McVey, he say, 'I go with you.' An' he ride his horse. Soon I put the horses in the corral an' he need to rope one horse. One of those boys, one of the cowboys, said, 'I'm gonna rope it.' Jack said, 'No, I'll rope it. I'll rope it.' An' he take his horse an' they go to rope that horse. When they rope that horse, Jack's horse, you know, start to buck an' he goes straight to the fence. An' when he close to the fence, that horse step back an' throw Jack off an' break the neck.

"An' that Ramon Ahumada, he was a good cowboy [Ahumada, a legendary figure, was one of the first to be named to the Cowboy Hall of Fame]. He always ride good horses. Ramon, got better than a hundred horses, but in roundup one horse get away an' Ramon, he said to me, 'I like to ketch him. You help me.' So we go an' pretty soon I say, 'The horse is over there. Right there's the horse. He's a brown horse.'

"Where the horse is there is a big pasture an' I go, you know, to push the horse straight to the little pasture. An' Ramon help to push him to go in the gate inside. He wants to beat the horse before he go outside that little pasture, but he can't do that."

Luis described how Ramon Ahumada fought the horse along the fence up into a canyon and then Luis lost sight of his boss.

"I don't see nothin' and I get kinda nervous. Soon I go aroun' to that canyon an' I see two horses in the pasture. An' then I found Ramon. He's on the ground, you know, with the hat down. An' lots of blood. I have lots of trouble tryin' to make him straight 'cause he's a big man. I speak with him; he can' speak nothin'. I go an' get a blanket an' I make a bed for him. I run to get water from a well and a little kid is there and I tell him to go to old man Campos on the little ranch and tell him Ramon is hurt pretty bad.

"They take Ramon in to Tucson to hospital. He get well, Ramon, but he's one man don' speak much, he don' live much after that. When he came home he kinda laugh all the time an' he forget everythin'. That horse in the corral he forget."

Luis Romero sat at the edge of the sofa and pointed down to his ankle.

"This ankle he broke twice. An' this arm, pull out of socket four inches. Fourteen times I break bones. Horse fall with me twice. Last time horse she fall an' then get up high as can an' she fall again. When she fall again she hit my foot right here an' ankle he broke again. I couldn't use boots any more. I couldn't use nothin'. I'm crazy to ride the horse. I like to ride, but I can't do it."

We asked Romero about the hard work of cowboying and whether he liked the work.

"You know the cowboy work is one hard work. The cowboy he needed to ride horse, to ride buckin' horse, need to know how to rope wild animals, need to know how to tie in the tree, need to know how to lead, how to do the brandin's an' lots of things."

We pressed the question: But did you like this work as a vaquero?

"Did I like? Well, I was raised in that thing. I didn't have so much school. I can do nothing else. Just to cowboy."

Early Days of a Flagstaff Doctor

THE FRONTIER didn't attract professional men in great numbers in the early days, and doctors found themselves working round the clock with staggering patient loads.

Martin George Fronske had planned to settle down to practice in Saint Louis where he was born in 1883 and where he went to medical school. Where the promise of riches and adventure had lured the early settlers of the Southwest, it was poor health that sent Dr. Fronske away from the comforts of midwestern living. He arrived in Flagstaff in 1914, and he practiced for more than a half-century. Flagstaff residents gave up counting after Dr. Fronske had delivered more than 2,000 of their babies.

It was Dr. Fronske who attended the famed astronomer, Percival Lowell, on his death bed. Lowell, known for his discovery of "canals" on Mars, is still considered Flagstaff's most celebrated citizen. But the city has heaped its highest honors on Martin George Fronske, the frontier doctor.

THE TERRIBLE FLU EPIDEMIC OF '18

Martin George Fronske was not far from his ninety-third birthday when he sat for this taping in the comfortable home of his son and daughter-in-law in Flagstaff. The morning sun came through the windows and glinted off the thick glasses he wore. His eyes had gone bad, but at ninety-three, he said, that had to be expected. His memory was not in any way impaired.

"Well, I was born and raised and went to school in Saint Louis, Missouri. My father was a blacksmith and my family needed all the help they could get so in the summertimes I worked in a big department store.

After the second summer, I told my mother, I said, 'Now I'm not going to work in any store. I'm not going to work and have everybody boss me.' We talked things over and my mother said, 'What would you think about being a doctor?'

"There and then I made up my mind I was going to be a doctor and I did it. I graduated in medicine from Washington University there in Saint Louis in 1907 and I had a pretty good practice going when I took sick. I was told I would have to go west, so I went to Albuquerque in the spring of 1912 and then went out to work at a lumber camp in the Zuñi Mountains as a doctor. Well, soon I thought I could go back which I did. I got back to Saint Louis and right away I started to work again. I think it was 1913 when I broke down again. I nearly bled to death from hemorrhages."

The young doctor and his wife headed west again. They were in Albuquerque in 1914 when a Flagstaff doctor, R. O. Raymond, offered him a position.

"Well, I arrived in Flagstaff that year after one of their big blizzards had just finished blowing. The snow was knee deep and the porter helped me off with my luggage. I remember I stopped at the Commercial Hotel, had breakfast and I walked over to the corner of Leroux Street. I looked up toward the San Francisco Mountains and it looked to me like the mountain was just beyond the hill. Well, I started to walk that way and the mountain wasn't getting any closer. I realized the clear atmosphere of Flagstaff had just made the mountain seem so close.

"Getting started in Flagstaff wasn't easy. Dr. Raymond had a pretty well-equipped laboratory, but you had to do all the work yourself—urinalysis, blood count, bacteriology, blood cultures— everything. In our days doctors did a lot of things that they won't do any more.

"To see a patient in the middle of the night was nothing. I've tramped through the snow nearly hip deep and I have gone out in a buggy after the snow was so deep you'd ride right over the top of the fences. Later on when the main roads were plowed, I'd go to a certain point, maybe eight or nine miles out of town, and somebody would be waiting there for me with a sled made of railroad ties hammered together. And they'd take me out to a ranch house where a woman was bleeding to death with a miscarriage. Well, I would do the best I could; that was all we could do then.

"And, I want to tell you my wife was the best sport you ever saw. When I was over in the Zuñi Mountains in New Mexico she came out to

Dr. Martin Fronske poses among the tools of his trade of an earlier day, on display at the Northern Arizona Pioneers' Historical Society in Flagstaff.

join me. She got off the train in the middle of the night and she needed some place to stay. She asked the agent how to get to where I was staying. The agent told her he couldn't leave the station and he motioned towards a hill where there were some residences. He said, 'I'll give you my six-gun and you can walk up there and find a bed. Then in the morning your husband will come on over and pick you up.' She was a great sport, my wife, for it was crude living those days."

Some of the most difficult days were during the flu epidemic of 1918.

"We'd heard about it hitting all over, but nothing happened until the fall of '18 when Winslow High School came over to play the university football team in Flagstaff. One of the players that came had just recovered from the flu. Well, they played an afternoon game and in the evening they had a dance. That was a Saturday night, I remember. Well, the next day they called me to the university and said there were some sick boys there. Well, pretty soon the number of sick grew so high the school was quarantined. We brought in nurses from Los Angeles. They were supposed to have been immunized, but they all took sick after two days. I stayed with it and we didn't have a single death at the school.

"The epidemic died out at the university and then it started in the city. And that was something. I never saw anything like it. Everybody got sick; everybody, even the other doctor. I was the only doctor in Flagstaff left standing, besides the public health doctors. It got so bad the Health Department took the desks out of Emerson School and put in cots and brought in the sick people. And I would go all over the town taking care of people. When I'd park my car in front of a house and then come out from treating a patient, there were two or three people waiting to take me up to the house next door or up the street.

"And the deaths started to come. There were quite a few pregnant women in Flagstaff and any pregnant woman that got the flu died. I don't think there were any that lived through the flu. I remember where the Chamber of Commerce building is now there was a carpenter shop run by a man by the name of Sullivan. They couldn't get enough coffins, so he started making coffins and soon he had a stack of coffins on the outside of his shop. He'd build them and put them out there and they'd take them as fast as he could put them out there.

"I don't remember how many died, perhaps a hundred, more or less. Whatever the number, it was plenty. It was an awful thing. I'd see a young man in the prime of health in the morning, and the next morning he'd be dead.

"I worked day and night almost during those two months of that epidemic. I never did get sick myself. I smoked a pipe all the time during the epidemic. I'd light my pipe and get in the car and go to the home of the patient and I'd just keep my pipe puffing all day and night. I don't know whether it did any good, but I didn't get sick with the flu.

"The worst thing was that we didn't really have anything to work with. We didn't even have enough whiskey."

Not enough whiskey?

"That's right. You see by 1918 there was a lot of bootlegging and there'd been a lot of stills out in the forest around Flagstaff. And the county attorney and the sheriff would bring in this liquor and they'd store it in C. B. Wilson's safe. He was the county attorney. Well, when the epidemic got real bad they allowed us to use that liquor as medicine.

"I'll tell you, some of that liquor was anything but good. But that was all we had. In fact, we didn't even have enough of that to treat those patients in that awful flu epidemic. We didn't even have enough of that liquor."

ERNEST W. McFARLAND

Governor, Senator and Judge

ERNEST W. MCFARLAND has been all of them, and at the age of eighty-one when he sat for this interview in the office of his Phoenix television station, he was quick to point out that "I'm the only one to have served in the highest office of each branch of government in this state."

McFarland was a United States Senator from 1941 to 1953, governor from 1955 to 1959, and justice of the Arizona Supreme Court from 1964 to 1970.

"Mac" was one of those "newcomers" who settled down in Arizona after World War I. He had come west from Oklahoma where he was born to W. T. and Keziah McFarland October 9, 1894, near the town of Earlsboro. He had been ambitious even as a youngster. From the family farm he had gone on to East Central (Oklahoma) State Teachers College, taught in a country school, and then, by doing janitorial chores, working in a grocery, selling insurance and filling in as a law librarian—all of that—the young McFarland was able to earn an A.B. degree at the University of Oklahoma.

McFarland's legal and political career started in Casa Grande, Arizona, where he became Pinal County Attorney. From that start he went on to become Democratic Majority Leader in the United States Senate. In the taping he tells of some of his days in Washington where he became a close personal friend and advisor to President Truman. The senator takes the reader behind the scenes of big government to detail the inner struggle to gain approval of Truman's nomination of Dr. Philip Jessup as United States Ambassador to the United Nations during a very difficult time in American history.

A COUNTRY LAWYER IN WASHINGTON

"The Judge"—McFarland reveres that title above "Senator" or "Governor"—sat upright at his desk talking with animation as the interview began. When we noted that he still had not lost his Oklahoma accent, he grinned and said, "Oh, yes, I'm still an Okie."

"My father and mother made the run in Oklahoma when they opened the Potawattomie Strip. That would be about in eighteen 'n ninety-one, I believe. It was an old, rolling prairie and, of course, it should have always stayed in prairie grass. There wasn't too much money in those days. My folks were settlers on the land and worked very hard. But I came from a wealthy home in one respect: that was that my father and mother gave me ideals that was worth more than money. They encouraged me to get my education and that wasn't always easy because you'd have droughts and crop failures.

"I'd always heard quite a bit about Arizona and when I got out of the navy after World War I, I got on the train and headed this way. I was kind of short of money and we stopped down there at Bowie—the train did a little while—I went out and thought I'd get a sandwich. I had only ten dollars in my pocket, and they wanted seventy cents for a sandwich. That's cheap now, but it wasn't then. You'd think if you paid twenty-five cents for a sandwich that's a lot. So I just thought I'd do without it.

"I came to Phoenix and I got a job. They had an employment agency for ex-servicemen in the old Monroe block where the school used to be set right in the center there. And Arthur Esgate—he was cashier of the Valley Bank at the time—asked me what I wanted to do. I said I'd like to work in a bank. I don't know why I told him that 'cause I'd never worked in a bank, but I got a job with the Valley Bank working on the books. Well, Charlie Whiteman was a friend of mine and we worked on the books. You worked one ledger and a statement book and you checked each against the other. I said to Charlie one time, I said, 'Charlie, we belong on the other side of this bank. I don't think I'm ever going to get there. I'm sure I won't, so I'm going out to Stanford University and finish my law.'

"People in Arizona had been very good to me and I was able to save a little money from my job. So I went out to Stanford and finished up with two degrees in about two years.

"How did I come to go into law and then politics? Well, you know, the dean of the Stanford University Law School, Dean Charles Houston, said to me one time, he said, 'I consider politics an avocation and not a vocation.'

"Well, starting in as a lawyer in that day and time was pretty rough, but I tried to keep my work—my governmental work—in the legal profession. First I was in Casa Grande and I started in playing a little politics. In nineteen 'n twenty-two, in particular twenty-one 'n twenty-two, I got in as assistant county attorney and I spent two years there, and then I ran for county attorney. And, of course, you had to work mostly, a lot of times, without a deputy and it was pretty nice work. You were legal advisor for the Board of Supervisors, and you had enough to keep you busy with your criminal work, and so forth . . . yes, and civil work, too."

In those earliest days in politics, did you dream you would go so high in politics?

"Well, of course, you always have a lot of dreams that maybe you don't expect to realize. I never expected to do all the things that I've done, if that's what you mean. Never thought, I guess, in those early days that I would become Democratic Majority Leader in the United States Senate.

"And, you know, those days back in Washington, those were pretty rugged days. President Truman had what he called a Big Four meeting each Monday morning. That was the vice president, Alben Barkley; and Sam Rayburn, Speaker of the House; and myself as majority leader of the Senate, and John McCormack as majority leader of the House. We had those conferences every Monday morning, and the first one I went to, why, General Omar Bradley came in and gave a report on what was going on in Ko-re-a. He told us that we could be pushed in the water, that we would have to be very strong.

"I knew what it meant to our country to have to go through that, and when I went back to the Capitol I met Bob Kerr—Senator Bob Kerr of Oklahoma—who had been an old schoolmate of mine down at East Central State College. And Bob says, 'What are you looking down your nose so much about?'

"And I says, 'Bob, it's the Ko-re-an War.' I guess the proper name is 'conflict,' but I always thought that where you're killing people it's war. I says, 'It's bad at the best.'

"He says, 'I say it's good at the worst.'

"Of course the reason Bob said that was, he says, 'Well, I'll tell you why I can say that and you can't . . . because I've got a son who will be there next month. I say it will prevent a third world war.'

President Harry Truman sat for this picture with his Big Four. Seated at his left is Vice President Alben Barkley with Sam Rayburn, Speaker of the House, at the right. Standing at the left is Senate Majority Leader Ernest W. McFarland with House Majority Leader John McCormack at the right.

"Well, of course, things changed and turned out there in Ko-re-a where it wasn't so bad. But probably one of the things that was really bad for us was the MacArthur hearing. General MacArthur—I don't think there was any doubt about it—he pictured himself as becoming president of the United States. And he made a mistake. He had challenged the president and was trying to take over the running of everything, including the military when the Constitution makes the president the commander-in-chief."

McFarland agreed with Truman that he had no choice but to fire General MacArthur. The Judge then went on to talk about the dispute over the nomination of Philip Jessup—a nomination the Red-baiting McCarthy sought to block.

"Harry Truman, President Truman, was a fine man to get along with. It was very nice to work with him. He had situations pretty well under hand almost always. I'll just give you a little example. Jim Webb, who was under-secretary of state, called me one day and said he wanted to have a little talk with me. I said, 'All right.'

"He says, 'I'll pick you up. I've got a car.'

"And I says, 'Well, you're on my way home. I'll pick you up.' So on our way home he told me the president wanted to send Dr. Philip Jessup to be our delegate to the United Nations and he wanted to know what I thought about it. 'Well,' I said, 'I'd like to think about it overnight. I'll get in contact with you.'

"Well, I thought about it, and I called him up, and he came out and I said, 'I don't think we ought to do that.'

"He said Senator Joe McCarthy was making a fight [against the nomination of Jessup] but 'we just can't give up to McCarthy.'

"And I says, 'No, Mr. Secretary, that isn't the point. When a man goes as a delegate to the United Nations we need a man that the people in other nations will feel speaks for the people of our nation, that we're in back of what he says. For that reason I don't think we ought to approve Dr. Jessup.'

"Well, the thing came along, and I got Tom Connolly up in my office; he was chairman of the Foreign Relations Committee. So I said, 'Tom, I want you to call up Secretary of State Acheson. Talk to him about this.' He did. Of course, Old Tom, he had a little wicked tongue, and he could really tell them off—which he did.

"In a day or two we got a call from the White House wanting a meeting of the Big Four in the middle of the week, and that wasn't usual so I anticipated what it would be about. I got ahold of Alben Barkley and I told him, 'Alben, I want you to stand behind me on this thing. I'm sure this is what the president is calling about.'

"So I went down to the White House a little early, and Sam Rayburn came in and I told Sam the same thing. He said, 'Oh, that's a Senate matter. We don't have anything to do with that in the House.'

"I said, 'No, Sam, now don't say that. This is a matter that involves the whole nation, not just the House and Senate. Now I want you to speak up.'

"So we went into the meeting and the president opens it up—I tell you this little story because it gives you an idea of the true character of President Truman. The president said to us, he says, 'I understand that there's some objection to my sending Dr. Jessup's name up for confirmation to be a delegate to the United Nations and I don't like it.'

"And then he looked at me and he says, 'And this is the first thing that you've ever done that I've objected to.'

" 'Well,' I said, 'wait a minute, Mr. President. Mr. Webb came and talked to me about this, and I thought that he was asking me to give my best judgment as to what should be done, and I thought I did that. That was my opinion then, and it's my opinion now.'

"So then he called on Vice President Barkley. Barkley made rather a long talk about it, but he recommended that we not send the name up. So then he came to Sam Rayburn and Sam says, 'I think there'll be trouble.'

"Well, the president rather calmed down and he says, 'Well, I'll think about it.'

"Knowing Harry Truman, I figured he'd send up the name of Dr. Jessup anyway, and he did. Well, we had a rather long session in the Senate. We'd had this McCarthy thing and we'd had other difficult things. It wasn't an easy time in the history of our country. When we got through with the other business I went to Harry Truman and said, 'Well, Mr. President, there's one thing I would like to discuss with you just a little bit. You know we've run into some trouble with Dr. Jessup out there. I can get the name out of the Foreign Relations Committee. I can't say whether it will be with a recommendation to confirm, a recommendation not to confirm, or no recommendation. We could get his name out and then we can recess, and you can give him a recess appointment.'

"Harry Truman, he kind of grinned, and he says, 'You told me there would be trouble on that nomination.' And he said, 'What do you want me to do?'

"I said, 'Well, Mr. President, I'm tired. I want to go home.'

"He says, 'Well, that's good enough for me.'

"Well, we recessed without taking any action which enabled the president to make a recess appointment. You see, Harry Truman didn't expect you to do everything that he suggested. He recognized that you had views, and he was agreeable to work with. He was, in the first place, a gentleman. And he was fair.

"I rate him as a great president because he had the nerve to stand up for what he thought was right, regardless of whether it was going to be popular. Harry Truman was one of the nicest fellows to sit down and visit with I've ever seen."

After being in Washington through the Truman era, was the Judge upset with the revelations of corruption and immorality in the Nixon White House?

"Well, I'm disappointed with some of the things that have occurred. It looks like every time you pick up a newspaper you see someone that's done something they shouldn't. I don't think it was like that in Washington when I was there. If it was, I didn't know about it.

"I would still encourage—even now—young people to go into politics and government. I would urge young people to remember that there are pitfalls in government, but the man who is really successful and has the happiness is the one who has the high ideals and lives up to them. We'll never be perfect in our government, but high ideals, I think, can predominate. If they don't why our government won't last. But I've always been an optimist. I surely am an optimist, even now."

As governor of Arizona what do you see, looking back, as your major accomplishments?

"The thing that I wanted to do the most and what I worked on hard might surprise you. You see, you've got various duties as the governor. You are administrator, you have the executive position of visiting and handling all of these departments, and you have to work with the legislature. But the work that I enjoyed the most really was trying to help the youth of our state. I was interested in the young people.

"As governor you can't do everything that you want to do. You don't accomplish everything. But if you can build a little bit for the youth, I think that's more important than building a highway—and we built plenty of highways. But we made a lot of advancement in building the universities and colleges. I remember we had some battles with the legislature over our schools. My first job was to get more money for the schools. We had a deadlock between the senate and the house, and I went before the legislature and impressed them about the needs. I recommended a compromise and they accepted it. Legislation is just one of the things you work with as governor, and you're going to win some battles and lose some, no matter who the governor is.

"You know I had this theory in government and I tried to carry it out. I said that we should conduct our affairs on the money that we get, and the increases and the improvements that we make should be based upon the increase that we make in business and the taxes we give for additional income. That is the ideal and, of course, you're never going to completely follow it. But with that ideal you can keep your state, your government, on a good financial basis."

When you look at Arizona today and compare it to the Arizona you came to homestead, is it all that you hoped this state would be?

"Well, I would put it this way. My brother Carl, my youngest brother who is now deceased, said to me just a few years ago, he said, "Well, Ernest, where could we go to find a place like Arizona was when we came here?'

"I said, 'Carl, you couldn't find one. It's still the best state in the Union.' "

BOOK FIVE

A SOCIETY IN CHANGE

*By 1900, the Southwest had emerged
predominantly Anglo-American in
population and culture; yet this region
also had acquired some large and
influential minority groups. . . . All of
them had contributed much of the labor
which had transformed the Southwest
so remarkably in the brief span
of one century.*

LYNN I. PERRIGO IN
The American Southwest

Bigotry Doesn't Bow for a Governor

THE YOUNG TERRITORY OF ARIZONA attracted people of many skin colors, heritages, and religions, and that mix did not always result in harmony. Prejudices, perhaps fanned by the struggle to succeed, even to survive, in a harsh area, developed rapidly. And many of those prejudices did not end with statehood.

The Spanish and then the Mexicans were the earliest arrivals in the area. When their domination ended, they often became the target of prejudice. Raul Castro knows its sting. He was born in Mexico, came across the border as a youngster and then as a naturalized citizen embarked on a remarkable career. One of fourteen children, he pushed his way through school until he had his law degree. Six years after his graduation from the University of Arizona College of Law, Raul Castro began his public life. He was elected Pima County Attorney in 1955, then served as judge of the Pima County Superior Court from 1959 to 1964.

Castro, hard-jawed and barrel-chested from his days as a boxer and football player, was named United States Ambassador to El Salvador in 1964 and four years later was ambassador to Bolivia.

In 1974 Raul Castro was elected governor of Arizona, the highest office in the state won by anyone of Mexican heritage.

A LIFETIME OF FIGHTING PREJUDICE

It was a typical governor's day when we made this tape in Tucson. Raul Castro had come to Tucson to speak to a luncheon club and sandwiched in the taping before going back on the road for other meetings. In his patterned machine-gun style of speaking, he rushed into the interview.

"Let me just start. You know I was born in the mining community of

Cananea, Sonora, Mexico. It's about 60 miles south of Bisbee and about 100 miles west of Douglas, Arizona and Agua Prieta, Sonora. My father as a young man was rather active in different revolutions and political plots as most people in Mexico were in those days. There were thirteen boys and one girl in our family and I can remember when we came across through the border town of Naco, Arizona.

"The thing that impressed me when we came through was that the Salvation Army wasn't there to greet us, or the Red Cross. Nobody took us to a camp to give us three meals a day, and nobody was sending us tutors to teach us English as they have with the Vietnamese and other people. They just said, 'You're in America. This is your problem. You scratch for yourself.' And that I think has stayed with me since then. It's a question of everyone taking care of their own dilemmas and their own problems.

"My family came to a community called Pirtleville, out of Douglas. Pirtleville is a town maybe five miles from Douglas. Mostly a hundred percent Mexican families worked in the mines, or in the smelter, and that's where we lived, and that's where I grew up. I think my first negative aspect was when I had to walk to school from Pirtleville to Douglas, and bus service was furnished to the Anglo children that lived in the valley in the area. They would be picked up by bus and taken to schools in Douglas. And the Mexican kids, we were not picked up; we had to walk. The bus would pass us on the way to school, and the kids would wave at us. We walked and they rode. And those early impacts, of course, raised the query with me: Why should it be that we're both going to school, and yet they get rides and we don't?

"I think something else that made an impact on me was when I used to go from Pirtleville to Agua Prieta to buy sugar, meat, potatoes and other basic foods; they were cheaper on the Mexican side. And invariably going from Agua Prieta to Douglas I'd be stopped at the immigration border. A man in uniform would ask me where I was born. I would say, 'In Mexico.' That in itself was enough to create suspicion and I was jostled and hustled. And I would ask myself: Why should it be that two peoples, two contiguous countries . . . why should there be this aura of suspicion that exists one with the other . . . and why should I be subjected to this type of abuse?

"All of these factors, of course, I think have been things that more or less molded my life and motivated me to try to improve relations between peoples of different parts of the world.

"After I graduated from Arizona State College in Flagstaff and got my teaching degree, there were people who did not want to accept it. I returned to Douglas, which I considered my home town, to get a teaching job, and I remember being called in, of course, by the superintendent, and he told me the school board had met the night before and had passed a resolution that no one of Mexican-American background would be hired as a school teacher."

What year was that?

"Nineteen hundred and thirty-nine . . . so therefore my dreams of coming home to teach school and use my education went out the window. It was then that I caught a freight train and started traveling and doing some boxing, some professional boxing, to make a living. Later, of course, I returned to Arizona. All these things have been, to some extent, things that have led to motivating me to try to jet-propel myself into something else.

"The fortunate part is that these bumps that I had in my life have been good for me; I think they made me charge ahead. But unfortunately I find that ninety-eight percent of the people aren't built like I am. There are too many good students in the Douglas-Pirtleville area, too many people much superior than I was academically or intellectually who became winos and drunks, and made penitentiaries for the very reason that nobody tried to claim them. They just sort of were cast adrift, cast aside, and no one made any effort to put them back into the mainstream.

"And I sort of regret this because in many instances some people use me as an example. Bill Mathews [the former editor and publisher of the *Arizona Daily Star*] used to say, 'He did it with his bootstraps.' Well, maybe I did, but I was the exception to the rule. There are too many people who did not use their bootstraps who could have been very productive to society, been very useful to our country, had someone taken the pains to put them on the right path. And we just didn't take that effort."

The governor paused here and returned to the days of his youth.

"My father died when I was thirteen and left fourteen kids, so my mother had to make her way by serving as a midwife. She delivered about every Mexican kid in the Douglas-Pirtleville area in those days, and she was paid with a sack of beans, or a chicken, or tortillas, or whatever they could find. And that's the way the family was raised.

"I received a football scholarship to college in Flagstaff and I remember I hitchhiked my way up there. In those days a football scholarship consisted of working three hours in the kitchen peeling potatoes, or working some other way for your meals. And that's how I went to college. I just hitchhiked up there, got a job working in the kitchen. In four years I graduated.

"I had been very determined about getting a college degree. I felt that education was the way to go. I just couldn't conceive of seeing generation after generation of Mexican kids in the Douglas and Bisbee area spending all their lives in the mines like their fathers had done. The only way out of that was to go to school. Going to school was an outlet; it was a way out, a way out to another life."

After you were turned down for a teaching job by the Douglas School Board and after your boxing tour, then what did you do?

"I came back to Douglas and that's when I got a job with the State Department working in the American consulate on the Mexican side of the border in Agua Prieta. My paycheck was ninety-five dollars a month. I left that job after an incident with the consul-general. I was ready for a promotion I thought, but the consul said to me, 'You're a great guy, a lot of potential, a lot of possibilities, except that you're not typically American.'

"I said, 'What do you mean typically American?'

" 'Well, you were born in Mexico of Mexican parents and we can't very well send you abroad. It's hard to send you to Europe because you don't typify the Anglo-Saxon type of culture.'

"I realized it was time for me to leave the State Department, and I quit. That was in nineteen and forty-one. From there I went to the University of Arizona where I received a teaching job and also went to law school, and that's another story.

"You see, I didn't have any money when I came to the university. What I did, I went over to the university to look for a job. The man in charge of the employment office, a fellow by the name of Dr. Victor Kelley, looked at my name and said, 'Castro, you know we can't get you Mexican kids a job. It's tough on the border; we just can't get you jobs. Let me send you to the Mexican consul.'

"I said, 'Well, I'm not a Mexican citizen. I have nothing to do with the Mexican consul.' So I left the office and went across to Dr. Richard Harvill who was then dean of Liberal Arts. He was in his office—I recall very vividly—and I gave my name; by that time I had enough bravado about me. And I said, 'Dr. Harvill, I think I can give a service to this university. I'm a language major. I speak Spanish fluently; it's my native tongue. I can teach here at this university.'

"He looked at me and said, 'You know, you sound awful confident, very cocky. How are you going to prove your ability?'

"I happened to have my transcripts in my pocket and I gave them to him. He looked at them and said, 'You've got a job. One of the teachers got married, or was ill, or failed to report, and we start classes tomorrow and I need a Spanish teacher badly.'

"Right there I signed a contract, and on the way out of the office I ran into Dr. Kelley and he stopped me and said, 'Castro, I've got a job for you.'

"I said, 'What's that?'

" 'Working at the Commons [the university dining hall]. I got a job for you washing dishes for your meals, three meals a day.'

"I said, 'Well, thank you very much. I'm an old pearl-diver, but I don't have to do that any more. I'm now a member of the faculty. I'm one of your colleagues.'

"He said, 'I don't understand you.'

"I said, 'Well, you never asked me what I could do.' And then I explained to him that I had gotten a job as a Spanish teacher. We've been very close friends since then."

Castro's troubles didn't end there. He was told he couldn't go to law school and work as a teacher at the same time.

"The dean said that was just impossible and furthermore he said he found that some of the Mexican youngsters that applied were never able to get out of law school because they just couldn't adapt, that it was too difficult for them. Well, I called the president of the university who then was somebody from Montana [Dr. Alfred A. Atkinson] and he saw to it that I was admitted. I finally made the grade, taught and got into law school, but you can see that the doors were closed every time I turned.

"Well, I came out of law school in 1946. I borrowed $200 from John Favour, a lawyer in Prescott I knew, and opened an office on Church Street in downtown Tucson. The office was in an old rickety building. I lived in the back, cooked in the middle and had my office in front. I had an old typewriter that I brought from Mexico. If I had to leave to file a document in court, I'd put up a sign, 'Be Back in Twenty Minutes.'

"About a year later Dave Wolfe came in with me and we started getting clients and began to prosper."

Why did you decide to leave private practice to enter politics?

"Well, I always felt that there were some inequities in politics, and I felt the time had come for part of the Mexican community to be represented in government, to have some voice in it. I considered running for county attorney, and, of course, I was told by everyone that I didn't have a chance, that it was beyond my reach because I was born of Mexican parents, and never in the history had there been a Mexican county attorney in Pima County. My answer to the doubters was, 'Well, who ever tried it? You never try it, you never know. I'm going to try it.' So I tried it and found out; I won by sixty-five votes.

"And from county attorney, of course, I went on to run for superior court judge. Same old story again—that I didn't have a chance because of my ethnic background. But I was elected, and I was the first judge of Mexican background to be elected to the bench in the whole state."

Castro now moved ahead to his appointment by President Lyndon Johnson to become ambassador to El Salvador. Again Raul Castro's name and background presented problems.

"Senator Carl Hayden had recommended me to Johnson and the president said to him, 'My gosh, Carl, of all the people in the world, why would you recommend Raul Castro?'

"Now keep in mind that Lyndon Johnson was up for election and he was deathly afraid that the name of Raul Castro might boomerang on him because of the situation in Cuba where there were some other Castros.

"Well, I was asked if I would consider changing my name, using my first name, my father's name in the middle and my mother's name at the end—Raul Castro Acosta—as is traditional in Latin America. But I refused. I said, 'The good Lord gave me that name. I don't intend to change it now.' "

Raul Castro got the ambassadorship, but signals were changed and instead of being assigned to Bolivia he was sent to El Salvador. His second assignment was in Bolivia.

"I think it was better sending me to El Salvador at the time. My name did cause some consternation even in El Salvador; after all, Raul Castro was Fidel's brother and there were a few jokes about my appointment. But it wasn't too bad. I was well received really, and the fact that I spoke Spanish and mingled with the people was a tremendous help.

"But later when I was assigned to Bolivia it was more difficult. Che Guevara [the Cuban revolutionary] had just been killed and there was a

Raul Castro chats with President Lyndon Johnson prior to being sworn in as ambassador to El Salvador.

tremendous aftermath in Bolivia. The students and teachers were on the streets, bullets were flying and there was pandemonium all over the place. And right in the middle of all that Lyndon Johnson sends me to Bolivia. The people there were saying to themselves, 'Here we've got this Che Guevara situation, we've got a revolution going full blast and we get an American ambassador called Raul Castro!'

"Well, that was quite a thing, but after a couple of months this quieted down and everything worked out well."

It worked out well until Richard Nixon took office and Castro lost his political appointment. After trying life in Washington, Castro found he missed Tucson and he returned home and soon was back in the political swim.

"I couldn't stay out. You know, I'm one person that likes people. I'm sort of an extrovert. I enjoy crowds and enjoy people, meeting people, seeing people. And again there was going to be another first; no one of Mexican background had ever run for governor of Arizona. I thought the time was right for people to be receptive to some one of other than the Anglo-type. It was on that premise that I felt I could make a contribution. I knew Arizona well. I understood the people. And I figured I'd be able to unify the state, bring people together, and I think that's really the reason I decided to run for governor.

"Of course, there were people again who said I was wrong to try to run for the post. They said I wouldn't have a chance for the governorship because of my background, but I decided to try. And there were some nasty incidents during the campaign. For instance, when I would appear on television the first thing they would ask me was, 'Where were you born?' I would answer, 'Born in Mexico.' Well, that was supposed to defeat me.

"It takes a thick hide; you know, there are a lot of prejudices. People say awful things. I remember hearing someone say, 'I'd rather vote for a dog than vote for a Mexican.' I just barked.

"You know, you walk into bars and saloons during the campaign and sometimes the remarks coming at you are hard to accept. But you have to learn that that's part of the campaign, part of political life. And you have to realize that wherever you have one scoundrel, you have ten others that aren't scoundrels. Somebody knocks you down, there'll be four others to pick you up. And you have to remember, too, that there's a foul ball in every crowd. Well, just don't judge everybody by that individual.

"And I think the American way of life is like that. I think Americans basically are always for the downtrodden. Americans always support the guy that's the underdog and will support one who is making an honest effort to get there, to reach his goal. If he conducts himself properly, with dignity and decorum, they'll support him. I think that's always been true and I have found the American public has been very responsive to me."

Now Castro remembered the time he first decided to run for governor in 1970 and lost in the general election.

"You know, I'm one of those people who has never done any planning. I've never planned any of my life at all. I just go from day to day, year to year and things come up and develop. If I think it's something I want, I'll do it.

"The funny part of it, the first time I ran for the governorship, my wife Pat didn't know about it. I didn't consult her on it. I felt she was opposed to it. Four years of diplomatic service had given her a fill of being in the limelight and the social life. So I decided to run and then make amends with her afterwards. She later joined the campaign trail."

So in 1974, he was elected Arizona's first governor of Mexican-American descent. Why had it taken so long for a Mexican-American to rise to high political office?

"Psychological barriers. I think Mexican-Americans have a defeatist attitude. For instance, the feeling in law school that no one could graduate from there if they were Mexican-American. They said it was difficult, that it was impossible, and therefore don't bother to try. And they said the same in the engineering schools and the medical schools.

"People of Mexican background could see only one goal in school—becoming a teacher or a coach, and that was the maximum glory for the average Mexican-American. I think the barrier has been broken; now they recognize that it can be done, that psychologically it's all within their reach now, the other schools, and the high public offices, too."

As governor do you still find prejudice?

"Oh, yes, I still see prejudices. Not long ago I went on a trade mission to Europe and Russia with a group of Arizona farmers. Keep in mind that most of these farmers employ Mexican 'wetbacks.' To them it was rather hard to conceive that I was their leader on this trip, that I was the man in charge of the group. . . . 'Here is a wetback; here is a guy born in Mexico leading us.' Some looked upon me with disdain. . . . 'How could it be possible that this guy would be in charge of our group?'

"Very carefully I told them, 'Look, I play with four languages, Italian, Portuguese, Spanish, some French and some German, five languages. When you try to communicate in Italy, you can't. I can communicate for you.'

"So then they began to realize, 'You're not what we thought.' So when we returned home, they said, 'You know we voted against you. [They were all Republicans.] We didn't support you. But we'll support you now. We think you're a great guy.'

"It's this feeling that I don't have horns. It takes time and then people gain respect for you. It takes time."

The Forgotten Jewish Pioneers

IN HISTORICAL ACCOUNTS of early Arizona much space is given to the early contributions of Spaniards, Mexicans, Chinese, Japanese, Mormons and, of course, the Anglos of diverse national backgrounds. Too often little or nothing is said about the contributions of the early Jewish pioneers, and when there is mention the description centers on "pedlars."

The Jews who came into the territory of Arizona included merchants and traders, freighters and cattlemen, bankers and miners, sutlers to the military posts, lawyers and judges, mayors of frontier towns and members of the territorial legislature. They were, historically, involved in almost every area of the territory and state's development.

It is factual, too, that because there were so few Jewish women in the territory that many of the Jewish pioneers intermarried and were assimilated . Yet in 1910 the first Jewish house of worship, Temple Emanu-el, was established in Tucson. In Phoenix the first synagogue was built a decade later; it evolved into Temple Beth Israel. Today the major centers of Jewish population are still in Phoenix and Tucson, but throughout the state the marks of those early pioneers remain, if blurred by historical omissions.

GROWING UP WITH BARRY GOLDWATER

As throughout the state, Jewish pioneers in Phoenix were involved in many fields. Among those families were the Goldwaters and Rosenzweigs. This tape by Harry Rosenzweig, son of one of those pioneers, relates the story of growing up in Phoenix and an interesting partnership in politics with Barry Goldwater, also from a pioneer Jewish family, but not Jewish himself because of his father's intermarriage.

"My dad was born in 1869 in a little village near Lemberg in Austria, which later went back to Poland. And when he became sixteen years of age, although his family was poor, enough money had been saved to get him out of the country because, you know, in those days the young boys were forced into military service for five years. So he caught a freighter and started for America. He said that he was in the hole down about three decks and he said for three weeks he was sick. He landed first in Montreal, Canada, where he was taught the art of cigar-making in order to make a living. But from Montreal he wandered to Winnipeg, and from Winnipeg to Duluth, and then he was in Saint Paul before he went to Fargo, North Dakota. He moved back to Duluth and he told me that when he was sitting in a hotel around a pot-bellied stove during the winter he read about sunny California. He knew that was for him.

"About four days later he was on a train for Los Angeles where he started a little cigar stand somewhere down where the city hall is today. He said he did very well and saved a few dollars. One of his friends, a Louis Baswitz who was one of the early settlers of Phoenix, convinced my dad to go with him and look over Phoenix. He said he understood Phoenix was going to get water and it looked like it had some promise.

"Well, later on my dad sold his cigar stand for $400 and came to Phoenix. That was in 1896, and he opened a little pawn shop and jewelry store down about the 300 block on East Washington, right where the civic plaza is now. He said he was immediately successful. They used to call my dad 'Honest Ike.'

"After, oh, three years, he decided he needed a wife. Well, he heard that the woman who would become my mother had come over from the old country and landed in New York. Although he didn't know her, he had a cousin back there who helped set things up. And I guess my father used a little subterfuge to get her out to Phoenix; he sent word that there were two prospects—Charlie Korrick and Baron Goldwater—as potential husbands. But the real idea was that he wanted to look before he jumped. So he went down to Maricopa—that was the nearest the train came to Phoenix in those days—and he met her. He liked what he saw and after a year of courting her they got married. I think that was in 1903. My brother, Newt, was born in 1905 and I came along eighteen months later. My mother always used to say that her present for having me was a new electric fan which was a great gift in those days. About four years later my sister Anna came along.

This was downtown Phoenix around 1900. It was at this time that Harry Rosenzweig's father, Ike, established himself in the Phoenix business community.

"There wasn't any Jewish community at all. But a funny part of it was that many of the early settlers, when you get to checking them out, were Jews, like Mike Wormser, probably the first Jew in Phoenix, and then the Goldbergs, Goldwaters, Melczers, Diamonds, Korricks, Goldmans, Oberfelders and Emil Ganz, just to name a few.

"You know, Barry Goldwater and I grew up together. We lived at 504 North Central Avenue and Barry lived at 710. And in the early days we were rather inseparable. I remember Riverside Park used to be our summer vacationland. The Goldwater family had an interest in all the Rickerd and Nace Theaters so we went to the movies for nothing, and Rickerd and Nace owned Riverside so our swimming didn't cost us either. And Barry's mother was very good about taking us kids on overnight picnics to Granite Reef, to Cave Creek and to Blue Point.

"In the earliest days we didn't have any temple or synagogue. Then about 1920 my dad helped organize a temple with about fifty people. My dad was one of those people who was not religious, but he had been well trained and continued to believe in how he was raised and what he was born into. My mother also was old country, so although we had no basic religious training we were always taught of what we were and not to forget it.

"I guess maybe the first real prejudice that hit me was when I went to school at the University of Arizona. My brother, Newt, had gone to the University of Michigan and he told me, 'Now don't expect to make a fraternity; you're not going to make it.' But I remember the day we got off the train at Tucson and there were fraternity boys, Kappa Sigs and Sigma Nus, to pick up the guys who had gone to Phoenix Union with me and were my close friends. But I stood alone until finally Spence Woodman came along and he said, 'You got a place to stay?' I said, 'No.' He said, 'Well, come on over and stay at the Sigma Nu house till you find a place to stay.'

"Well, I moved into Cochise Hall and pretty soon some of the Jewish boys got together and we all started what later became the Zeta Beta Tau fraternity.

"But going back a bit, you know, our families, the Goldwaters and Rosenzweigs, used to go over to the beach in California in the summer together. Every summer we'd spend a month there, and Barry and I would do the normal things teenagers would do. I remember that at the end of Barry's freshman year in high school, his father didn't think Barry was doing very well. And then my father didn't think I was doing very well. So they were going to send us to military school. Barry and I applied for the same school, but they didn't think the school was big enough for both of us. So Barry went to Staunton Military Academy and I stayed home in Phoenix.

"Even so we vacationed together. We used to make trips together all over the state. Barry, you know, only had one year of college. His father died in 1929, and Barry decided to go to work in the store."

The narration moved ahead to 1949, the start of politics for Barry Goldwater.

"Well, in July of that year a gentleman by the name of Alfred Knight and others, I don't remember who, came to see me at our jewelry store in downtown Phoenix. They said they were forming a ticket to run on the Charter Government slate. In those days Phoenix had, I guess, about thirty-five city managers in thirty years and corruption was supposed to be running rampant in the city. They wanted me to run on that first Charter ticket and I told them, 'No, I wasn't interested,' because my father always used to tell me that anybody that got into politics was going to get in trouble. Well, about a week later they called me to a meeting to a room that was on the top of the Title Building and they had about fourteen people there. Well, I finally gave in and I said I would run.

"They had picked most of the candidates, but then they started wondering who they could get for the seventh person. I said, 'I think I know a person who would be good.' And they said, 'Who do you have in mind?'

"I said, 'How about Barry Goldwater?' They said they had asked him before they asked me, figuring he was a Jew and they wanted to put two Jews on the same ticket. Barry had turned them down, but I said I thought I could get him. So I invited Barry over to dine with me. Barry loves Old Taylor so I got the biggest bottle I could find. We sat around and talked and about ten o'clock he's going out the door and he said, 'Well, what did you invite me over for?' I said, 'I want you to run for city council with me. I've got to have somebody I can trust.' He said, 'Okay,' and went out the door.

"Now ever since then when something goes wrong, Barry says to me,

'You S.O.B., you're the one that got me into this.' "

Harry Rosenzweig now began chuckling as he remembered those early days with Barry on the Phoenix City Council.

"When they were seating us, they put me next to him, because he would talk off the top of his hat so much and that way I could kick him and shut him up. He says the reason they put him next to me was so he could keep me awake.

"Well, it's true, Barry could make some of the wildest statements, just like in his first years in Congress. He'd shoot from the hip and I'd be reading about what he'd say. I would call him up and ask, 'What did you mean by that?' He'd say, 'Well, it came out a little different than I expected.'

"Anyhow we did a good job on the council and I knew Barry had gotten the political bug. Later on after he had managed Howard Pyle's campaign for governor, Barry said, 'Well, I think I'll run against Ernie McFarland for the Senate. It'll tune me up for the governorship in '54.' Well, I became his fund-raiser [he was later to be state chairman for the Republican Party] and Barry just worked like a dog. He flew his single-engine plane three times around the state. It was a small plane and he could land it any place, and he did, at every little village and hamlet.

"I remember, the Sunday before the election he said, 'Rosie, I'll win this thing by 8,000 votes.' I think he won by 7,000, and everybody was surprised. Well, I was an alternate delegate to the Republican National Convention when Barry was nominated in '60 and withdrew. He said to me then, 'Rosie, if Nixon stubs his toe, maybe I'll make a run for it in '64.' And Nixon stubbed his toe. So we started laying a little groundwork and getting in a little seed money.

"And then in December of '63 he called me up. It was December 27, I'll never forget it. He said, 'Come on to the house, I want to talk to you.' I went over and he took me back to his bedroom. He told me the pressure was on for him to run for president. A group of conservatives wanted him. I said to him, 'Well, now that Kennedy just got shot—Kennedy was killed in November—I think I would wait for the next go-round.' But Barry said, 'I don't know whether I can resist the pressure or not.' But it wasn't long before he made the decision to run and I guess I raised almost a million dollars for him.

"Well, you know how it turned out. He lost and when he came back to Phoenix I remember Barry and I were sitting back there in that same bedroom in his home and he made a classic remark to me. He said, 'Rosie, maybe we were a little early, but there'll never be another time. I've had it.'"

The Blacks Who Pioneered

WHEN THE DEFINITIVE BLACK HISTORY of Arizona is written there will be raised eyebrows, and some more stereotypes will be put to rest.

It is generally believed that the blacks who came into the territory of Arizona were only cooks and servants. The truth is that there were blacks who were cowboys, miners, soldiers and landowners.

And more startling is the historic possibility that the first non-Indian to journey into what is now Arizona was the black slave and explorer, Estevanico, or Esteban. Esteban, a dark-skinned slave of Moorish background, guided Fray Marcos de Niza into this area in 1539. But while it is accepted by many historians that Esteban was a black man, Jay J. Wagoner, writing in *Early Arizona*, raises the question of whether he was a Negro, an Arab, or a "moreno," a brown man.

Nevertheless most artists who depict the discovery of Arizona are prone to give Esteban a handsome, black face.

At any rate it was before the turn of the nineteenth century that blacks came into the territory in some numbers and among them were land homesteaders, some of whom did quite well financially. One was William (Curly Bill) Neal, an intimate of William F. (Buffalo Bill) Cody. Neal had come to Tucson in 1878, starting as a cook but soon becoming a successful freight hauler. In 1895 he and his wife established the fashionable Mountain View Hotel in Oracle, once a health spa in the Santa Catalina Mountains north of Tucson. Buffalo Bill frequently visited his old pal at the hotel and the guest list carried the names of many famous persons including European royalty. Neal died at the age of eighty-seven in 1936, but his wife continued to run the hotel until her death in 1950. The grand old hotel still stands there in Oracle, now a gathering place for Baptist religionists.

Curly Bill Neal (left) *posed for this picture with his personal friend Buffalo Bill Cody before the old Mountain View Hotel in Oracle, Arizona. Curly Neal was one of the earliest successful black businessmen in Arizona.*

Many black families in Arizona can trace their start back to their fathers and grandfathers who were stationed at Fort Huachuca. That post in southern Arizona was the headquarters for the legendary Buffalo Soldiers and it was from there that General John Pershing rode out with the Tenth Cavalry against the Mexican bandito, Pancho Villa. The unit was made up of blacks.

The records show the contributions of blacks to Arizona in frontier days, but it is factual that prejudice—demonstrated in segregated schooling and Ku Klux Klan terrorism—kept them from playing larger roles in Arizona.

Even today many "firsts" are still being established. Hayzel Daniels was one of Arizona's first black legislators and the state's first black judge.

A MAN OF FIRSTS FOR HIS PEOPLE

Hayzel Burton Daniels, Phoenix City Magistrate, sat in the living room of his modest house. He looked to the mementos around him as he searched back to his beginnings.

"My grandfather and father used to tell me how they left Florida and traveled into Mexico and then how, after agreements were reached, they came back out of Mexico to Fort Clark, Texas. That's where I was born. These people were Seminole scouts; you see, there had been some intermarriage between the blacks and the Seminole Indians in Florida. It was 1907 when I was born down there in Texas. In 1913 they broke up the scouts and my dad came out here to join the Tenth Cavalry at Fort Huachuca.

"My dad was a bugler in the scouts and a bugler in G Troop of the Tenth Cavalry. When the First World War broke out he went overseas and afterwards he transferred into the Twenty-fifth Infantry.

"Well, I grew up around the fort when I was a kid. But when it came time to go to high school, my mother moved the kids to Nogales so I could get better schooling. She was my real inspiration to pushing ahead in education. You know, she never wanted us to be soldiers. Now don't ask me why; she just never wanted us to be soldiers. Maybe it was because my father never got to be an officer, or anything like that.

"But I think my mother had ambitions that my father didn't realize in those days. There were five of us children and she had this terrible desire for her children to have education."

This picture was taken at the International Bridge in Carrizal, Mexico, June 21, 1916. The Tenth Cavalry, a black unit, was stationed at Fort Huachuca. It was at that post that Hayzel Daniels's father served. PHOTO COURTESY LT. COL. JOHN H. HEALEY

Actually Hayzel Daniels had twin ambitions: an education and a career in football. After a disagreement with the football coach at Nogales, Hayzel went to Tucson High School.

"You see I had asked the coach down there at Nogales to put me in the backfield and he said, 'No, you're going to play end.' And I said, 'No, I'm not going to play end. I'm going to Tucson.' And I went to Tucson. My mother said okay and I moved in with a Mrs. Hart in Tucson. Now Syl Paulos was the coach at Tucson High. He was a good coach and I wanted to play for a good one. How did I get along by myself? Well, my mother and father took care of me until my senior year; then I began to earn my own livelihood. And people began to help me because they knew me from my football.

"Well, then I started at the University of Arizona in '27, but it took me until—what was it?—'37 to complete a bachelor's degree. You see, my older brother, and another fellow and myself were living together, supporting ourselves through college. But when the Depression came along, well, that threw me out of school and I went back to work in Nogales as a jackhammer man for the W.P.A. After I saved up enough money, I came back up to the university, and I was determined to play football and finish my education, too.

"It wasn't easy making it, but I would get jobs, not easy jobs, but working as a waiter, or janitor, yard boy, errand boy. Working and going to the university, and, in the first place, being black, was tough. The professors at that time weren't as liberal, as considerate, as they are today. They were clouded by discrimination and the segregation that was rampant throughout the community. So they gave you a bad time and it was discouraging.

"Well, as you might remember, I had been an All-State halfback for Tucson High School and, in fact, All-American honorable mention in my senior year. So the university just couldn't say, 'We don't want you. Go away.' They had to give me a uniform, even though I was black. I remember what Mac [University of Arizona Athletic Director J. F. McKale] told me, bless his heart. He said, 'Now I want to tell you I'm not going to treat you any different from anybody else. You go out there. You do what the rest of them do. If you get hurt, you stick it out.'

"When I hurt my knee, I couldn't go to Mac. I took the doctor's advice to give up football."

And so Daniels missed a chance to become the University of Arizona's first black to win an athletic letter. That "first" had to wait until many years later; in fact, it was 1950 before the U of A awarded its first varsity letter to a black person.

"Anyhow, I stuck it out with school, finished in 1939 and then I went over to the law school to register. J. B. McCormick was the dean at that time and when he saw that I was working—I was cleaning up at the Thomas-Davis Clinic at that time—he rejected my application and told me to get a full-time job and then come back when I had some money. Well, then I got my master's degree and went down to Texas as a teacher in a little country town out from El Paso. It was a little school—one teacher and about fifteen or twenty students. You taught them from the first to the eighth grade. Now the furniture was cast-off from a white school. And the books were cast-offs. The room itself was an oblong sort of thing about twenty feet by twelve. When it rained, it rained inside the building and it leaked outside. And come cotton-pickin' time you didn't have anything to do because all the children were gone cotton-pickin' or cotton-choppin'.

"All those children in a one-room building like that, and with one teacher . . . how the hell do you teach?

"Well, that experience had a lot to do with my understanding of discrimination in education. Later when I was teaching at the high school at Fort Huachuca I saw more of that. The white children at the fort were being transported to another school, but the black children were kept in a crowded little situation with the elementary and high school together, and that's a mess. At that time I was doing some advanced work at the University of Arizona in education and I wrote a couple of nasty seminar papers on this business of segregation at Fort Huachuca. I remember the dean calling me and saying, 'You mean to tell me you're teaching in this school and still you would write these papers? Do you want to lose your job?'

"I said, 'Yes, I want to lose my job so some kids can get some education.' And in my mind I was beginning to get the idea that I really couldn't help the situation by teaching. I said to myself, 'I have to know what the law is. That's what our problem is; we don't know what the law is, whether they are actually administering the law fairly.' You can't tell me that down there in Texas where I had taught, they were supposed to treat children that way. There should have been a truant officer or someone who took care of the Negro children and kept them out of cotton patches. They were entitled to their education as well as the whites. I mean there were, in those days, differences in everything, and the blacks always came up short."

Daniels was determined to turn to the law, but before he could return to school World War II came and he served overseas. The G.I. Bill helped him return to the University of Arizona.

"My wife Grace—by the way, I met her when she was doing graduate work at the University of Arizona in 1937—she suggested I go back and try again to get into law school. I went to see Dean McCormick and asked if he remembered me. He said, 'No, I don't.' I said, 'Well, I'm the fellow you told to come back when I didn't have to work while studying law. Well, now I don't have to work because I've got a very rich man (Uncle Sam) that's going to pay my way.' Well, he laughed, and I laughed, and we were good friends up to the day he died.

"Why was I so persistent in trying to get into law school? Well, I don't know. I do know that as a youngster I saw a movie in which there was a black lawyer and the story was that this community was not very well represented, and I was impressed with what that lawyer did to try to help his people. Later as a teacher I found out that blacks were not getting equal education and that they never could get equal education until something was done with the laws. And I knew I wanted to do something to help.

"In fact, when I finished law school I was planning to go to Texas where I had seen those problems in education. But my friends in the law school—Mo and Stew Udall, and Raul Castro and Shelley Richey, who is now a lawyer in Douglas—convinced me that I was needed in Arizona, that I should practice in Phoenix where I was needed.

"And so I became Arizona's second black lawyer. There was another black lawyer who had come from Oklahoma. He was admitted by motion back in Oklahoma and he came to Arizona during the time you were able to be admitted by motion. So actually I was the first black lawyer who passed the bar in Arizona and practiced in Arizona."

It was not very long before Daniels realized he could do even more for his people by getting into the state legislature and changing the laws.

"At that time old man Wade Hammond was the big honcho in the black community of Phoenix. He was what they called a 'backdoor lawyer,' who, if some black got into trouble, could go downtown and maybe resolve the problem without court action. My dad had soldiered under

Hammond down at the fort when Hammond was bandmaster. And Hammond knew me as a little kid and he just couldn't understand why this 'little boy, this bare boy' wanted to run for the legislature. Mr. Hammond, you see, wanted to be the first black legislator in this state. Well, he got a lot of people worked up against me because I had had the audacity to challenge segregation in the schools. But I won anyway and I went in as a representative in 1950, and Carl Sims and I were the first two black legislators in the state.

"You see, I felt that by going to the legislature I could get the laws changed. Earlier I had read a case where the judge had declared it unconstitutional to segregate Mexicans in the schools in Glendale. I made friends with that judge and he explained to me that it was different for blacks. There was a specific law that permitted the segregation of blacks in the schools and he said if that law could be changed that would be another thing. So I tried to do that; that was my purpose in going to the legislature.

"And in the legislature we did get the law changed; we got the wording of the law to fit the language used in the Glendale case and now we had to go attack the entire thing. And I led that attack. Let me say this, I didn't make friends of every black in the state. Black teachers, you see, feared they would lose their jobs if the schools were desegregated. But that didn't stop me. I knew there was a big job in front of us.

"But I remember how the opportunity came. Representative Jim Ewing from Tucson came to see me and Carl Sims on a Sunday morning. It seems they needed two votes from Maricopa County to get the speaker they wanted re-elected. We were the two votes they needed, so Ewing asked us, 'What do you guys want? Do you want some good committee appointments?'

"I said, 'I'll tell you what. I'll come in, if you're interested in integrated schools.'

"He said, 'Don't want to hear about that.'

"But finally I got to him when I said, 'I want your assurance that we can introduce a desegregation bill on the floor and that your administration will at least give it a chance to pass.'

"He said, 'Well, let me talk to Raymond Langham.'

"Langham was the speaker they wanted to get re-elected and he told Ewing, 'Yeah, let's promise him that. Let's give him that. And we'll do better; we'll give him a vice-chairmanship on the Judiciary Committee.'

"I don't imagine they really intended to go that far. But I did have some strong people on my side—Nielson Brown, the representative from Santa Cruz County, and Hubert Merriweather, the senator from Santa Cruz. I knew them personally when I was working at the Old Pueblo Club, working there as a waiter in Tucson. They knew me and liked me; they were proud that I had come so far.

"Well, I wrote up the bill and we submitted it to a committee, the Committee on Highways and Bridges. I don't know what that committee had to do with a bill like that, but they said that was the place to put it. The real reason was that Frank Robles of Tucson was chairman and he could bring it out of committee. Then we got it out of two other committees and on to the docket of the Rules Committee. And believe it or not, there was enough pressure from the public, enough pressure on the representatives that we were able to pass the bill in the house in modified form and send it on to the senate. I think the house was saying, 'Let the senate be embarrassed with this bill.' But they hadn't reckoned with my friend Senator Merriweather. He was the one who got it carried through the senate, I think, nineteen to one, or eighteen to one.

"The governor signed the bill and we had this modified thing with the words 'they may separate.' On that basis we filed the action, seeking to declare the law unconstitutional. But our action in federal court was aborted because the Los Angeles lawyers who were working with me came and said they wanted it filed before a three-judge court and that would put us together with the five other segregation cases coming up across the country. That would allow us to go right to the Supreme Court.

"One of the lawyers from Los Angeles was a big labor lawyer and the other two—they came into it through the NAACP—were outstanding constitutional lawyers. But they overlooked the one point that you have to have the state declare this constitutional before it could go to the federal court. Well, there had not been a state court decision on this new legislation and we were thrown out of the three-judge court and told to go seek remedy in a one-man court. So we came down and Judge David Ling heard the case and he ruled the same way, deferring us to the state court. I guess this big lawyer who had wanted the three-judge court had been so anxious to get up before the Supreme Court and argue the case, that he was disappointed that it didn't go that far.

"Well, the California lawyers abandoned us and Herb Finn [a Phoenix attorney] and I were left. So we filed in Superior Court and Judge

Fred Struckmeyer declared the new law unconstitutional, but he did it from the narrow point that there were new standards set and therefore it was unconstitutional for that reason. That put us back under that Glendale school case and that didn't satisfy us. So we decided to file against a little elementary school out at the edge of Phoenix and brought them into court. This time it was Judge Charles Bernstein on the bench and he met the issue. He said the law was unconstitutional, a violation of the Fourteenth Amendment. That was a year before the Supreme Court handed down its decision in the Brown case in 1954. I was told that Bernstein's papers may show that the Supreme Court clerk had written and asked for Bernstein's opinion on school desegregation as a guide for the Brown decision."

Hayzel Daniels had been the first black to practice law in Arizona under the Arizona Bar standards. He and Carl Sims were the state's first black legislators and he was Arizona's first black assistant attorney general. Now came still another first in 1965.

"Well, when I came out of the attorney general's office I applied twice for the position of city magistrate in Phoenix. There had never been a black on the bench in the state, and they just wouldn't appoint me. Well, finally as things changed in the city, they figured they needed a black man. The mayor of Phoenix agreed to that and I was offered the job.

"At the time I had a good practice so I thought seriously about giving it up and going on the bench. I discussed the offer with my wife and she said, 'Here we go chasing windmills again.' But she added, 'You can do some good for your people there.'

"So I took the bench in 1965, and I am still there. I'll be there until I retire."

A Chinese Success Story

ESTHER TANG and her family live in a fashionable home high in the foothills north of Tucson. She is one of Tucson's most-honored citizens, a member of the Pima College Board of Governors, a volunteer in dozens of community organizations and a popular figure in every section of the city.

Where she lives she can see down and across the sprawling city to where she grew up in the barrio. What is left of the barrio is a shambles of old adobe homes and a few blocks of restored buildings saved for historical purposes. Esther Tang lived the history of the barrio. She remembers the Chinatown that once stood close to Tucson's downtown business section and she can recall the stories her family and relatives told of the harsh treatment Chinese received in another time.

The Chinese first began coming into Arizona in the 1860s. Esther Tang's father, Don Wah, came before the turn of the century. He was typical of the Chinese immigrants who sought a new life in America.

For the pioneer Chinese the days in the territory of Arizona were difficult. They were treated with curiosity and indifference at the best and with brutality at the worst. They were hated aliens, tolerated only because their hands were needed. They came as railroad workers, cooks and farmers and they were rarely well received anywhere in the territory. In Clifton a public outcry forced a mining company to abandon its plans to bring in Chinese workers. In Tombstone a businessman offered to put up $1,000 to get the Chinese out of town.

Yet the territory of Arizona, and later the state of Arizona, was a haven for the Chinese. In 1876 they were expelled from California and they found new lives, although not easy ones, in the territory. And when Mexico, jealous over the success of Chinese businessmen, pushed them across the border in 1932 and 1933, many settled in Arizona.

The prejudices died slowly; even after World War II many Chinese-Americans found they could not buy homes in certain areas of Phoenix and Tucson.

But over the generations it has been a story of success— a Chinese success story.

GOING TO THE MOUNTAIN OF GOLD

Esther Tang can remember the days when there were areas restricted to Chinese, and, going back further, she can recall growing up in the city's barrio.

"My father was born in San Francisco and he came to Tucson in the late 1800s. His name was Don Wah and he went to work in the Santa Fe Restaurant cooking for railroad workers. And then in 1908 he went back to China to get a wife. When my mother and father came back to Tucson they opened one of the first bakeries in Tucson. It was down on Simpson and Convent. Later we moved to Convent and Jackson, down in the area where they now have that beautiful community center.

"My father really wasn't much of a businessman and so my mother took over. She would tell me how, when I was just three months old she would wake up at three o'clock in the morning, strap me on her back and go into the bakery to wrap bread. We had a grocery store there, too, and since we were living in the barrio, most of the customers were Mexican. So mother had to learn English and Spanish in a very short time, even without going to school to learn. My folks used to tell us about how my father lost his first batch of bread. He had loaded the bread on his wagon, this little wagon, and I guess the horse reared and the bread was all over Simpson Street. You know, the neighbors really had a treat that day.

"As I said, my father was not a good businessman. He was a happy-go-lucky person. There were many days he would leave my mother at the store and go off to Chinatown to play Fan Tan. That was very popular and the men would tease my father: 'Oh, your wife's got you working at the store? How come you're not playing Fan Tan?' Well, off he would go.

"They told us the story of how one day he went to the barber shop to get his queue cut; my father was a small man, but he was very handsome. Well, that day they were voting as to where to build Drachman School and there was a tie. My father said they pulled him out of the barber shop. He voted, and this is why Drachman School is where it is today.

"Chinatown in those early days was immediately west of Meyer Street, not far from the main streets of Broadway and Congress. I can recall they had a complex of apartments there, dilapidated little apartments. They were mostly single men who came from China, living by themselves and sending their slim earnings back. And their families in China thought, gee, we have to send all our sons and husbands to the United States. Literally they called it the 'Gold Mountain.' They didn't realize their poor husbands and sons were really struggling. They didn't know of the prejudices. Oh, I can remember those prejudices, too, when I was a kid. When we went to the old Lyric Theatre, the Chinese couldn't sit in the main area; we had to sit up in the balcony. And the Chinese were not allowed to go to those two swimming pools, the Mission and Wetmore, in those days. There was a big joke going around saying the reason they didn't allow the Chinese to swim there was because they always took soap along to take their baths.

"And our parents used to caution us, 'Now, don't forget you're a Chinese and you mind your manners. You go to school and you try to do your best.' They were cautioning us as children to never expose what they had gone through when they first came. And so when we went to school we tried to do our best. But I remember, even though we were at the head of the class, even though we played together with the other children on the school grounds, when they had parties at their homes we were never invited. And when it came to a dance or a social then we just didn't go."

There has always been curiosity as to how the Chinese persevered here through all of this, how they became successful in businesses. Esther Tang smiled. . . .

"Well, one relative would help another come to this country and to start them off in their little business. The newcomers would work as apprentices, you might say, for a year or two, actually not getting any salary, only enough to buy clothes and possibly a few extra dollars. The pay really was in room and board. And that's the way it was—one relative helped another. That was the way it was with my family.

"I can still remember vividly those early days in our little grocery there in the barrio. We were a big family—nine girls and one boy—and we all had to help. The store itself was small, perhaps twelve feet by twelve feet and immediately at the back of the store there was a cloth curtain and, as you went in, there was a bedroom. We didn't have many rooms and there were about three of us, I remember, in one bed and my

These rare photos of early Chinese in Tucson were taken by the pioneer photogra-pher, Henry Buehman. The photos were taken, it is believed, in the early 1900s. The Chinese first began coming into Arizona in the 1860s. ARIZONA HISTORICAL SOCIETY BUEHMAN MEMORIAL COLLECTION

oldest sister, Rose, she had some sort of boxes with a plank board and a mattress on top of that. And, of course, we used chamber pots during the night, because we didn't have any toilet facilities inside the house.

"If any of us had to go at night we'd take a candle and walk outside. Sometimes we'd escort our mother. Two or three of us would go and we'd sit outside and wait for her. It's funny now, looking back, that in those days we never complained about those things.

"And we all helped in the store. It didn't matter how young you were. When we started school we also stocked the shelves, we dusted them and when we got a little older we would make change. In those days, I remember, we had a little notebook and it was called a *cartera* and any charge purchases that the people made was put down in that book. The funny thing is we always gave that noteback to the customer; the Chinese grocer never kept account. There was a tremendous trust.

"We didn't have much and we worked hard, but we never had a shortage of food. I think it was for this that so many Chinese went into the grocery business. You see, what they couldn't sell they ate. If we were selling fresh meat and there was some left over that was just beginning to turn bad, we salvaged it. And it was the same way with the vegetables. We were never short of food.

"Sometimes we would nag our mother about our shoes, but sometimes it would be months before we could get them. Meanwhile we'd cut cardboard and put it in the soles of our shoes.

"I remember we would get up early, help our mom do some of the cleaning and then we would run off to school. Then when we got home we did what we had to. If there was a younger child that had to be fed or bathed, we'd do that. Or we dusted the shelves, waited on customers or sacked the beans and sugar. And we also would go to Chinese school for about two and a half hours and we'd get home then about eight-thirty or nine o'clock at night. We would study and then help put the younger children to bed.

"There were times when I was a little girl that I would go with my father to the farms around Marana, the cotton fields. It was just a little, old truck that he used to go to Marana, to Sells and to the mining towns to sell groceries. I remember one time the fields had been flooded at Marana and our truck bogged down. So we were stuck for the night and my father would make a little fire along the roadside and broil a piece of meat. And I spent the night sleeping across the front seat of the truck.

"And there were many times when the customers could not pay and the honest ones would say to my father, 'Chappo'—they called him that, the Mexicans, because he was so short—'we can't pay you so we can't buy any groceries.' But because they had children, my dad would always say, 'Oh, come on. Go ahead. Don't worry about it.' And some times, just out of necessity to find work, some of these people moved away and never paid him. But he never went after them."

Was it from this attitude of your father that you have spent a lifetime working for others?

"Yes, yes, I believe so. You know, my father always said, 'I don't care if you kids ever make a nickel, or ever have a nickel, as long as you keep a good name. Keep a good name and serve the community.' And, of course, when I went to school I was always interested in helping and I think the combination of the teacher that I had and my dad are what pushed me on. I can remember even now that when I brought back good grades from school, my father would hold up his thumb and he'd say, 'You're Number One.' "

HIRO NOMURA
WILLIAM KAJIKAWA
MARGARET KAJIKAWA

And Suddenly Behind Barbed Wire Fences

WHEN IT CAME to the mistreatment of Orientals, the Japanese were not
left out in Arizona. There were few Japanese in the territory of Arizona—
only 2 in 1880 and perhaps 100 in '97, and they were brought in to work
on a farm in the Tempe area. When California passed its Alien Land
Laws of 1913 and 1920, Arizona followed in 1921 with an enactment that
forbade the Japanese from owning land.

By 1934 there were about 120 Japanese farms in the Salt River Valley,
many purchased under the names of children who had been born into
United States citizenship. Even when the population of Japanese was less
than 1,000, whites in the Salt River Valley felt threatened. In 1934 Japanese families had their homes bombed, they were shot at and their crops
were flooded out. There was even a day in 1934 when 600 whites gathered
for anti-Japanese demonstrations.

There are expert historians who believe that the handling, or the mis-
handling, of the Japanese in the Western United States was a factor in
building up the anti-American sentiment in Japan that led to the attack
on Pearl Harbor.

After Pearl Harbor the situation worsened for the Japanese in this
country. Japanese citizens living here and even Japanese-Americans were
herded into what were called "relocation centers" in Arizona. There, suddenly behind barbed wire fences, the nisei, those American citizens of
Japanese background, found an even greater hostility in the United States
than their pioneer forefathers.

Hiro Nomura, a master photographer now living in Phoenix, was
taken behind the barbed wire with his family. Margaret and William
Kajikawa worked as interpreters in the relocation program. They recall
how it all came about in 1942.

208

LOOKING BACK WITHOUT ANGER

In the Kajikawas' home in Tempe near the campus of Arizona State University, the three Japanese-Americans talked of darker days in the treatment of their people, but never once would they look back with anger.

HIRO NOMURA: "My grandfather came before my father. He couldn't come directly into Arizona, so he came across to Peru and practically walked across the continent into Arizona. He established himself as a farmer on the west side of Phoenix, in Glendale,. in 1908 and then he called his three sons over. The middle son was my father. That's how we became established over there west of Phoenix."

BILL KAJIKAWA: "Well, my people came into Arizona in 1929 from Oxnard, California. My father, he was really my stepfather, because my father had passed away, was a barber and he came over here in the hottest part of the summer of '29 and started a little barber shop in downtown Phoenix. We lived down around Madison around Second or Third and there was a real mixture of people there—some blacks, some Mexicans, some Indians who came off the reservations, and there were some Chinese chop suey houses, too, I remember.

"I think because we lived in that mixed section, we didn't have any troubles, any troubles as far as being Japanese, I mean."

NOMURA: "Well, I remember, back in 1934, 1935, there were troubles. There was an anti-Japanese rebellion. They—the white farmers—threw bombs and flooded the fields. I think there was only one person that was hurt, though. You see, the Japanese were farmers in the valleys around Phoenix and the white shippers decided they could grow their own produce and they wanted to take over the farming. So the shippers got together with the white farmers and they tried to get all the Japanese out of the area.

"We had trouble at our farm. I don't know who it was, the attorney general, the sheriff, or somebody, came out there and wanted to serve a paper on my uncle, my oldest uncle. And my young uncle was driving a tractor, grading a road from the main road to the house when they came up there and tried to serve the paper on him. My youngest uncle says, 'That's not me.' And they said, 'You're a liar. This is you. It says right here on the paper.' He says, 'No, that's not me.' Well, they dragged him off the tractor and almost bodily harmed him. Finally he convinced them they had the wrong person and they went away.

"There was only one accident where they threw bombs. One bomb went into the window of a Japanese farm house and this kid was sleeping under the window and the glass shattered and it fell over him and he was cut on his head. I don't remember how long those demonstrations lasted but they happened throughout the whole Salt River Valley."

The Japanese farmers survived the demonstrations and continued to farm in the Salt River Valley. But then came December 7 and Pearl Harbor.

MARGARET KAJIKAWA: "Well, when the war broke out what happened was that over the air, over the radio station, KTAR, or whatever it was, came Governor Sidney Osborn, and he said, 'Bill Kajikawa, come in to see me. I want to get in touch with you.' It was something like that. And then maybe a few days later Howard Pyle came on the radio and said something like, 'Bill Kajikawa, we are behind you. We're your friends.' Well, the Japanese people in the area had been trying to get to see the governor, to see what was going to happen. But the governor told them to get Bill to bring in a delegation from the two groups that were trying to see him, the Buddhists and the Free Methodist Church group. Bill, you see, already was coaching at Arizona State College at Tempe and the governor knew him.

"So Bill brought the delegation in to see the governor. What these people wanted was protection. We were afraid what would happen to them in the moments of hysteria, that innocent people, Japanese who were American citizens, would get hurt."

BILL KAJIKAWA: "Soon we were the liaison, getting information from the government and giving it to the Japanese-American people. We would get the directives and we would tell the people what they had to do. I tried each of the three branches of service, volunteering to join, but they turned me down."

MARGARET KAJIKAWA: "At first, I remember they said they'd take you. Then they called you back and said, 'We're really embarrassed, Bill. We can't take you.' Bill, you see, was very popular. He had been an All-State football player at Phoenix Union, and also played baseball and basketball. And he was an All-Conference football player at Arizona State. He had many friends."

BILL KAJIKAWA: "We escaped the internment in 1942, the evacuation of the Japanese to the relocation camps because there supposedly was a ruling that had a line drawn all along the coast and then inland, and the

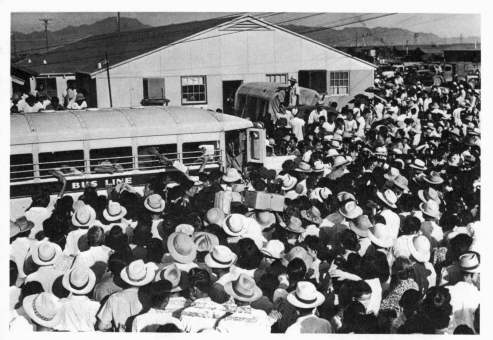

On August 24, 1943, internees at the Poston, Arizona, camp gathered to bid good-bye to friends who were being shipped off to Japan. The group interned at the Colorado Relocation Center, as the camp was officially called, included many Japanese-American citizens. UNIVERSITY OF ARIZONA LIBRARY SPECIAL COLLECTIONS PHOTO BY PAULINE BATES BROWN

line, of course, came through Phoenix. But it went through Glendale and took the northern city limits of Phoenix rather than coming through the city itself. And then it came across the Tempe bridge. If you were on the side of the highway we lived on then you didn't have to go to the camp; you could remain if you wished. [At the time, Bill was president of the Japanese-American Citizens League of Arizona.] So when I couldn't get into the service, Margaret and I were doing the interpreting for the people who were being evacuated."

NOMURA: "I had graduated from Phoenix Union High School in 1941 and I guess it was May of '42 when they took us to camp. There were seven of us in the family and I remember that before they took us we tried to get some answers as to what would happen. We went to the district attorney's office. We went to the FBI. They couldn't give us any answers. It was just confusion after confusion. Nobody could promise us that if we moved across the line we could stay out of the camp permanently. . . ."

MARGARET KAJIKAWA: "At that time, too, the Arizona Legislature passed a bill that the Japanese people couldn't buy anything but food."

NOMURA: "That's right. I went to Sears to buy a bar of soap, but they said they couldn't sell a bar of soap to me."

MARGARET KAJIKAWA: "At this time I was handling the payroll for Arizona State College and I went to Mrs. Gammage—she was the wife of Grady Gammage, the president of the college—and I told her I could not buy anything because I was Japanese. She said that was ridiculous. So then I went and I bought up sheets to take to the Japanese people in the camp. I asked the people in the store why they could sell to me and not to other Japanese. I said, 'That's discrimination. Something's wrong.' They said, 'Well, you're Mrs. Kajikawa, aren't you? You can buy. We've got orders to let you buy anything you want.' So then I went to see Dan Garvey, who was secretary of state, and I told him that he was going to have to sue me 'because I'm working for the state of Arizona and I'm breaking every law.'

"Well, all I can say is the Gammages were terrific. Dr. Gammage could have gotten into trouble, but he stood up for me. He said, 'Margaret, don't ever hate. Governments might make mistakes, but don't ever hate the people.' Anyhow, I wanted a test suit so our people could buy things, things like oil for their heaters. We got the test case; Simpson Cox represented us, and we won."

BILL KAJIKAWA: "About this time some of the Japanese-American

Citizens League members got together and decided to form this special unit, the 442nd Regimental Combat Team. I wanted to serve, too. . . ."

MARGARET KAJIKAWA: "You've still got the letter you wrote to Senator Hayden—'I don't care how I serve, I want to serve. You can't give lip service, but must give real service.' "

BILL KAJIKAWA: "When I finished the school term in 1943 I went and our unit fought in Italy first, and then in France and from France we went to Germany. Two of Margaret's brothers also went overseas with the unit. I was the only one of our family to come back."

The 442nd was one of the nation's most decorated units in World War II. It brought much honor to Japanese-Americans who were behind the barbed wire of the internment camps.

NOMURA: "For our family it was all very confusing. Our parents had made this their home; they never thought of going back to Japan any more. At first, when they were ordered to the camp, they thought it was something of a joke—'it's not true, it can't be.' But we were assembled in Glendale and taken to the processing camp at Mayer, up near Prescott. Just a suitcase and a bedroll, that's all we could take. From Mayer we were taken to Poston I, and my father, myself and my brother we come out in about a year, or a year and a half because they needed us for manpower on the cotton fields and produce fields. My mother, two sisters and another brother, they stayed until the camp closed down in 1945."

We asked about the feelings of the people once they were in the camp.

NOMURA: "Well, there were different groups. There were some who eventually were deported back to Japan. But for most of the people, they adapted to the conditions pretty fast. The Japanese, well, are a little different from other people."

MARGARET KAJIKAWA: "If you can't change it, why look back?"

NOMURA: "Yeah, it's just like they used to teach us: Be like a bamboo. You have a strong back, you know, bend with the wind, and when it goes over, you come back, the same way."

Mr. Nomura, when you and your father and brothers came out of the camp to work, what did you find at your home?

"Well, we were lucky 'cause we came out early. The car was still there; we just had to buy tires and batteries. They were stripped off the car. We had bolted the garage, boarded it up, but they broke in and stripped the car. We knew who did it, but you couldn't prove a thing. And they took a little console radio that was bolted down and they also took all kinds of farm equipment. Afterwards we filed against the government. We were able to file a loss claim, but we got very little back."

MARGARET KAJIKAWA: "My parents were living in California when they were taken to camp. They lost their personal property, too."

NOMURA: "Yeah, that is what happened, and in addition our parents had bank accounts which were frozen. We got back part of the money, but there was no interest for the time the money was held and they deducted ten percent or something like that for the attorneys' fees for processing. You can't win. You can't win."

MARGARET KAJIKAWA: "I didn't know they did that, but I did know about the land problems, because after the war I decided that Bill had been in service and he should have every right to own land. Well, I found that when it came down to the deeds, if you wanted to get into a first-class subdivision, you had to be white, of the Nordic race. Well, we found this subdivision close to the college and the people who had bought land there didn't know about the restrictions and they said, 'We want you as neighbors.'

"But the restrictions were still there—this was about 1948, '49. I was angry. I said, 'We'll fight it.' I said, 'How can a man serve his country, how can my parents come to this country in 1898 and have this happen?' Well, it was a long struggle, but we finally built the house under Veterans Administration approval. It was some fight."

After all the torture what were the attitudes of the Japanese-Americans?

MARGARET KAJIKAWA: "Well, I remember when we went to visit my folks. We were eating around the table and my mother said that in the last war [World War I] the German-Americans were mistreated. And my parents said, 'We chose to come to America. Now this is your country, the place where you live. And no matter what happens, just don't look back. You serve your country.' "

NOMURA: "I don't think these things that happened could happen again, not to the Japanese-Americans. But I fear for the other people. I pray for this country that some crackpot won't get hold of things in Washington and put us all under a dictatorship. It could happen."

MARGARET KAJIKAWA: "It can't, if we all speak up. We're all too timid; we don't want to rock the boat. If there is some injustice being done, then we have to speak up. We can't just be afraid for our own security.

"And let me say this, it does none of us any good to look back and be bitter. My mother used to say in those days of trouble, 'Don't become bitter.' And I would say, 'But what about our home?' And she said, 'I want to teach you something, Margaret. Don't ever cry about material things; they're just material things. And remember if you become bitter you just hurt yourself. Don't look back at these things that have happened to us.' "

They were, the Kajikawas and Nomuras, not looking back. Hiro Nomura was pushing ahead in his photography, a business that was given a tremendous boost when he was selected to be the pool photographer for the marriage of Senator Barry Goldwater's daughter. Bill Kajikawa closed out forty years of coaching at Arizona State University in 1977 with great homage paid to him. And the Kajikawas were beaming at the appointment of one of their daughters as director of admissions and high school–college relations at Arizona State.

The Woman's Role

IN THE FALL OF '99 Pearl Hart and Joe Boot held up a stagecoach at Cane Springs, between Globe and Florence. And it wasn't long afterwards that eastern newspapers and magazines romanticized Pearl as the Bandit Queen of the West. Sympathy followed her through her court trials, her escape and her term at the Yuma Territorial Prison.

To western buffs Pearl yet may be the most romantic figure of Arizona's pioneer women. But her story is only indicative of the wide roles played by women in territorial days. They came West to stand alongside their husbands and they shared in the adventures and in the development of the state.

There was Sarah Bowman, the first American woman to settle in Yuma (1852). She went on to serve in the Mexican War, finishing with the rank of colonel. And there was Josephine Brawley Hughes, who in 1878 helped found Arizona's first daily newspaper (now the *Arizona Daily Star*). When her husband became territorial governor, she edited the paper, probably the first woman editor in Arizona history. And Josephine was a relentless fighter, first for temperance, and then for women's suffrage (Josephine would be shocked to find the fight for women's rights continuing in Arizona in 1977).

Nellie Cashman opened Delmonico's Restaurant in Tucson in 1879 and thus became the first Main Street businesswoman. She went on to become known as the "Angel of Tombstone." In that early mining mecca she ran a boarding house and grubstaked a long list of men trying to find their fortunes in silver and gold.

The difficulties of those early days were shared by other pioneer women. Larcena Pennington Page Scott worked with her husband lumbering in Madera Canyon south of Tucson. One day in the year 1860

A contrast in women leaders: At the left Josephine Hughes, whose husband was an early publisher of the Arizona Daily Star *in Tucson and later became governor. Mrs. Hughes perhaps was the state's first woman editor and suffrage leader. At the right is Lorna Lockwood, who became the nation's first woman to sit on a state supreme court.* MRS. HUGHES PHOTO FROM UNIVERSITY OF ARIZONA LIBRARY SPECIAL COLLECTIONS

Apaches attacked the camp while her husband, John Page, was out lumbering. She was kidnapped, stabbed and thrown over a cliff. All of that she survived, a testimony to her pioneer strength.

In the northwest section of the state the surviving village of Oatman holds the story of Olive Oatman, who with her brother, had been captured by the Mohave Indians after a massacre. Olive survived seven years of captivity.

There were many firsts for Arizona women. Sara Herring was said to be the first woman lawyer, Ida Genung the first trained woman doctor. And there were women who were pioneers in teaching, in politics and in the building of the state.

Lorna Lockwood was the first woman to become a judge in Arizona and the first woman in the nation to sit on a state supreme court. Her battle to gain that position is a milestone in the fight for women's rights in Arizona.

ONE WOMAN'S LEGAL BATTLE

Honorary certificates and plaques surrounded Lorna Lockwood in her modest home not far from downtown Phoenix. In miles she had not come far from her hometown; her achievements, however, are historic mileposts.

"I was born in Douglas in 1903 and I had my early schooling there. My father was city attorney in Douglas. I didn't think much of what was going on outside of school in those days, but I do remember my father had promised to get me anything I wanted if he was elected. I wanted a gun, so I got a gun.

"We moved to Tombstone in 1913 and stayed there until 1925 when my father was elected to the Arizona Supreme Court and we moved to Phoenix. I recall that I used to go down and visit my father's law office and I used to think how wonderful it would be if I could some day practice law with him. Father thought that was interesting but he had an idea that girls should learn housekeeping and so he kept me out of school one year. But I fooled him and made up the year.

"When it came to college I was going to go to Pomona in California because that was the family college, but they didn't have the law course there so I switched to the University of Arizona. My father went with me to see the dean of the law college and I told him that I wanted to enter the school. And, oh, he did his best to discourage me. He couldn't say no, but he did his best to discourage me. He said it was no place for a woman. But I said I wanted to go to the school and, well, finally, he capitulated and said, 'All right.' So I went into the law school and I was very timid. After all I was the only girl in the class and remember that this was right after World War I and there were a lot of returning soldiers and they were considerably older than I.

"But as it turned out they were very nice. They took me just as I was, and I was just another student. When I finished law school I went to Phoenix and was secretary to my father who meanwhile had been elected to the Arizona Supreme Court. That didn't last very long because I became ill and was ill for about a year. I had been going strong, active in politics and civic affairs, so I was slowed down for a while. When I recovered I went to work in a large Phoenix law firm and they gave me the opportunity of going over and filing papers and so I acted as secretary there and learned a good deal.

"And then I decided to run for the state legislature and I went in to see the attorney who headed that firm and told him I was resigning to go into politics. Well, he was, I won't say horrified, but he was a little reluctant and finally he said, 'Well, you can do that, but remember you'll always have a place here if you want to come back.'

"There had been a few other women in the legislature, Nellie Bush, and one or two others. Well, I campaigned hard, going on foot throughout the district. My opponent was a well-known agriculturist and he was sure he had the election in the bag because he knew so many people. I didn't say much. I just campaigned until I think I reached every house in the district, and then I decided to go to California. I bought a little second-hand Ford and drove to California. My opponent heard that I'd gone to California and, well, that was fine with him. So he decided to go also, but I came back fairly soon and then I really campaigned. Yes, I guess I had faked him out."

Lorna Lockwood served from 1939 to 1942 and was re-elected but instead of continuing she decided to find a way of serving during World War II. She went to Washington as secretary to John Murdock, Arizona's representative.

"It was a very interesting experience that year and a half in Washington. I learned a lot about Congress and how it worked and learned about Washington. There wasn't any Watergate in those days. I came back to

Phoenix in 1944 and served in the Office of Price Administration as price attorney. And then in 1947 I decided to run again and was elected to the legislature for a third term. After that I was appointed assistant attorney general for the state. And two years later I ran for the judiciary and I began breaking the ice as the first woman to sit as a superior court judge in Maricopa County.

"People were surprised, but the lawyers were the ones that were a little bit against it. They didn't think that a woman belonged on the bench. One of them said he knew I was a good lawyer, but he just didn't believe women should become judges. After I was elected, he changed his mind and we became very good friends. There weren't any real valid reasons given, just that a woman hadn't been there and therefore they shouldn't be.

"I have to tell about one thing that occurred after I had been on the bench for a little while. I decided that I would run the court in accordance with the law and there were two lawyers, rather prominent lawyers, who were very contentious. And they would jump up and interrupt each other, they would talk to each other. I knew that wasn't proper. And I reprimanded them, but they continued. Finally I rapped the gavel and said, 'Gentlemen, I find you both in contempt and fine you five dollars. You may pay the clerk.'

"Well, that stopped everything. One of them stepped up to me and said, 'Well, I don't have the cash. Could I pay later?' I said, 'Yes.' There was a room full of lawyers and they all laughed, and it was all over. I never had any trouble after that.

"And when I joined the supreme court, as far as being a woman, I never had any trouble. I was just a member of the court. And I became the first woman to serve as chief justice of any state supreme court in the country. The others on the court had served their term as chief justice and they decided it was time for me to serve, so they elected me.

"Looking back over my career on the supreme court I have a great deal of satisfaction. I think I acquitted myself very well, and helped to make some of the laws. The courts are accused of making the laws, and in a way they do because they have to interpret them and, of course, the interpretation is what makes the law. And I felt that there were several cases that I ruled on that were very important. There was one case in which I held that a woman could ask for damages if her husband had been injured and disabled. It had never been that way. We had to overturn one of the laws that said a man could ask for damages but a woman could not. I saw no reason why the law shouldn't work both ways.

"And there was a fairly recent case where an Indian was elected in the northern part of the state and the people there did not want him to serve and they wouldn't certify him. And, of course, the Indian brought action and it came to our court. I held that since the United States had made the Indians citizens they had the right to run for office and had the right to election."

In the recent battle to get the Arizona Legislature to ratify the Equal Rights Amendment to the United States Constitution, Judge Lockwood stood up to be heard. We asked her why she felt the legislators were so reluctant to pass on equal rights to women.

"For the same reason they were reluctant, that the lawyers were reluctant to have a woman as a judge. Women hadn't been there before and they didn't think they should be. I think that the men in some way feel that the ERA is going to emasculate them, if I can use that term. They believe that women will no longer be feminine. And I can't see that at all. I don't think that when I served on the supreme court that I was any less a woman. And in my own intellectual capacity I had no question of femininity or masculinity. I was a judge, a judge of the supreme court."

BOOK SIX

FROM A
DIFFERENT PERSPECTIVE

*Before coming to the American West
my vision of it was composed partially
of a hill over which a long line of
horsemen suddenly appeared, and partially
of a telephoto view of Highway 66 with
the·billboards and hamburger stands
looming up into the lens. This
combination of the movies and* Life
*magazine did not prepare me for the
truly vast stretches of open country,
awesome and lonely, that still make up
the biggest part of the West.*

THE NEW ZEALAND ARTIST,
PETER MCINTYRE, WRITING IN
Peter McIntyre's West

Arizona for the Artist

WE HAVE LOOKED at this land and heard its voices. They have told of the ways of those first settlers and they have narrated the tales of those who came afterwards to this land which is now Arizona, a name that evolved from the Papago words meaning "place of the spring."

In this last section we turn to those whose eyes are trained to observe and whose fingers translate to canvas and paper a view of Arizona from a different perspective. The voices are those of artists, editors and historians.

The dean of Arizona artists, the painter who started earliest and is still active, is Lew Davis. Davis grew up in the town that is slowly slipping down a mountainside, Jerome. Although Davis left that mining town to study and work in New York, he never lost his attachment to Arizona. First, it was his penetrating representation of the mining men of Jerome that brought him national fame. And second, as he narrates in this taping, he found he had to return to Arizona to paint.

Little Boy Lives in a Copper Camp, one of his most famous paintings, was shown at the World's Fair in New York and was taken on international tour. Among the honors won by Lew Davis are the Tiffany Fellowship, Mural Award, Denver Art Museum Awards in 1938 and 1940, California Watercolor Society Awards, Pasadena Art Institute Award and the Arizona State Fair Award.

Lew Davis also holds the Legion of Merit, an award he received from General George C. Marshall for his work for black soldiers during World War II. But that is another story that this remarkable man narrates on the pages ahead.

THE LIFE AND TRAVELS OF AN ARTIST

Lew Davis had come in to Scottsdale from his home north of Phoenix at Pinnacle Peak to do this taping. It was just a few days before his sixty-sixth birthday which fell on election day. Davis pushed a drink back on the table and began. . . .

"Well, I was born in Jerome on November 2, 1910. That was in territorial days. My dad was a carpenter up there. This year in celebration of my birthday they're closing the saloons until seven o'clock at night.

"Now, I've got to predicate any description of my life by saying that if one seems to be born an artist, you're born into a great minority. I mean that's the real minority group in the world. Therefore, you're never like anyone else and your life is never like anyone else's and your feelings and reactions are not like anybody else's. When I read today about the minority groups, I keep thinking all the time, 'My God, I'm one.'

"Jerome—anywhere—when I was young, an artist was not only a minority, he was a sissy. It was a disgrace to be an artist and I wouldn't even admit in those days I was an artist. I used to say until I was about twenty-five that I was a signpainter, because being a signpainter was a respectable trade. Being an artist meant that you're a sissy; that was clearly understood by everybody including myself. Although I wasn't a sissy, of course, I knew how everybody else thought about it.

"I turned to art very young because I failed all my school classes, only I didn't know what an artist was. I'd never seen one, and I associated art with the covers of the *Saturday Evening Post* and the illustrations in the *Post* and that's all I knew about it. But I wanted to be an artist whatever it was, and I simply wasn't interested in what you had to do in school to pass tests and that sort of thing; so I never passed them. I made a bargain at that time: you do what you want and I'll do what I want. So the teachers did what they wanted; they failed me all the time."

When he stopped laughing, Davis remarked, "Which I may add has never handicapped me in the pursuit of my career or my life.

"Now I was about sixteen when I knew it was pointless trying to get through school. I knew that I wanted to go somewhere to learn to be an artist. Now if I'd grown up in Iowa, I'd have gone to Chicago, but I didn't know about art schools there, never heard about them. I grew up in Jerome which was New York–oriented because all the capital came from New York and all the mining companies had their headquarters there. So

I knew something about that city, and that is where I decided to go to.

"My mother was very sympathetic to all my foolishness; my father ignored it. He failed to teach me how to saw straight lines with a saw, or hammer a nail on the head. He gave up on me when I was quite young; he thought I was hopeless. Anyway, I took off for New York with very little money. I was sixteen years old, bewildered by the big city—which I still am, incidentally—and determined to go to art school, but I didn't know what art school to go to. I began making inquiries and found that the Art Students' League charged certain fees and I couldn't afford the fees. It wasn't much, but I couldn't afford it.

"Well, I found I could support myself with odd jobs. I was a rather clever soda jerker and could get work because I knew how to toss a scoop of ice cream in the air and catch it in a glass. I'd also get work at short order counters because I could flip flapjacks or fried eggs and catch 'em in a skillet. And I apprenticed in sign shops and learned to do showcard writing. So then I could go out to grocery stores with a couple of pots of paint and a couple brushes and paint signs for their windows for a couple of bucks. I managed; I never was hungry.

"Then I discovered there was a school called the National Academy of Design which was the oldest art school in New York, second oldest in the country, and that you didn't have to pay a fee there. All you paid was a ten dollar matriculation fee, which I gave them. And then I found a loft on Twenty-third Street, four stories high with the lower stories being occupied by small machine shops, sewing shops and the most notable thing was an exterminator's place of business. The rent was fifteen dollars a month. It had running cold water and that's all. The toilet was in the hall.

"Well, this apartment was a block away from the Chelsea Hotel and in the old days, I mean even before my time, Chelsea was for the artist. And this studio had once been occupied by Daniel Chester French, the sculptor who did Lincoln and all that sort of stuff. And the legend was still being passed on that when French had that loft he had the job of doing a man on horseback. And one day he led a horse up those four flights right into that studio."

Again Lew Davis broke into uncontrolled laughter. When he returned to his narration he noted with pride that he had moved ahead very quickly in the art school and was considered its outstanding student.

"One day at the art school there was a notice on the bulletin board that said, 'Employment, Art Dept., N.Y. Sun.' I got my coat and headed for the newspaper office. I must have gotten there about two hours later than all the other applicants. The *Sun*, at that time, was in a very old building. I guess it was the original building: wooden floors all scuffed up; offices with those frosted glass doors, and when you passed through a door there were those mahogany railings with swinging gates. When I got to the art department I knocked on the door. Nobody answered so I opened the door and went in. I stood behind the rail; nobody looked up. Finally I got impatient and I spoke up in I guess what you would call a hillbilly accent today, I said, 'Is this where you want somebody to work?'

"The man at the far end sitting behind a desk looked up and said, 'Come in, son,' in exactly my accent. And he started to talk to me. He told me that he was raised on a ranch in Oklahoma, been in New York for ten years or something like that and he was kind of homesick for the way I talked. Well, he put me on the payroll. The Depression had already taken place in 1929, but the New York *Sun* organization was so goddamn backwards it took them a year to recognize they were paying pre-Depression salaries. I got an enormous salary—seventy-five bucks a week. I didn't need to spend that; I put it all in the Dime Savings Bank on Eighth Avenue and Twenty-third Street.

"I never did a thing on that paper except erase guidelines for these other guys and be a messenger boy which I found to be very interesting because I learned all about the newspaper. And my boss would take me to lunch at his private club, you know, that sort of thing, and I felt I was very sophisticated. I didn't know how to use the cutlery, but I was very sophisticated.

"Well, I worked on that paper for a year until I thought I had enough money to keep me going through the rest of school. So on Christmas Day I resigned. My boss had a friend on the paper who was a columnist. He came from Arkansas and he had gone home before Christmas and brought back a jug of 'white lightning'—this was during Prohibition, of course. Well, he gave that jug to my boss for the Christmas party. I'd never had a drink in my life. That stuff looked like water to me—water in a paper cup —so I drank it, and when I started burning up I started drinking water which made it worse. So I was instantly drunk and I made a big speech about resigning and everybody wept because they thought I was a nice kid—and, of course, they were all drunk.

"Well, so then I could go to school—this was about 1930—without having to work. But, you know, I never planned to live in New York. I always wanted to come back to Arizona. I know now that I am much older that I can't stand cities, any city. It wasn't just New York; I can't stand Phoenix.

"I was anxious to get out, but I knew by this time that to come back to Arizona where there was absolutely nothing in art was the most risky thing a man could do with his career—ditch something to go back to nothing. At that time there wasn't a gallery in Arizona. There wasn't an art supply store in the state. Frame shops they had where you could get a diploma framed, or wife's picture, but that was about all. I was well aware of that, but I thought I wanted to risk it. At that time the federal government had all sorts of work programs, you know, WPA and all that. There was one program called the Treasury Department Art Project. Its purpose was to get people out of New York and back where they came from so that New York wouldn't be full of starving artists. The idea, you know, was to spread it around the country.

"Well, I managed to get on the program. You were obliged to send four pictures a year back to Washington and anything else you did you could keep, which was a very generous deal. I got back to Jerome and six months later I started getting my checks. But even before this I'd been saving money. You see, when I got out of school, before I came home to Arizona, I got a job in Plainfield, New Jersey, teaching in a private art school which today is known as the 'menopause school.' It was for amateurs, ladies whose children had grown up and had nothing to do. I worked at that job for three years and saved every penny to get a car to come back home. Finally after three years I had enough money, got a second-hand Ford station wagon—a wooden one with those isinglass curtains—and I came back to Jerome, which was the only place I wanted to come back to.

"Now finding a place to live and work in Jerome was a problem because when you are painting you have to have light—north light preferably because sunlight will destroy what you're doing by color change. Well, the Jerome Hotel which had been *the* place, simply had no guests in the Depression days. Below the street level there were two levels of basements and they let me have the sample rooms as my studio and a room upstairs to sleep in. For weeks at a time I was the only guest there, and I began working, first to fulfill the obligations to the government and second to try to make as many things as I could for myself—not that anything was marketable in those days. Nobody, not even famous painters, were selling, and for a beginner like me it was useless. But I did quite a lot of work."

It was there in Jerome that he began to paint the figures and shapes of the miners, and those paintings won him international fame.

"People misunderstood what I was painting in those days. They called it 'proletarian' painting. If they want to call it that, well, that suits me fine, because I don't care what anybody tries to categorize my painting as; I can't categorize it myself. But I can tell you I wasn't interested in proletarian painting; I didn't think proletarian. Of course, I was class conscious; if you lived in New York in the thirties you knew something. But what I was trying to do there in Jerome was trying to paint something I knew and I knew the mines and those miners. Because my father had worked for UVX [United Verde Extension Mine Company], they would let me go down in the mines. They always had a supervisor go with me because you could get lost underground, which I did once when my carbide lamp went out.

"What I was trying to do was to put down this experience as a work of art, not as a pictorial record. Well, I fulfilled my obligations to the government and in 1937 I began getting bored so I decided I'd drive down to Phoenix and get some intellectual companionship. I knew a couple guys about my age who were painters down there. To me they were rubes, you know, but they were the only ones I knew. Well, they took me down to Pueblo Grande where they had a museum there, at that time run by a woman named Odie Halseth and she was the mover and shaker of art events in Phoenix. She was giving a tea, of all things, that afternoon, to which she invited all the Tucson artists and all the Phoenix artists. I went to that tea and I saw this girl there. I fell instantly in love with her. I finally got to talk to her, and she said she lived in Scottsdale. I never heard of it, but she told me how to get there.

"I was staying in the old Ford Hotel, which is no longer, in Phoenix and the next morning I decided to go visit her. I forgot her directions so I asked the hotel desk clerk, 'How do you get to Scottsdale?' He said, 'Hell, I don't know; never heard of it.' I went out on the street and started asking people and I finally found someone who said, 'Well, you go east, out Thomas Road.' So I went east on Thomas Road and never got anywhere. Never saw a town. I got within two miles of Scottsdale before anybody knew where it was.

Thirty Minutes for Lunch, *a painting of early mining days in Jerome, was executed by artist Lew Devis in 1936.* COLLECTION OF MR. AND MRS. JOHN MCGREEVY, NORTH HOLLYWOOD, CALIFORNIA

"But I finally did find her. She was a sculptor. I decided we'd get married. I didn't tell her; I just decided it right there. So I went home and I told everybody in Jerome that I was going to marry this girl named so-and-so, lived in Scottsdale. Told them I was getting married, told them the date. Then I came down to Scottsdale to tell her the date. I wouldn't get married in Maricopa County; it was so strange to me. She agreed to getting married, and I insisted we go back up to Yavapai County and we got married there in the court house.

"Mathilde was a city girl. She'd lived in New York, Chicago, Memphis . . . actually, Scottsdale was her first rural residence. My friends, you know, said we could stay in their ranch house up near Oak Creek Canyon. So we stayed up there and Mathilde, as I said, had never really lived out in the country. And up there we had a kerosene-operated refrigerator; it never worked. We got our water bailed out of the creek. You could drink water then; this was 1937. And we had to go thirty miles away to Flagstaff to market. But she got used to it very rapidly.

"She smoked as I did, but I was rolling my cigarettes and I'd buy Prince Albert in cans. So I tried to teach her, but she couldn't do it. So one day I decided, 'Well, by God, I'm going to have her learn how.' And I said, 'I've got to go to Jerome. I'll be back about five o'clock.' I left her at home with a can of Prince Albert, eight packs of Wheatstraws. When I came back, she was rolling cigarettes."

Davis laughed until the tears rolled from his eyes. Mathilde Schaefer Davis had learned to rough it the hard way.

"Well, you know, she really didn't want to live up there and I didn't blame her. So we moved down this way around Phoenix and stayed ever since. And we were married for thirty-six years until she died of cancer . . . thirty-six years and that day I made up my mind, it wasn't a mistake."

The artist struggled with the memories and then he continued his narration.

"I got on WPA as an executive, not on a pauper level. I was the assistant director of the Phoenix Art Center. I stayed with it for about a year and then I resigned because it took too much time from painting. You see, I made only one painting that year. About 1939 I began painting full time and I accumulated enough paintings to get a dealer in New York. Even at this time some of my paintings had been widely exhibited. As a matter of fact, I was in *Who's Who in American Art* in their 1938 edition.

"Well, my wife and I loaded our station wagon full of paintings and drove to New York and I got a dealer there. But we ran out of money to get back home. Well, there was a man that we knew who arranged with his bank that we could borrow the money as long as I put the paintings up for collateral with the arrangement that when the gallery sold something they pay the bank, not me. So we got home and they did begin to sell these things. They paid off the bank and presently I got some money.

"You know, I was always high-priced. Yes, I was always high-priced. My prices today are outrageous, of course. Considering my status—you know, my youth, and the times—they were outrageous then. The first painting this gallery sold was to Mervyn LeRoy, the director, producer or whatever he was. I forget what that painting was, but it drew a pretty decent price.

"And then in 1939 I come to the conclusion, and Mathilde did, too, that we really ought to get out into the desert. So we found eighty acres for sale in Paradise Valley at the outrageous price of ten dollars an acre. Mattie and I built the house. Took us a year and I didn't paint much during that year. It was an experience that I thought was valuable; she did, too. And we lived in Paradise Valley for ten years. We had the only place in Paradise Valley for ten long years until I got in the army.

"I was in for three years, you know; until the end of the war. Never left Arizona; I was at Fort Huachuca all that time. I had a very unusual position. First of all, Fort Huachuca was a Negro post and this was during the segregated army. And I was an enlisted man. Well, I came up with what I thought was an absolutely necessary program for them. I proposed that where the army was sending, frankly, propaganda posters, with smiling blond white men on them out to posts, that that was meaningless to the 30,000 Negro servicemen. My idea was that I would set up a silk screen poster shop, do the posters with Negroes. Anyway the post commander, a man by the name of Colonel Hardy, was very sympathetic to this idea, sympathetic to artists, too, and he liked me. You know, I was a Westerner and his wife was from Montana. I was a horseman, my wife was a horsewoman. He liked the whole idea, and he liked artists because his mother had painted."

We asked Davis to go back and explain how he had gotten to Fort Huachuca in the first place.

"All right, I'll tell you that story. The head of WPA that year was a Major General Fleming in Washington. He had been a classmate of Colonel Hardy's at West Point. When Hardy came West he went first to the Ninth Service Command Headquarters at Salt Lake City. They had their headquarters then in a building that had been decorated with WPA murals. When Hardy got to Fort Huachuca there was nothing like that down there and he thought, 'I'd like to have some murals down here.' So he called his friend Fleming in Washington and said, 'Hey, you got a WPA out here in Arizona. Get me some murals.' And Fleming called headquarters in Phoenix and said, 'Get a mural painter down there to the fort.' But there weren't any art people on the payroll there at all, and the administrators didn't want to lose their jobs. So one day a man named Sidney Curtis who you may have heard of—he was involved with Colorado River water for years—he was head of what was called the Women's Art Project.

"He knew where I lived out in the desert and one day I saw out my east window—it was after a rain and that road which came into the ranch, which was called the Doubletree Ranch . . . well, I looked out and saw a guy walking, pants rolled up above his knees . . . squish, squish through the goddamn mud, and it was Sid Curtis. And he came in and said, 'You've got to take this. We'll put you in our top bracket you know, pay all the top salary we're allowed. You've just got to go down there and see this man, this post commander, because General Fleming ordered it. We'll lose our jobs if you don't do it.'

"So he got in touch with Colonel Hardy and said that I would come down. Colonel Hardy sent a staff car for me and I got driven down to Fort Huachuca in a staff car driven by a colored sergeant. And I stayed at the White Officers' Club as a guest of the post by order of Colonel Hardy. Then he had me driven to various buildings to see what I could do. I stayed there five days and for those five days the only thing I could see was absolute demoralization of the troops and the waste of ten percent of the army which was the figure they drafted Negroes on, you know, ten percent.

"I felt I understood something about minorities because I was one. And I knew Indians well; I'd lived among the Hopis since I was very young. I knew Mexicans and all that sort of thing. I knew what were called minority groups and I didn't see why the Negro would be any different."

So the artist went back to his ranch and drew up a five-page proposal. The radical idea of doing posters with black faces had to be approved by General George C. Marshall. After getting the approval, Davis went back to the fort, found a black soldier with silk-screen experience and soon Lew Davis posters were being sent to all the Negro posts. Davis didn't stop there; he started a world-wide newspaper for the Negro servicemen.

"It became a very good paper. We had it printed at the Douglas *Daily Dispatch*, on the old flatbed press they had there. It was a weekly, tabloid size. Then I went on to paint a mural that was a great success. It was maybe forty feet long and it was called *The Negro in America's Wars*. It began with the Revolution, you know, with Crispus Atticus, and came up through World War I. It was a very good mural, by the way. The mural was sent all over and displayed with a light and music show.

"You know, when I got to Fort Huachuca the Ninety-second Division was there. The Ninety-third Division had left. Now the Ninety-third was a failure; the Ninety-second was great. My propaganda, the posters, the newspaper, the mural, had instilled the spirit in the Ninety-second.

"The Ninety-third? It was a failure because there was no motivation; they were 'niggers,' you know; they hadn't been prepared. But the Ninety-second, I prepared them. Incidentally, General Marshall agreed because I got the Medal of the Legion of Merit from him.

"That mural? I think it went to Howard University after the war and still is there. The ones I did for the White Officers' Club, *The Founding of Fort Huachuca*, had one long panel of Geronimo surrendering to Lieutenant Crawford and it had Whitside, who was in charge of the troops that founded the fort—put the flag down and said, 'This is where it'll be.' And I did two murals, one big one about Captain Whitside with lots of horses and troopers, you know, and the Huachuca Mountains behind, a couple Apache scouts on the side panels and one long panel of the Apache band with Geronimo in the center and then Lieutenant Crawford accepting his surrender.

"The state claimed the murals and they were in the State House until Fort Huachuca was reactivated. Then they claimed them back down there and what they're doing with them, I don't know."

The artist now turned to talk about the period after World War II.

"We lived out at the ranch then, which really was pretty remote, out a dirt road from Scottsdale. While I was in the army, my wife had started a pottery works. She'd been carving stone, wood and so on, but she figured she'd make some money potting. And she made tableware, ash trays and that sort of thing. Then after I got home I wanted my studio back that she'd been using for the pottery, so she decided she'd start a pottery in

Scottsdale. I started to try to paint, but I found the three years I was in the army had thrown me off. I had had a theme for my painting before the war; after the war that was all gone because the world had changed around me. So it took me a couple of years before I really could get back to painting. In the meantime I'd go down and hang around the pottery and decorate pottery for my wife. Then one day, fortunately, the pottery burned down, and she didn't have to fool around with that.

"I decided that I'd open an art school—remembered that one that had been very successful in New Jersey, and there were plenty of menopause ladies around Phoenix. So a friend of mine built me a building, and I had a rather handsome, large building and began getting students. If they didn't drive up in a Cadillac, I wouldn't accept them because I really didn't expect, or want, to make artists of them. I wanted to teach them about art, to appreciate it; not to paint. And it was a very successful school; we made money out of it. Then because we had too much building for the number of pupils I decided to get various people together in a club to which they would pay dues and I would provide organized exhibitions for the gallery. They would be supporters of it and so I changed my club and called it the Arizona Art Foundation, had it incorporated and tax exempt.

"I had many friends around the country, friends in every major museum. I got together some really remarkable exhibitions. I got twelve paintings out of the Metropolitan Museum in New York. Actually I put together some of the most astonishing exhibitions that you ever heard of. Schools would send busloads of kids. We had a big patio in the place and they'd have lunch there and have a good time. Now this was all started in 1950 and I ended it in 1957.

"We limited the membership to forty because that was as many as Mathilde could handle. But they were all very rich people. I didn't take any money; I just wanted money for the insurance, packing and shipping of the art. We had opening parties. We felt these people would enjoy a party more than they would art, and you could force art down their throat. Well, we started forcing it and presently we didn't have to force it any more. Those parties were great. We'd have punch bowls with some innocuous stuff—cheap champagne—but loaded with vodka. And so people would have two innocuous drinks and get drunk; the parties were great. Everybody thought the Arizona Foundation was more fun than anything else.

"But then we got tired. We decided to leave Paradise Valley and lease out the school. And so we bought forty acres up on Pinnacle Peak, where we built a house in 1957—been there ever since. Well, I've been there. Mathilde died three and a half years ago . . ."

Davis's voice trailed off. After a few moments we asked him why, if he could have lived anywhere in the world, had he chosen to remain in Arizona to paint.

"Well, the only thing I can say in answer to that question is one word —everything. First, to me Arizona is the only place I loved and understood. Every place else was strange to me, and I don't like to be a stranger anywhere.

"You know, even in New Mexico I feel like a stranger, but once I cross into Arizona I feel at home. Looking back, I guess returning to Arizona was fulfilling a personal need and I suppose in a way a challenge. I was going to run counter to what was considered the necessary thing for an artist: to live in an art center, establish your name in New York, you know, that sort of thing. And I said, 'Hell, I'll beat them at it.' And for a long time I did. I had a big reputation in New York even from out here. After the war I stopped sending things to New York because insurance expenses got too high. And then a lot of Easterners started moving into Arizona. I found I didn't have to send things to New York; they could buy them here. And from about 1950 I started earning a very good living by selling paintings."

Lew Davis began talking about the importance of his painting in Arizona.

"I've never painted a thing that wasn't related to Arizona. When I was in Mexico one summer I did five or six paintings. I didn't do them down there; I did them when I got home. I'll tell you why the light in Arizona is so important to me. For forty years I haven't painted a shadow in any of my paintings. I've depended entirely on the color and the intensity of the pigments, on the arrangement of color to give the sense of light, and not light and shadow giving the sense of light. To me that was literary.

"Now even when I get into New Mexico that light, that light I am familiar with here, disappears; I don't have the feeling for it. I mentioned light because that's the first thing that occurred to me, but it's not merely light. Recently, well about two years ago, I began painting horses again. I hadn't painted a horse in twenty years, and I began painting them after

I lost my leg [an arterial occlusion forced the surgery]. That meant I couldn't go out and look at horses, you know, go out there and sketch. But I remember, because I know something about horses. I remember not through my mind, but through my hand, how everything felt and whatever part of the anatomy of the horse I'd come to, I'd remember the feel and would paint from feel.

"Now a horse is not exclusively Arizona. You can find horses in Central Park in New York City. So I'm not a cowboy painter; to be a cowboy painter you have to come from Westport, Connecticut, or some place back there.

"And I'll tell you something else. If I had stayed in New York I'd have been a different sort of painter. I might have been more famous, but I wouldn't have been what I wanted to be."

The Little Ones Are His People

ETTORE (TED) DE GRAZIA is everything that he has made himself become, but he is not all that he has led people to believe.

De Grazia is the artist with more than nine million reprints of his paintings already published. Because of this there are some art patrons who sniff the air and say De Grazia is only a commercial artist, no more. Artists who have followed his career will tell you something 180 degrees away from that; many admire him, not for his becoming a millionaire through art, but for his sheer talent and artistry.

De Grazia's fame is international and it is true he has enhanced that fame by his eccentricity. Once he told a newspaper interviewer that he had sixteen children, but he didn't know where they all were. De Grazia explains, "Look, I say those kinds of things because they make me look eccentric. They all expect artists to be eccentric, so I am eccentric; it sells more paintings."

He has a right to his whims—even to burning his paintings to protest taxes (he won spots on national television for that bit of eccentricity). For there was a time when De Grazia couldn't sell his paintings in exchange for more than food. There was a time when he lived on five cents a day while he studied under the great artists of Mexico.

And even now he can take you onto the campus of the University of Arizona and point to huge trees and say, "See that one, I dug the hole for that one, and that one over there. . . ." That was how he worked his way through school. De Grazia lived and worked among the poor and he learned to love the "little people" and they made their way into his paintings. The simplicity, the raggedness, the sensitive beauty of his little figures have a universal appeal that has brought him international success.

Today De Grazia is the maestro, holding court in his Gallery of the

Sun below the Santa Catalina Mountains north of Tucson. He sits, autographs and philosophizes, and the visitors go out with their arms filled with De Grazia reprints, cards, dolls and trinkets.

THE GOALS OF AN ARTIST

From the very outset it was obvious the De Grazia taping would be different. This is how it began . . .

"Everybody, you know, likes to begin with the beginning. I'm going to begin at the age I am today because I'm really not too interested in the beginning any more. Sure I had identity, but I'm no longer that one segment. Now I'm part of everybody—part Italian, part Indian, part Mexican, part Jew, part everything. I think when you get to a certain age, you begin to realize that you are a part of everybody and everything that's around you. You begin as a seed and then you keep on rolling and rolling like these damn thistles. You roll all over hell and then when you get to about the end—where I'm at now—you realize that you are just part of all that you've been through, all that has been around you.

"I like to think that the very best things that can happen to any human have happened to me—but also the very worst. Through a lifetime a guy has a terrible lot of breaks and I have had them. So that's the way I feel—sixty-seven going back to sixty, going back to fifty, to forty and that's where I'd like to be now, thirty-five to forty years old. That was the time—when I was thirty-five years old—that I was struggling, when I was trying to get there. Struggling to get there, that was a good time. I was touching base with every damn thing then in order to live better. I'd like to turn the clock back to that time.

"If I could get back there I'd say to hell with the world. But, you know, I don't really know what made me want to get where I am today. If I made it, I got in through the back door; nobody let me in the front door. And if I'm a success in Tucson, it's in spite of Tucson. I was never the darling of society here. I know what made me come to Tucson in the first place; they shut down the mines in Morenci and there was a guy asked me if I'd give him a hand loading a truck and the truck was coming to Tucson. So I got on that truck with fifteen dollars in my pocket and I came to Tucson.

"I looked at Tucson and liked it. And I liked the campus at the University of Arizona, and there I was a freshman in college at the tender age of twenty-three. I didn't have anything so I got a job digging tree holes on the campus. And there were three of us—all poor, poor as hell—and we got a place to live for seven dollars a month each. I had been in a dormitory for a month, but in a month I was out; didn't have enough money. But I remember we used to go down and buy stale bread and that bread was so hard we had to dunk it in the coffee. But there was one thing that kept you going; you don't want to go back into that mine!

"It wasn't all bad. At the time it was rough, but I was young and I was with other people who were poor so I didn't feel the whole class thing. And then finally I put a few bucks together and got a bicycle. I used to pump that bicycle to Club La Jolla down in South Tucson and I used to play trumpet there. That was before it became a real high-class club. And I used to relate to a place in the barrio called the Beehive. It was a rough place, but I hung around there. I guess I was just killing time then.

"You know, I wasn't too good in school. I never did like school. I like learning, but I don't like school and I never liked the attitude of the professors. To me it was that they were way up there and their attitude was that you were way down there, dumber than hell. And they're feeding you so much medicine and you take it and you don't talk back. Any time that I was asked to leave the campus I would go to Mexico, to Indian country, anywhere I didn't feel too dumb any more. There I was just another guy; I didn't have to prove myself. In school you have to prove yourself. So it was a struggle and it took me a long time, like thirteen years, to get out of the university."

De Grazia grew up in the mining camp of Morenci. He began to talk about the early influences on his life.

"Near this mining camp was another town called Milltown, full of cathouses and somehow or another I always got around those damn things when I was young. It was a hard town, where I grew up, hard liquor, hard living. Fights and killings? Well, nobody paid attention. I think I saw three guys when I was a kid who had their bellies ripped open in fights. They would take them off to the company hospital and I never knew whether they survived or not. It was a hard town, very hard. But, you know, I never knew about class consciousness until I came to Tucson. Where I grew up you never cared whether a guy was a German, Italian, Mexican or Negro. Sure there were the company bosses who had nice houses and a little piece of lawn, but the rest of us were down there together and you kind of ignored the way the bosses lived because it didn't touch your life.

"When I was young, very young, I used to go down to Mexico, to Chihuahua, to Sonora, where I came in touch with people who were human beings, people who were always scratching for a living. They didn't worry if you were dressed right, if you had on a shirt or not. Now at this time I was thinking of my painting. I was searching. I knew I was fond of El Greco and Van Gogh and Gauguin, but I said to myself 'these guys are dead.' I was looking for somebody alive and at this time Orozco and Rivera were big in Mexico. So I went down there to Mexico City like a dummy, but they treated me like a human being.

"I didn't have any money—I guess this was about the middle 1930s—and I used to live with the Indians, sleep beside them on the sidewalks. And I got along on about five cents a day. Get an ear of corn about twelve to fourteen inches long, roast and eat it—eat all of it, the shuck, the whole damn thing. And you could buy a little pulque to drink; it was very cheap.

"Well, I heard Diego Rivera was doing a mural not far from the Palace of Fine Arts. He was painting way up high on a scaffold and I would just hang around. I just hung around until, I guess, he finally noticed this dumb shirt hanging around there and he'd come down from the scaffold to have a sandwich and talk. We'd sit around and talk and he'd give me some of his lunch. Then he'd go back on the scaffold and I'd follow him like a little puppy, I had so much respect for him. One day he asked where I was from. Somehow he knew where Arizona was. And I told him I like to paint. He said, 'We'll see what you got. We'll see your work.'

"And Rivera and Orozco did everything for me. I was so damned hungry to learn I must have been a sponge. I soaked up everything they taught me. They didn't give me theories like up at the university; they showed me what to do. They were giants, both of them, Rivera and Orozco, and they were great human beings, too. I would spend two days with one and then two days with the other. I got to knowing them both pretty well. When I was with one, he would call the other names, and then it would reverse when I went to work with the other painter. And each one would ask me to tell him all about the other.

"They were great human beings, though. I remember one time Orozco saying to me, 'You know, whatever you want to do, you can do.

This painting by Ted De Grazia was selected for the United Nations Christmas Card in 1960. It is entitled Los Niños. PETER BALESTRERO WESTERN WAYS PHOTO

Whatever you want to learn, you can learn. But you have to learn it; nobody can do it for you. And if you want it bad enough, you can do it.' I have never forgotten those words. Then they got me a one-man show at the Palace of Fine Arts, there in Mexico City, and the exhibition was a success. I took that exhibition back to Tucson and I showed my paintings to the museum, but the director turned me down. He said that I didn't belong to this certain school of artists so he didn't want to show my work."

De Grazia began talking about the development of his art style.

"In the art world all you want to do is get along. You're not really in there for money. You're not thinking of big money; I never was. All I wanted to do was get by, to do what I wanted to do. That's why I would be satisfied being thirty-five again, because I was doing what I wanted then. Had a big pot of frijoles, and coffee was there all the time . . . and that satisfied me.

"When it came to my painting the subject matter was people I had known and people I know. I don't paint the sea because I don't know anything about it and I don't like it. I never painted the president of a bank, or a university professor, because I don't know those people. Anybody out of my class I don't paint. I paint the people I understand.

"And I like children—they're so innocent, so beautiful. I don't feel too bad about somebody over sixty who dies. But the other day I heard about a couple of kids got killed in an accident. I didn't know them, never heard of them, but I felt bad. You don't have to know the people to feel bad.

"There was a time when my colors weren't nice, not brilliant; they were sombre. I was painting beggars, people sleeping on the ground, *borrachos* and cathouses. One guy in Tucson, Ted Sayles, called that the 'De Grazia God-awful period.' As I got older I think my views of life changed and my palette lightened. Hell, it was the same style of painting, but I was lightening the colors instead of making everything so damned drab. I used to do a lot of studying of kids and kids are joyful, so my colors became joyful.

"You know, I used to paint pink horses and if I drew a horse and the proportions weren't just right, I would get scolded. To hell with that. If I want to stretch the neck of a horse, I'll stretch it. If I want to paint a pink horse, I'll paint it. That is what it's all about—not doing the way they want you to do it, but doing it your way."

Why has the Southwest been the only place De Grazia has wanted to stay and to paint?

"Well, I love the Southwest, specifically Arizona, and I love the Indians and the Mexicans and the horses. I love this country but things are changing. A lot of things have disappeared. When the Spaniards came to Mexico they destroyed what the Indians had and that's bad. They imposed on the Indians what they had—Christianity.

"And when the white man came to Tucson, he imposed his style on the cultures that were already here. All you have to do today is to go into downtown Tucson—one of the oldest cities in our country—and see what they've done. They had to build on top of where the old barrio was, where the old walled city was. They literally covered that historical area with concrete and now it's the government complex and the Tucson Community Center.

"It's the imposition of the men with power who destroy things that are very beautiful and then they are gone forever. Whoever is in power does it and that's the way it's always been."

A Passion for the Indian

PAUSE FOR A MOMENT in the gallery of artist Paul Dyck. There behind the striking coloration of his paintings of American Indians and their way of life is much of the story of Arizona.

Dyck, himself, is a relative newcomer to the state and that matches him to the majority of Arizonans. But Paul Dyck is from the "old country," his roots going back to Europe which sent so many of its people to explore and then to settle the New World. And, trained in the master painting techniques of the Old World, Dyck has translated that style into a brushwork that elegantly records the glories of the American Indian.

In effect, Paul Dyck is the transition, the bridge between the Old and New Worlds. He is a descendant of that great Flemish family of painters, the Van Dycks. The "Van" was dropped after Haddon Sundbloom, an illustrator for *Saturday Evening Post*, remarked to him, "Kid, you sure got a good art name, but can you paint?"

It was during the 1930s that Dyck left South Dakota and explored Arizona. He rode a motorcycle across the state, sold little paintings for twenty-five and fifty cents in order to eat and then found the land near Rimrock where he lives today.

To understand why Paul Dyck has such a love for Indians, his story must be traced back to his early days when he lived among the Plains peoples. Those days remain as vivid experiences to the man and the artist. And today he is not only artist but recognized ethnographer of the Plains Indians. He has collected many old ceremonial objects which had been taken out of this country and scattered around the world as curiosities.

Like Davis and De Grazia, Dyck has very strong views about people and about the way of life in Arizona.

THE ARTIST AND HIS THOUGHTS

Paul Dyck settled back in the hide chair. His wife, Jean, had poured drinks and the artist turned his thoughts to the Old World and his family beginnings.

"Historically the family goes back to Anthony Van Dyck. There have been painters in our family for over 300 years; it is an old family tradition that one of the boys is always a painter. In my own case it was rather accidental because my older brother was the student in the family so my mother didn't have much of a problem in making the decision. She just pointed a finger and says, 'You're it.' I was eight years old at the time, but fortunately I was apprenticed to a man that I really fell in love with, Uncle Johann Von Skramlik, who was a very prominent European painter.

"Uncle Johann was in his seventies at the time and, you know, being a Dutchman, he had a very strict regimen. At ten o'clock sharp, whatever city we were in—Paris, Rome, Prague or Florence—we would promenade on the boulevards. He had this big flowing black hat and cape, and, of course, a cane, and people would bow to him from the waist and say, 'Good morning, Master.' This was very impressive for a little snot-nosed kid, an American kid. Uncle Johann was a very kind man and for me that was something because I was rather distant with my own father. Father was up in years, fifty-five, when he married my mother who was sixteen, and there never was this father and son thing, or slapping him on the back.

"Anyway Uncle Johann was a very talented painter, an art scientist, and I was fortunate to have been apprenticed to him. Of course, that didn't mean I painted right away; I spent most of my time hauling coal, and over in Florence that meant two big, heavy buckets for a little kid to haul up three flights of stairs. I had to keep the models warm. And I had to clean up. But I learned by observation, and later when I started to paint my uncle would look at my work and say, 'Well, now, I've done this when I was fourteen.' And I'd say to myself, 'What am I doing here? I like horses.' The fact is I didn't have the slightest inclination of wanting to be an artist; at that time I wanted to be a doctor. Actually I didn't really want to be an artist until I was thirty-six years old. Yet, by God's grace, I have somehow made a livelihood at art since I was twelve years old.

"At the time my father was with the United States Information Services. He was retired and consequently we kept moving from country to country. We started out in Prague, then went to Berlin, Paris and Rome. Well, by the time I was twelve I finished my apprenticeship and my father, being a very strange man, just gave me my little hat and he says, 'Adios. You're a man. Go out; make your living.' So officially I was an artist and I was, you know, plunked in the middle of Europe in the days just before World War II. It was a very tough place then. To be an American in Europe with money is one thing; to be an American there without money is another thing. And then my family had a very bad reputation for being revolutionists and democratic revolutionists at that. Consequently, the minute somebody would see my name they'd say, 'Oh, we're going to fix that one. He can clean the toilets, the pisserie. . . .'

"Then in the early part of 1934 all American citizens were ordered back home because of the Hitler problems; at that time we were in Berlin. And so I came back to Chicago where I had an aunt who graciously loaned me two hundred dollars to get home. But let me make an interjection here; you see it was in Dresden, Germany, in 1932 that my association with the Sioux people began. There was a German writer by the name of Karl May who from 1870 to 1914 wrote about cowboys and Indians in America. He wrote about Old Shatterhand, forerunner of the Lone Ranger, who had a silver-tacked Henry shooting silver bullets, and his sidekick, Winnetou, was a famous Apache chief. And May wrote about the San Carlos and Whiteriver country and described it to a 'T.' Maybe he had never been to America, but he described the country to a 'T' and this is how I first became conscious of the mysterious Southwest.

"Well, when we were in Dresden the famous Haggenbeck Circus came to the city and they had some American Indians riding in a big, open bus. They were parading through the city, so I pushed my way through to get close to the Indian chief. Behind the chief sat some Sudanese camel drivers and they were talking in English. They saw a pretty girl and one of them tapped the Indian on the shoulder and said, 'Hey, did you see that chicken walking there? Boy, that's something.' And the chief just shook his head and said, 'Boys, I'm too old for that.'

"Well, I couldn't resist it, and I said to him, 'You don't look so old to me.' The chief said, 'It's an American.' And he started hugging me. He was One Elk and he had his whole family with him. Well, that was one time I broke the rule—the strict rule of behavior in our family—because

I just brought them all, all ten of them, home for dinner. I expected an explosion, that my father would throw them out. But it was the reverse and my father was delighted. That day the old Sioux, One Elk—he was a holy man—predicted that some day I would come to live with him, to become part of his family.

"Two years later I made a beeline for Standing Rock, South Dakota; that was Sitting Bull's country.

"I was seventeen when I came home. You see, I was born in '17 and I came home in 1934. Well, I worked around Chicago for about three weeks doing odd jobs. You see, there was no way that I could get into art at that time. When I managed to scrape up thirty-five dollars I took the Greyhound bus to Dakota, got to Cannonball and from there I hitched a ride to where One Elk lived. He lived a mile from where old Sitting Bull was killed. One Elk had been one of Sitting Bull's guards and was there at his assassination.

"One Elk at that time was close to eighty, but in fine shape. I married his girl who was about sixteen and that's how I got involved with the Indians. And pretty soon I needed money for groceries. Commercial art seemed to be the only avenue. I worked in Chicago, Detroit, and then in New York. And, I guess, the first job I got five bucks a week. Fortunately, I had a half-uncle who was half-Bohemian. His name was Ignatz Dycke, but he became an Englishman and put an 'e' on the end of Dyck, and he was one of the founders of modern American advertising art in 1921. The contact helped me, but I could only get menial jobs because my uncle wasn't too sure that this far-out nephew of his was 'kosher.' And to this day he doesn't know whether he should be ashamed of me or congratulate me.

"But the old weakness caught up with me. The minute I got thirty-five dollars together I took off and went home to the family on Grand River. Well, my wife died having a child; this was in a year and a half. And that broke up the whole thing when Fawn died. It was a very sad affair. I felt quite responsible. I could have stayed right there, but there were too many bad memories.

"By this time I had a motorcycle and I took off across the country. I think if One Elk had been younger he would have come with me. So I came to Arizona like 1936, just on an adventure. How I made it financially was chopping wood, making little watercolor sketches. And I got down to Tucson that year and made some of those sketches for Porter's store windows. These sketches averaged about twenty-five cents; the most expensive was like two-fifty.

"So I just gravitated from one reservation to the other. And I went to the West Coast and then back East and then I broke into fairly decent commercial art. But, you know, my father had raised me up a certain way, that a man wasn't a man without land or without a horse. And I kept coming back to Arizona, and up in Joe City [Joseph City] between Holbrook and Winslow, I met a fabulous character, 'San Diego' Rawson, a beautiful man and an exact physical double of Mark Twain. He wrote poetry, stories and he was about eighty-six years old. When he had been younger he had traveled through the early Colorado mining towns as 'Professor Rawson and his Trained Mule.' He recited Shakespeare and he had the mule trained to sit down every time he wanted a drink of water. Of course, he kept that mule pretty thirsty.

"And he was the one who told me about this land down near Rimrock. When I finally came over to look—there was no road and I had to walk over the ridge. Well, the sun was just going down and there I was up on the top of that ridge looking down in the canyon. I said to myself, 'My Lord, this is it.' "

For a broke artist, pulling off the purchase of the half-section was no little trick. The asking price had been $1,200; when he finally raised the money the tag had been raised to $1,500.

"But I finally made the deal and I got here to Rimrock in 1938, and it was a very good set-up. I would stay on the land, then go back to do commercial art, and I was still going from reservation to reservation. I had four lovely years before I went into World War II as an artist with the navy.

"When I came out it was still a while before I became the artist I wanted to be. As I told you, I was thirty-six years old before I really wanted to be a painter and I guess this happened roughly about 1951. What happened at that time are things that are rather on the intimate side. I had reached the end, I thought. I had a bad marriage; things just didn't work out. I hit the end of the road and I was going to blow my brains out. It happened that the gun clicked but it didn't go off. And in that one moment came a vision that what I really wanted to do was to paint."

Paul Dyck, of course, has had many subjects for his paintings, but he

Artist Paul Dyck entitled this painting Dear Mr. Catlin, I Love You . . . *when the work was done in 1966. It is in the collection of the Whitney Gallery at the Buffalo Bill Historical Center in Cody, Wyoming.* PHOTO BY PETER L. BLOOMER

is known best for his brilliant representation of the Indian way of life.

"Actually I had been painting Indians all the way back in 1933. You see, I had been born with an attraction for the Indians. My father had pioneered among the Blackfeet in the late 1880s and I grew up hearing their stories. My father had fallen in love with those people when he was fairly young. Even the short time I spent as practically an infant at Calgary has a lot to do with it. My father had collected many Indian artifacts and since my brother never had those interests they automatically came to me. In fact, when I came back from Europe to New York in '34 I had two huge steamer trunks full of Indian stuff and one suit of my own clothes and five dollars of borrowed money in my pocket.

"Of course, One Elk left a fantastic impression on me, an impression on the spiritual side of life. My father's values, too, as hard a man as he was, were very straight. So I found out very early that what he said was quite valid, as tough as it was. For an artist to survive in America you had to be on something solid. If you had money, maybe you could call that something solid. If you didn't have money, you had better be somewhere where you could eat.

"And you have to preserve your freedom. Without that there is nothing. For myself I have to be on Mother Earth to be able to have any sincerity in my art. If I can't touch earth with my hands, I'm nothing."

Could you have painted as you have if you had lived on Park Avenue in New York City?

"No. I could have made a fortune in the East or living in Hollywood. But that wasn't my direction. And don't forget that at the time when I was painting Indians everybody hated Indians. Today the situation is ridiculous. Today you don't make the grade if you don't paint Indians. You must paint Indians.

"Let me say here that a lot of people who see my work get very confused of my purpose, of why I am painting what I am. Well, I'm a flag-waver Number One, because I believe in only one thing and that's Americanism. Through my intimate experiences with the Plains Indians I found out they were the only constitutional Americans I ever met, if you take our Bill of Rights and the Constitution word for word and for what they are supposed to mean. Of course, if you put double meanings, or it's a closed country club, then it's a different story. But I think times have changed to the point where we insist on true and valid meanings.

"There is today much more respect; I think that the American Indian is 'in' today. But that still does not alleviate the problems. What most people don't realize is that the Indian problem is basically a social problem. If you get a group of people down so low economically, they are going to have all kinds of problems."

Paul Dyck, Indian ethnologist and painter, worries about the future of the people he loves so much. He would like to see practical solutions to their problems and he scorns the "do-gooders."

"My favorite question is, 'When have you taken an Indian to lunch?' You'll be surprised how few whites who say they love Indians can answer that."

Some Closing Words from Arizona Editors

A STATE AS DIVERSE as Arizona—its physical picture ranges from the sandy and cactus-spiked deserts to snow-capped mountain peaks and its social structure is built on a mixture of Indian, Spanish and Anglo cultures—brings widespread opinions.

And so on these final pages of this personal and social history of Arizona we have recorded the opinions of three men whose eyes and minds have been focused on the development of the territory and the state.

At eighty-seven Craig Pottinger was, perhaps, the oldest living editor in Arizona at the time of this taping in his Nogales home. Pottinger came West from his earliest days in Kentucky and Indiana to settle first in Phoenix in 1910. He worked as a reporter in Phoenix, witnessing the inauguration of Arizona's first governor, the impressive George W. P. Hunt. Pottinger founded the Nogales *International* weekly newspaper in 1921 and operated it for forty-three years before selling out and retiring.

Harry Montgomery, alongside Pottinger, is a newcomer. He came to the state to direct the Associated Press in 1934. In that position and later as associate publisher of the state's most powerful newspaper, the *Arizona Republic*, Montgomery has an inside view of the state's progress—and the problems of that progress. Montgomery calls the late Eugene Pulliam, former publisher of the *Republic*, "the last of the great individualists among metropolitan newspaper owners in America." And he rates the late William R. Mathews, former editor and publisher of the *Arizona Daily Star*, "one of the strongest editorial voices" the state has ever known.

And finally comes the voice of Bert Fireman, both newsman and historian. Fireman came to Arizona in 1916 with his family. He was a reporter, an editor, a popular columnist for the Phoenix *Gazette*, and the writer and voice of a state-wide radio show on Arizona history. Today

Fireman heads the Arizona Historical Foundation, an organization pledged to preserving and presenting the true picture of the state's history through research, education and publishing.

Craig Pottinger's home sits high above downtown Nogales. He can look into Mexico, or, by turning in the opposite direction, view the Santa Cruz Valley, the path of many early voyagers into this territory.

"I came out to Phoenix on a Santa Fe train in 1910. Phoenix was a terrible place then. Wheee . . . it was hot and there was no paving; dust about a foot deep. I'll tell you I was mighty homesick for the green of Indiana.

"Well, there were three papers in Phoenix then—the *Republican*, the *Gazette* and the *Democrat*, and the *Democrat* was on the west side of First Avenue between Washington and Adams. It was run by an old man named John O. Dunbar. I asked him for a job. I had been working on a paper in Marion, Indiana, making three dollars a week, and to tell you the truth I wasn't much of a reporter in those days, but I was very young. Well, he said, 'We only have one reporter. His name is Sidney P. Osborn [later to become governor of Arizona] but if you want you can have a job. How much money do you want?'

"I was afraid to say anything. I was too bashful then, too timid. And he said, 'Osborn has gone away for six weeks, taking part in the Constitutional Convention.' You see, it was territorial days. And he said, "We can't afford to pay over seventy-five dollars a week.' I didn't blink an eye. He says, 'Hows that?' I said, 'That's all right.'

"So I was the only reporter and I covered the city hall and the courthouse and the mortuaries and the hotels. But, wheee, it was hot and so I saved up money and the following spring I quit and went back to Marion, Indiana. I wasn't in Marion four days until I was homesick to get back to Phoenix. I got back and they gave me my job back."

George Wiley Paul Hunt was Arizona's first governor when statehood came. He was re-elected six times and stands even today as one of Arizona's foremost governors. Craig Pottinger, the young newsman, knew the governor from a close, personal relationship.

"I remember very clearly that day of the inauguration of Governor Hunt. It was February 14, 1912, and I remember I got in the line to walk down the road—the dirt road—from the old Ford Hotel to the Capitol building. The governor made a speech, but I don't remember what he said; I wasn't impressed.

"But I got to know him pretty well. He was a great big fellow. Wore a white suit. Gosh, he was so big when he got in an automobile it was kind of lopsided. He wasn't very well educated, didn't use very good grammar. Hunt was a self-made man. He came into Globe punching a burro as a young man and he became president of the Old Dominion Mine up there; became a very rich man.

"Hunt was one of the best governors we ever had. Remember all those terms he served? He was very friendly, social and he was particularly nice to newspaper men—even though they worked on papers that lambasted him. One day the *Gazette*, the paper I worked for, had an editorial lambasting Governor Hunt. It happened that I went into his office that same day and he said to me, 'I know it isn't your fault. It's who you're working for. You know what I have a notion of doing? Well, I'm thinking of going down there and horsewhipping your boss!'

"He didn't do that, however. In fact, the governor had a great sense of humor. One time he took us out to spend a weekend at Florence to see the conditions at the prison. We slept on top of the administration building; nothing but sky above us. And you know what he did to us newsmen that night? The governor put boards in our beds.

"He was a good old guy, that Governor Hunt."

Harry Montgomery is retired from his hectic days at the core of Arizona's newspaper industry, but he has kept an interested and critical eye on the changing state.

"I came to Arizona in 1934 with the Associated Press as chief of bureau for the state; I think I was the youngest chief of bureau in service at the time I came here. And, you know, it is odd but there seems to be a repetition of the major news stories from my earliest days here. When I first came to Arizona the three biggest stories in the state were the Winnie Ruth Judd trunk murder, the June Robles kidnapping in Tucson, and the murder of a social worker out on the Apache Reservation. The three big stories then were crime stories and you could almost say that's about the same today. Crime stories are the big stories in Arizona even today.

"The killing of *Republic* reporter Don Bolles was the worst crime we ever had in Arizona, in my opinion. Here was a high-type, clean, well-educated, good newspaper man. There was just no excuse in the world for a thing like that to happen, to have him killed for writing exposés. We do have a bad criminal element in this state and Arizona has to do something about it. I think we've gone through—and I mean the rest of the

Photographed with his staff in front of the Arizona Star *office in Tucson, L. C. Hughes, later to become governor of Arizona, poses at the far left with arms crossed.*

nation as well—a period of permissiveness and of compassion towards criminals. But I think the pendulum is swinging back the other way now."

And how did the former editor view government in Arizona and also the swift growth of the state?

"Well, I think Arizona government has been cleaner by far than in most states. Oh, mistakes have been made and I think that nearly all government in Arizona, as everywhere, is too big. I'm simply amazed these days to go out to the State House and see the growth that has taken place. When I came to Arizona the legislature met every two years for sixty days and they usually got through in sixty days, or sixty-two or sixty-three. Now we have a session of the legislature every year. They start in January and they're usually still going in May—and then they have to have special sessions.

"You hear a lot of conversation about stopping growth, denying the right of people to come to Arizona. But even if they built a wall around this state you couldn't keep people from coming. People in the country are migrating to the deserts and the sun country, and we have both. I think if we can just firm up our water and energy resources Arizona's growth will be unlimited."

The papers Harry Montgomery worked for are the largest in the state. Have they really influenced changes in Arizona?

"I think that some newspapers do have influence. When I came out here, for instance, Arizona was a one-party state. I can remember when there wasn't a single Republican in the legislature. Now it's pretty well divided between the two parties.

"I remember that the first time I ever talked with Gene Pulliam about working for the *Republic* and *Gazette* I told him that if he had in mind converting Arizona to a Republican state I wasn't interested. I didn't think it could be done. But he said, 'It doesn't make a bit of difference to me and that's not my intent at all. But I would like to see Arizona be a two-party state.' And I think that has happened and I think it has been due to leadership.

"I think, too, Arizona has been fortunate in having good leadership. You know, as many times as I've traveled around the country the one question people ask me is how Arizona could have as much national influence as it has had, seeing that it is a small state, population-wise. Well, we have good men running the state and we have been successful in sending good men to Washington. Of course, Arizona started with good men.

You go back and look at some of the territorial governors, you'll find they were outstanding men. I suppose you can say that the frontier breeds good men like them, but I think they had great native ability, and, of course, the opportunity. You know, when I look at the mountains and the forests and the deserts of Arizona I wonder how anybody ever had the nerve to get here to begin with. But are we glad they did!"

Bert Fireman's office is on the campus at Arizona State University in Tempe. He is surrounded with history and lore of Arizona. His views are not the run-of-the-mill evaluation of what made the Southwest.

"I've always believed that the sweat on some guy's brow who was a miner, or was running a wagon across the land, or an irrigator, or a soldier, that all this was far more important than all the gunsmoke at the O.K. Corral, all the violence in Pleasant Valley in the sheep and cattle fights. These people had to come out here and clear the land, put it under irrigation, build dams and homes, businesses, roads and railroads, and also to convince the Indians that the warpath was not a proper way of life.

"Wyatt Earp did not do anything but detract from the real achievements. The gunfight at the O.K. Corral was of no importance whatsoever compared to the great economic wealth produced in the silver mines of Tombstone. The great Pleasant Valley War—the so-called Pleasant Valley War that Zane Grey popularized in the *Last Man*—had no effect on the cattle or sheep industry in Arizona. It had no effect on that area; it was an isolated family vendetta, greatly overplayed at that.

"The violence, the gunfights . . . those things don't count. It's the people who go out and plant and grow, dig and mine . . . these are the ones who built the state. You know, Hollywood and its cowboy movies have distorted everything. They go by stereotypes. Zane Grey is the one who's mostly responsible for that mythology—that the cowboy was such a romantic character and that he was such a loving person. Inevitably every cowboy story in Hollywood has a person in a prominent position in the community—a banker or doctor or a merchant—who is a crook. And you have the 'good' girl; it's funny how all these girls hanging around dance halls are good girls.

"In actual life these 'good girls' are usually prostitutes. But in Hollywood they're all good girls; just misunderstood, fallen angels.

"And this business of always having a crook in a high place in community life, that's another Hollywood stereotype not true to life. Crooks usually end up in jail; they seldom achieve and maintain a prominent place in the community. But Hollywood is swept up with those stereotypes and so are chamber of commerce secretaries. Every time visitors write for information, they get the cowboy picture. So when they come to the West they expect cowboys. So everyone obliges and dresses up in boots that are hurting their feet. This is all nonsense.

"The cowboy? He was just a laborer on the cattle ranch. He was a laborer and he usually had the education, the talents, the poise and sophistication that you find in ditchdiggers; he was in an equivalent role. He was at the lowest level."

And the changes that came over Arizona from the waves of cultures, what have they meant?

"Well, we had a conflict of cultures. White men, Europeans—first the Spanish—then the Mexicans and later the Anglos . . . and they all came along and entered an area that had been inhabited by Asians for a long time. These Asians who had come over to this land now call themselves native Americans; these are the Indians.

"And so there was a conflict of cultures. A new group came along and tried to—and did—occupy the lands. They came, people from a very advanced civilization, into an area occupied by a few people who were still living in the stone age, who lived on a very meager subsistence, were barely living. And the more powerful pushed out the other ones. There was resistance; there was misunderstanding. There was poor communication because the white man didn't understand the Indian, and the Indian was not about to understand the white man. He saw him exclusively as an enemy.

"So there were inevitable conflicts, and I would say that the one thing I have learned from studying history is that people are people. The white man was not always wrong. The Indian was not always right."

Index